SWEET AND BLESSED COUNTRY

The Coronation of the Virgin, 1453–4, by Enguerrand Quarton.
Musée Municipal de Villeneuve-lès-Avignon, France / Photo Daspet

SWEET AND BLESSED COUNTRY

The Christian Hope for Heaven

John Saward

OXFORD
UNIVERSITY PRESS

OXFORD
UNIVERSITY PRESS

Great Clarendon Street, Oxford OX2 6DP

Oxford University Press is a department of the University of Oxford.
It furthers the University's objective of excellence in research, scholarship,
and education by publishing worldwide in

Oxford New York

Auckland Cape Town Dar es Salaam Hong Kong Karachi
Kuala Lumpur Madrid Melbourne Mexico City Nairobi
New Delhi Shanghai Taipei Toronto

With offices in

Argentina Austria Brazil Chile Czech Republic France Greece
Guatemala Hungary Italy Japan Poland Portugal Singapore South Korea
Switzerland Thailand Turkey Ukraine Vietnam

Oxford is a registered trade mark of Oxford University Press
in the UK and in certain other countries

Published in the United States
by Oxford University Press Inc., New York

© John Saward 2005

The moral rights of the author have been asserted

Database right Oxford University Press (maker)

First published by Oxford University Press 2005

British Library Cataloguing in Publication Data

Data available

Library of Congress Cataloging in Publication Data

Data available

Typeset by Footnote Graphics Limited, Warminster, Wiltshire
Printed in Great Britain
on acid-free paper by
Biddles Ltd., King's Lynn

ISBN 0-19-928009-6 978-0-19-928009-4

1 3 5 7 9 10 8 6 4 2

O sweet and blessed country,
Shall I ever see thy face?
O sweet and blessed country,
Shall I ever win thy grace?
Exult, O dust and ashes,
The Lord shall be thy part:
His only, His for ever
Thou shalt be, and thou art.

Urbs Sion aurea (St Bernard of Cluny,
12th century, trans. John Mason Neale)

Ad honorem Beatae Mariae
semper virginis Deiparae
Reginae caelorum
Dominae angelorum

CONTENTS

PREFACE

This book on Heaven, the sweet and blessed country of God and His saints, began its existence in the form of lectures at Pluscarden Abbey in Scotland during the Octave of Pentecost 2003. I thank Father Abbot for his invitation to give the Pentecost Lectures, as well as for many other kindnesses. The monastic buildings at present occupied by Abbot Hugh and his Benedictine brethren were for several centuries, during the Middle Ages, the home of monks of the now defunct Valliscaulian Order, which combined elements of both the Cistercian and Carthusian traditions. This makes the choice of a Carthusian painting as the subject of this theological meditation all the more appropriate.

I am also indebted to my friend and colleague, Dr Peter Kwasniewski of the International Theological Institute, for reading parts of this book in draft, and for innumerable enlightening conversations on this most beautiful of theological subjects.

Scripture quotations are from Bishop Challoner's revised version of the Douai-Rheims Bible; in some places I have adapted the translation.

May the Triune God, through the Precious Blood of Christ, grant us all at length and forever to live merrily on high with Him in the company of our blessed Lady and all the angels and saints.

J. S.

Oxford
The Assumption of our Lady, 2004

ACKNOWLEDGEMENTS

The author would like to thank the Municipal Museum, Villeneuve-lès-Avignon, for permission to reproduce Quarton's *Coronation* in the cover illustration and plates within the book, and the Lord Abbot of Maredsous for permission to quote from the works of Blessed Abbot Marmion. *The Collected Works of Abbot Vonier* and *The Catechism of the Catholic Church* are © copyright Burns & Oates, a Continuum imprint; they are used by permission of the Continuum International Publishing Group Ltd.

ABBREVIATIONS

AAS	*Acta apostolicae sedis*
CCSL	Corpus Christianorum: series latina
DCOO	*Doctoris ecstatici D. Dionysii Cartusiani opera omnia*
DS	H. Denzinger and A. Schönmetzer SJ (eds.), *Enchiridion symbolorum definitionum et declarationum de rebus fidei et morum*
DTC	*Dictionnaire de théologie catholique*
PG	J. P. Migne (ed.), *Patrologia graeca*
PL	J. P. Migne (ed.), *Patrologia latina*
ST	St Thomas Aquinas, *Summa Theologiae*
SC	Sources chrétiennes
Sent.	St Thomas Aquinas, *Scriptum super libros Sententiarum*

INTRODUCTION

Seeking the God of Heaven

Stand by a river in the highlands of Scotland, and you will discover what it means to have a goal. The rush of the water, the relentless movement up and over the rocks, makes it look as though the river is seeking something. That is how it appears, and that in truth is how it is: the lesser waters are heading for the greater; the river is seeking the sea. Here is an example of the purposefulness of everything in the universe, what Aristotle and Aquinas called the 'natural appetite', the tendency towards an end, to be observed even in the inanimate.[1] Fire tends to flicker upwards, rocks to sink downwards, rivers to flow onwards to the sea.[2] Senseless they may be, but somehow they have a sense of purpose.

Every creature has a particular goal or good or better state for which it is making, but there is also a universal good for which all things are making. In a certain way, every creature seeks God, the supreme and sovereign Good, the ultimate goal of the whole universe. 'All things', says St Thomas, 'in desiring their own perfection, desire God Himself, inasmuch as the perfections of all things are so many likenesses of the divine being.'[3] Of course, this longing for the Creator that pulsates throughout the universe is not a conscious desire in all things, because consciousness is not to be found in all things.[4] Rational creatures, made in God's image, can know and desire Him as He is in Himself. Non-rational animals know and desire Him through their sensitive knowledge and desire of some good that reflects and partakes of His goodness. Inanimate things, like our Scottish river, 'have a natural desire without knowledge, being directed to their ends by a higher knower'.[5] Rightly pondered, such beautiful consistency in natural bodies, their unfailing tendency towards their goals, leads the human mind to the natural knowledge of God's existence as Creator and Lord. St Thomas provides such an argument in the last of the Five Ways: 'Things without knowledge do not tend towards an end, unless they are directed by some being with knowledge and intelligence, as the arrow is directed by the archer. Therefore, some intelligent being exists by whom all natural things are ordered to their end; and this being we call God.'[6]

Almighty God, the wise and loving Creator, moves all His creatures to their proper ends; more than that, He *attracts* them to Himself, who is infinite goodness. In Dante's words:

> 'Tis this that draws the fire up to the moon,
> The mover this, in hearts of mortal things,
> This that binds up the earth and makes it one.[7]

The Christian monk also seeks God,[8] not by senseless instinct, as rivers seek the sea, nor by unintelligent feeling, as the salmon seeks the sea, but by acts of understanding and will, and not only by natural knowing and loving, but also by supernatural virtues perfecting his higher faculties. By faith enlightening his mind, and by charity enflaming his heart, he recognizes and surrenders himself to the attraction of the Supreme Good that is not an impersonal force but the Three-Personed God. The Father draws him, through the saving mysteries of the incarnate Son, and by the sweet impulses of the Holy Spirit. And the monk pursues his glorious goal, not by himself and with his own poor resources, but as a member of the Mystical Body of Christ, vivified by the share in the divine life that flows from the Triune Godhead through the manhood of the Son and into the Sacraments of the Church.[9] The monk may be 'single' (*monachos*) in his celibacy and solitude, but in every other respect his being and desires are Catholic, social, shared. He conforms his thinking to that of the Church Militant. He leans on the prayers of the Church Triumphant, of the Immaculate Virgin and all the angels and saints.

He seeks God with the help of the Holy Rule, in obedience to the abbot, his father in Christ, and in peace with the other monks, his brethren.

The monk seeks God, that is, to be perfectly united by charity with the Blessed Trinity, with Christ, the incarnate Son, and, through Him, with the Father and the Holy Spirit. His fellow-Christians have the same calling from their Baptism, but the monk has taken a course that leads more directly to its goal. Like all who sincerely follow the Lord Jesus, he keeps the commandments and thus renounces the evil deeds that destroy supernatural love and divine life in the soul; but he has also taken on the counsels, by which he renounces even certain good things, so that the journey to perfect charity be less encumbered.[10] In this way, too, his desires are social, for his vows serve as a sign, to remind the whole body of the baptized that before all things they must seek the Kingdom of God and His justice (cf. Matt. 6: 33).[11]

Seeking the Heaven of God

The monk seeks God and therefore Heaven, for it is in Heaven that God most perfectly dwells. Like the martyr bishop Ignatius, he hears living water saying within him, 'Come to the Father';[12] but he also knows that the Father, with the Son and the Holy Spirit, can only finally be attained, beyond all loss, in the Jerusalem above. And so he heeds the words of St Augustine, who looks for his final home in the safety of the Father's heart:

Let us, then, lodge in the inn of this life as passing pilgrims, not as permanent possessors. Eternal are the blessings that await us: life everlasting, the incorruption and immortality of flesh and soul, the fellowship of the angels, the heavenly city, honour without end, the Father and the Fatherland (*pater et patria*), the Father without death, the Fatherland without foe.[13]

In the Holy Rule, St Benedict presents the goal of the monk in this twofold form: the monastic journey is at once Godward and heavenward, a return to the everlasting arms, the long march home. On the one hand, Benedict urges his sons to turn their hearts simply to the perfection of charity: they must 'love the Lord God with all [their] heart, all [their] soul, and all [their] might, then [their] neighbour as [themselves]'.[14] They must 'prefer nothing to the love of Christ'.[15] On the other hand, the monk ought to 'desire eternal life with all spiritual longing'.[16] One of the motives of the monk's obedience should be the consideration that thereby he will attain 'the glory of life everlasting'.[17] He climbs the ladder of humility because it leads to 'heavenly exaltation'.[18] He 'girds [his] loins with faith and the accomplishment of good works . . . so that [he] may merit to see Him who has called us into His kingdom'.[19] The Holy Rule, this 'very little rule for beginners', is nothing other than a road map for those who 'hasten to the heavenly Fatherland': by accomplishing these instructions 'with the help of Christ', the monk can reach his final goal in Heaven.[20]

The Quietists of the seventeenth century thought that 'pure charity' was incompatible with the desire for a heavenly reward.[21] In contrast to this high but inhuman spirituality, St Benedict unites the two aspirations, the Godward and the heavenward, in one surge of the heart; and he does so rightly. Supernatural love presupposes and perfects natural love. Now natural love consists in wanting something good for someone.[22] This means that, when we love, our wills tend towards a twofold object: we love the something, the good we want (whether for ourselves or for someone else), by concupiscence-love; and we love the someone, the person, for his own sake by friendship-love.[23] We should not therefore be surprised to find among the Christian virtues both a supernatural friendship-love (charity), by which we love God for His own sake, and a supernatural concupiscence-love (hope), by which we desire the eternal happiness that God promises.[24] Now our hope for eternal happiness would only be perverse if it subordinated the love of God to itself, treating God as the means of obtaining one of His gifts.[25] But hope, when shaped by charity, does not disfigure itself in this way. It serves, in the words of an eighteenth-century Thomist, as 'a disposition and secondary motive for loving God more easily and fervently'.[26] Even without the reward we would love Him, but with the hope of reward we love Him more readily. God's good gifts, especially the good gift of Heaven, help me to see how good and lovable He is.[27]

The love of Heaven is both a disposition for, and a consequence of, the pure love of God. If by charity we love God above all else, then we want to love Him in such a way that no created good can deflect our wills from their most sublime object and goal. But such an unassailable perfection of love is possible only in Heaven. Therefore, we love Heaven for the sake of God, not God for the sake of Heaven.

St Benedict wants his sons to love God principally by the friendship-love of charity, cherishing Him for His own sake, on account of His infinite goodness. However, he also motivates his monks by reminding them of the blessings God promises and bestows. In the serenity of the Holy Rule, the monastic quest for God turns out to be a journey to that sweet and blessed country in which the angels and saints exult in the vision of the Trinity. As Dom Jean Leclercq has shown, the monastic 'desire for God' manifests itself spontaneously, in life and letters, as a 'devotion to Heaven'.[28]

Meditating on Heaven

Heaven is the goal to which the hope-strengthened will of the monk, indeed of every Christian, aspires. '[I]f you be risen with Christ, seek the things that are above, where Christ is sitting at the right hand of God' (Col. 3: 1–2). Now the will can only seek that which the intellect in some way apprehends; the more it knows of the object of its desire, the more it will yearn, the more it will love. Therefore, contemplation of the Catholic doctrine of Heaven is indispensable if we are to grow in our desire for Heaven by Christian hope, and in our love of the God of Heaven by Christian charity. As the Apostle himself concludes: 'Mind the things that are above, not the things that are upon the earth' (ibid.). In a conference on the Solemnity of the Ascension, Blessed Columba Marmion presents the same consideration within the dogmatic framework of the Mystical Body:

[W]hile awaiting our eternal union with the choir of the blessed, we should in mind and holy desires dwell in that Heaven where Christ, our Head, lives and reigns forever. We are upon earth only as strangers and pilgrims seeking our country; as members of the city of saints and the household of God, we may, says St Paul, already dwell in Heaven by faith and hope (cf. Phil. 3: 20). This is also the grace that the Church asks for on this solemnity in the collect . . . 'that we also may dwell in Heaven in our minds'.[29]

Thus speaks one of the greatest Benedictine spiritual masters to have been born in the British Isles, and in his voice we catch an echo of all the Church's saints throughout the ages. There is no more pressing ascetical task than contemplating, no more urgent pastoral duty than preaching, the four last things: death and judgement, Heaven and Hell. Whether our Christian state of life be lay or clerical, secular or monastic, the Apostle's words should resound in our minds with challenging force: 'If in this life only we have hope in Christ, we are of all men most miserable' (1 Cor. 15: 19). Our hearts were created for God, the infinite Trinity, and can only find their ultimate rest in Him;[30] any lesser goal will leave us miserably unfulfilled. As the Angelic Doctor says in his conferences on the Creed: 'Were the life of man only this one that we now live, there would be no great incentive for men to do good; whatever we did would be a small thing, for our desire is not for a good limited to a certain time, but for a good that is eternal. However, since we believe that by the things we do here and now we shall receive eternal goods in the resurrection, we strive to do good.'[31] Our end is Christ (cf. Rom. 10: 4), and so our only final resting-place is where Christ is: in His divinity, with the Father and the Holy Spirit, and in His humanity in its proper appearance, the delight of the saints. *[E]rgo exeamus ad ipsum*, says St Thomas, 'Let us therefore go off to Him.'[32]

Picturing Heaven

Moved, then, by the wisdom of the Church and her Doctors, I have chosen Heaven as the subject matter of this book. The goal is the understanding of the Church's sacred doctrine concerning Heaven, while the means is the contemplation and exposition of the theological content of a sacred image of Heaven: an altarpiece of the Coronation of our Lady painted in 1453 by Enguerrand Quarton for the Charterhouse of Villeneuve-lès-Avignon.[33] This work of art is like an icon of the whole Creed. All the dogmas are within its frame: the Blessed Trinity, the work of creation, the call of Moses, the Incarnation, Cross, and Resurrection of God the Son, the Blessed Virgin Mary, the Church, the Papacy, the Holy Sacrifice of the Mass, Heaven, Hell, and Purgatory. Moreover, the Villeneuve Charterhouse, through its agent, explicitly commissioned this theological content, as we learn from the contract drawn up between the painter and Jehan de Montagnac, the chaplain.[34] This is a painting produced expressly, by commission, for contemplation by monks.

Monastic Guides to Heaven

I am going to expound the dogmatic and spiritual meaning of Quarton's monastic painting of Heaven with the aid of monastic theologians. First among these is St Thomas Aquinas, who, though eventually a Dominican, was at first a kind of Benedictine, the child oblate of Monte Cassino, and who died among the sons of St Benedict, at the Cistercian monastery of Fossanova. In any case, by seven centuries of papal recommendation, he is the universal teacher of every student of Catholic doctrine, and so no special pleading is needed to justify his status here as an authority.[35] Secondly, I intend to press into service the Benedictine theologians of the British Isles from St Bede the Venerable to Blessed Columba Marmion and Abbot Vonier. The desire for Heaven burns with a blaze in the hearts of these holy men; each of them could make the words of the dying Bede their own: 'The time of my departure is at hand, and my soul longs to see Christ my King in all His beauty.'[36] Thirdly, as befits the exposition of a fifteenth-century Carthusian painting, I am going to draw on the work of a fifteenth-century Carthusian theologian, the *doctor ecstaticus*, Blessed Denys the Carthusian, Denys de Leeuwis. There is a pleasing fittingness about this choice of source, for Denys was an exact contemporary of our painter, born in Rijkel in what is now Belgium, in 1402.[37] He was educated at the University of Cologne, where he received a thoroughly Thomistic training in philosophy and theology,[38] and in 1425 entered the Charterhouse of Roermond, where he died, on the feast of St Gregory the Great, in 1471. In the breadth of their science, the *opera omnia* of this strangely neglected theologian are without precedent; only St Albert the Great comes near him.[39] There seems to be no subject in the sciences, sacred and secular, for which Denys did not pen a useful treatise. He was a prodigious commentator: on every book in the canon of Sacred Scripture,[40] on the Sentences of Peter Lombard,[41] on the works of Denys the Areopagite,[42] and on two classics of the Tradition, the *De consolatione philosophiae* of Boethius[43] and the *Ladder of Paradise* of St John Climacus.[44] He devised manuals for the instruction of his brethren: handbooks of philosophy and theology (the *Elementatio philosophica* and the *Elementatio theologica*);[45] a *précis* of the *Summa theologiae*;[46] and expositions of the rites and ceremonies of Holy Mass,[47] and of the hymns of the Divine Office.[48] He also wrote books on the various states of Christian life: monasticism, of course,[49] but also marriage,[50] widowhood,[51] kingship,[52] and the military life.[53] Of particular fascination to a twenty-first century reader are Denys's two works on Islam, which, like St John

Damascene[54] before him, he presents as a heresy, indeed as the summation of all the heresies of the Patristic age.[55] He made this judgement, not out of ignorance and prejudice but after close study of the Koran and the works of Muslim philosophers.[56] Denys lived at a time when it seemed that Islam, under the hegemony of the Turkish Sultan, was about to overwhelm Christendom. He wrote his books on Islam at the suggestion of Cardinal Nicholas of Cusa, whom, just a year or so before the fall of Constantinople, he accompanied on a journey to preach a crusade of defence against the external attacks of the infidel and of reform to root out internal abuses in the Church.[57]

I have invited Blessed Denys the Carthusian to join us in this book on our speculative journey towards the sweet and blessed country of Paradise. I have little doubt that my readers will find him a stimulating companion and a trustworthy guide. But I must warn them: he is not dubbed the *doctor ecstaticus* for nothing. He is an eager disciple of his namesake, the Areopagite, and so his prose abounds, as does his master's, with the vocabulary of eminence and excess: everything pertaining to God is *super-* and *-issimus*.

The Art of Immortality

The sacred art of the Church is a *locus theologicus*, one of the 'places' in the Tradition from which the journey of theology can make a start.[58] A painting such as our altarpiece utters no words, but instead, by sign and figure, bears witness to the dogmas of the Catholic religion. Moreover, when accompanied by meditation, it can lead to a better understanding of the faith, which is the business of theology.

The Villeneuve altarpiece portrays a truth, the Trinity of Persons in God, to which natural reason on its own has no access, for this most tremendous of mysteries is made known through supernatural revelation and can only be accepted by supernatural faith.[59] An unbeliever may admire the painting's material perfections, the brightness of its colours, say, or the proportion of its parts, but the fullness of its spiritual glories lie beyond his ken. However, by the providence of God, experiencing the sensible beauty of the image may dispose him to receive the infused gift of faith, which would open up the intelligible beauty, the splendour of the revealed truth. At the very least, admiration for this masterpiece of Catholic culture might move him to consider the claims of Catholic doctrine.

What can a painting do to help the man who has doubts about the immortality of the soul? Can the experience of art help convince him of the naturally knowable truth of the soul's survival after death? I believe it can. Art, even art considered in the abstract, can be an argument for immortality. Making a painting is a properly human act, the kind of thing only an animal with a rational soul can do, an exercise of the intellectual virtue of art.[60] Among creatures on earth, man alone is an artist. When swallows build their nests or bees make honeycomb, they act, not by any judgement of reason in themselves, but by the judgement of nature at work within them, that is, through powers implanted and sustained by the Author of nature.[61] The artistry of nests and honeycomb belongs properly to the First Cause Himself; the secondary causes, the birds and the bees, are not artists in themselves, but only the unconscious servants of the divine Artist. Man, by contrast, imitates the art of God more perfectly, by a true art of his own. Like his Creator, the rational creature employs intelligence and freedom in order to make beautiful things. Before he picked up his paintbrush, Enguerrand Quarton had an *idea* of the altarpiece, and so did the Prior of the Charterhouse, as we can see from the contract. In the chapel of the Holy Trinity, the *Coronation* existed in matter, shone out in line and colour, but in the mind of the painter it existed without matter, as an idea or intention.[62] Now from the immateriality of such an idea we can prove the immateriality of the intellect, or intellectual soul, that possesses it, and from the immateriality of the intellectual soul we can establish its incorruptibility. Thus thinking about the nature of human art—the virtue, its acts, and the products of the acts—can lead to the knowledge of the soul's immortality. It should be no surprise, then, to discover that metaphysics draws so many of its concepts and examples from art. From the four causes of artificial things the philosopher can rise to the understanding of the causes of natural things, indeed to the First Cause of all things.[63]

So much for the nature of art in general: the particular work of art with which this book is concerned can also furnish the elements of an argument for immortality. Like all paintings of the afterlife, the Villeneuve altarpiece is an expression not only of supernatural Christian hope for Heaven, but also of the natural and universal desire for unending existence. Now natural desires cannot be in vain, for God, the Author of nature, has established them, and He does nothing in vain. Therefore, the human soul is incorruptible, exists without end.[64] Even as expressing an aspiration, Quarton's *Coronation* manifests the spiritual nobility and indestructibility of the human soul. At their most bestial, men seem to desire only the goods that are sensual and temporal, but at their noblest, human yearning soars upwards to the Supreme Good who is spirit and eternal.

Attractive though it may be to argue from art to immortality, there is no need for our minds to follow this rarefied path. Humbler considerations will lead to the same conclusion. It is not just the artist's thoughts about his artefacts, but any man's thinking about anything, which displays the spirituality of the soul. When you know something intellectually, your mind lights up what is universal in the thing, its form, and you set aside all its material particularities. The idea of the thing thus conceived does not exist in your mind in a material way. The bodily senses provide the data with which the intellect does a work that is spiritual. You cannot gauge the length, or guess the weight, of any of my ideas, even when I am thinking of something robustly corporeal such as the Empress of Blandings. My concept of coldness is not cold, nor has thinking about wetness ever drenched me. Now if thoughts or ideas are not material, neither is the faculty from which they come. The intellect can operate in its own right, independently of the body.[65] But whatever operates in its own right, independently of the body, exists in its own right, independently of the body, for operation follows being. Therefore, the intellect or intellectual soul exists in its own right, independently of the body; it is not a body, nor a bit of a body, nor indeed anything material. Now something immaterial existing in its own right cannot be destroyed, because destruction is the reduction of something to its parts, and immaterial things existing in their own right have no parts. Therefore, the intellectual soul, by which man understands, cannot be destroyed; it is incorruptible, that is, immortal.[66]

Almighty God, in His wisdom and love, has not left the knowledge of the soul's incorruptibility to the unaided natural resources of the intellect. This truth has also been supernaturally revealed, and in the most glorious way, in association with the doctrine of the resurrection of the flesh, both Christ's and ours. In and through the divine Word incarnate, we have the hope for an immortality of the whole man, body as well as soul. If I want to grasp the immortality of the soul without any mixture of error, I must humble myself like a little child and accept from the heavenly Father the supernatural gift of faith in the risen Christ.

If one denies the resurrection of the body [says St Thomas], it is not easy, indeed it is very difficult, to sustain the immortality of the soul. The fact is, the soul is united to the body by nature and separated from it against its nature and *per accidens*. Therefore, the soul, when stripped of the body and as long as it is without the body, is imperfect. Now it is impossible for what is natural and *per se* to be finite and, as it were, nothing, and what is against nature and *per accidens* to be infinite—and that is what would happen, if the soul held out without the body. That is why the Platonists, in arguing for immortality, proposed reincarnation. But that is heretical. Therefore, if the dead do not rise again, we shall be men who have a hope for this life only. Again, it is a fact that man by nature desires his own salvation. But the soul is a part of man; it is not the whole man, and my soul is not me. Therefore, even though the soul may attain salvation in another life, *I* don't, nor does any man. Further, since it is man who by nature desires salvation, even of the body, his natural desire would be frustrated [if there were no resurrection of the flesh].[67]

Abbot Vonier holds the same view as St Thomas:

When he wants to have an irrefragable proof to the reality of eternal life, the Christian turns for arguments, not to philosophy, nor to the traditions of mankind, but he goes directly to Christ's sepulchre . . . To speak and think lightly of the mystery of Christ's bodily rising from the dead, and to rely merely on the philosophical grounds of belief in our soul's immortality, is indeed to sell our birthright for a pottage of lentils . . . I do not believe that faith in survival after death could have deep roots in a mind that recoils from the faith in Christ's Resurrection. All I need say here is that the doctrine of Christ's resurrection, being a specifically Christian doctrine, is of such a nature as to give us an unshakeable assurance of our personal immortality; so that for us temptations of doubt and despair are best overcome, not so much by investigations into the philosophical grounds of the soul's survival, as by meditating humbly on the Paschal mystery.[68]

A Theological Meditation on Heaven

Though organized around a painting, what follows is not an essay in art history or indeed any sort of history in the strict scientific sense. Although it is an intriguing possibility, there will be no attempt to prove a personal or literary connection between the Charterhouse of Villeneuve and Dom Denys of Roermond. This is going to be a properly theological book: the goal is the understanding of the Church's doctrine of Heaven, the vision of the Most Holy Trinity and the bliss of the angels and saints who enjoy it.

THE BLISSFUL SIGHT OF THE TRINITY

The first thing our painter was asked to do was to produce a picture of Heaven, with the Blessed Trinity at its centre: *First there must be the form of Paradise, and in this Paradise must be the Holy Trinity.* Quarton's altarpiece allows us to see on earth, by image and with our bodily eyes, what we hope to see in Heaven, by essence and with the eyes of our intellect made glorious: God, One and Triune. The invisible Godhead in itself cannot be represented in art, but Christian artists rightly make images of God the Son, who assumed a visible human nature into the unity of His divine person.[1] Images of God the Holy Spirit are also lawful, because, when the incarnate Son was baptized by John in the Jordan, God the Father sent the Holy Spirit in the temporary but visible form of a dove.[2] The artist cannot directly portray God the Father Himself, who sends but is not Himself sent, either in a visible nature or in a temporary form. Nevertheless, since the Son is His consubstantial Image and Expression, the Father can be indirectly depicted, as He is here, in the likeness of the incarnate Son. Of course, however lovely the created and material image, it falls infinitely short of the uncreated and immaterial archetype. 'Eye hath not seen,' says the Apostle, 'nor ear heard; neither hath it entered into the heart of man, what things God hath prepared for them that love Him' (1 Cor. 2: 9), a text that Blessed Denys expounds thus:

The bodily eye, indeed the spiritual eye, too, *hath not seen*, that is, it did not perfectly know, *nor ear heard*, that is, the bodily or spiritual ear did not hear from a mere man, *neither hath it entered into the heart of man*, that is, it cannot be thought or conceived by the human heart, nor can it be grasped by human affection, what things *God hath prepared for them that love Him*, that is, the eternal reward prepared for those who love God: uncreated Wisdom, the enjoyment of the Godhead, and the other goods to be granted to the elect. These indeed inestimably surpass all the knowledge and affection of man, nor are they known in any way except divine revelation.[3]

What God has revealed of Heaven, through the prophets but above all through His Son, the doctrine explained and defended by the Fathers and Doctors of the Church, is but a foretaste of the incomparably more glorious realities for which we wait in hope, the 'goods to be granted to the elect'. However, even the foretaste is precious and, as we see from the lives of the saints, a sufficient anticipation of the final beauty to motivate a man to take on the radical demands of a religious rule.

Beatitudo caelestis

The Names and Definition of Heaven

'Paradise'

'Paradise', the name used in the contract for our painting, is one of many names used by the Fathers and Doctors for 'Heaven'. 'Paradise'—a word, so it would seem, of Persian origin—is used in the Septuagint of the place on earth where Adam and Eve lived before the fall, the Garden of Eden. The name came to be applied to Heaven on the grounds that the place of original innocence was a type and promise of the state or place of final happiness.

Paradise [says St Thomas] is threefold. The first is the earthly Paradise, in which Adam was placed. The second is the corporeal heavenly Paradise, namely, the Empyrean Heaven. The third is the spiritual heavenly Paradise, namely, the glory of the vision of God; this is the Paradise to which our Lord was referring when He spoke to the thief [and said, 'This day thou shalt be with me in Paradise' (Luke 23: 43)], since, as soon as the Passion was accomplished, both the thief himself and all who were in the Limbo of the Fathers saw God by essence.[4]

As regards the promise made to the penitent thief, some of the Doctors argue that our Lord is using the name 'Paradise' to speak of the Limbo of the Fathers, into which, in His human soul, He descended after His death on Good Friday, and into which the soul of the penitent thief would also descend. Others, including Blessed Denys, say that 'Paradise' means the heavenly Paradise, and that our Lord is promising the penitent thief that He will do for him what He is going to do for the Fathers of the Old Testament: the soul of the robber will follow the soul of the Redeemer into the Limbo of the Fathers, but then, by the power of Christ's saving death, he will be taken up into the glory of Heaven.[5]

'Heaven'

Caelum in Latin, like its derivatives in the modern Romance languages and like the German word Himmel and the Anglo-Saxon heofon, means, first of all, that blue realm of the upper air in which clouds float and birds fly ('the sky'), and, secondly, the even more distant region of the planets and stars ('the heavens'), however we understand the nature of that region, whether according to the spheres of the ancients or the galaxies of the moderns. Caelum in Christian Latin comes also to mean the Heaven of God and the blessed, for, just as the sky and the heavens are above us physically, so the Heaven in which the blessed look upon the face of God is above us metaphysically, in some way beyond even the furthest reaches of the visible universe. Heaven in this theological, as opposed to meteorological or astrophysical sense, can be defined as the state and place in which angels and men or the souls of men attain perfect supernatural beatitude in the clear and intuitive vision of God. In the words of St Thomas, Heaven is 'divine beatitude itself, by which God rests in Himself, and makes others to rest in Him'.[6]

'Empyrean'

Heaven is called a place as well as a state, because it contains at least two glorified bodies, those of God-made-man and His

Blessed Mother. Where you have a body, you have space and therefore a place, for bodies are of their very nature extended in space. Now glorified bodies, despite the new properties given them in the resurrection, are still true bodies by nature. Therefore, as St Thomas concludes, 'the glorious body will always be in a place equal to it'.[7] When they think of Heaven as a place, the Schoolmen call it the 'Empyrean', the name first used by the monastic Doctors of the Church, St Basil the Great and St Bede the Venerable.[8] 'Empyrean' comes from the Greek word meaning 'fire': it is called the 'fiery' heaven, not because of its heat but because of its brightness.[9] According to St Thomas, following the Gloss, it is the Empyrean, not the visible firmament, to which Moses refers in the first verse of Genesis when he says: 'In the beginning God created Heaven and earth'.[10] St Bede adds that, 'as soon as it was created, it was filled with the angels'.[11] St Thomas offers a most interesting explanation for God's creation of the Empyrean at the very beginning of His works: the existence of a bodily heaven, from the first day, is a pledge of the glorification that the Creator intends, on the last day, to bestow upon the bodies of men and indeed upon the whole material universe:

[I]n the reward to come, a twofold glory is looked for, a spiritual one and a bodily one, which will consist not only in the glorification of human bodies but also in the renovation of the whole world. Now spiritual glory began with the beginning of the world, in the blessedness of the angels, equality with whom is promised to the saints. It was fitting, then, that even from the beginning there should be some inauguration of bodily glory in some bodily thing, free at the outset from the servitude of corruption and change, and wholly luminous, just as, after the [general] resurrection, we expect the whole bodily creation to be.[12]

It is to the Empyrean that Christ, our Head, ascended in His glorified flesh, in order to prepare a place for us, His members, and it is to the Empyrean, on the last day, that the just will rise in their bodies, conformed most perfectly to the glorified body of the Saviour.[13] Blessed Denys praises the visible beauty of this most exalted of places in words of light and fire:

'O Israel, how great is the house of God, and how vast is the place of His possession! It is great, and hath no end' (Bar. 3: 24f.). The Wisdom of the Almighty, reaching from end to end mightily, and ordering all things sweetly (cf. Wisd. 8: 1), adapts places to what is placed there, and places each thing finally in a place that is suitable to its nature or merits. Hence He placed the first man, whom He created in original justice, in the earthly paradise (cf. Gen. 2: 15). Since therefore the blessed, enjoying God fully and immediately, are incomparably more perfect, more worthy, and more rested in God than Adam was before the fall, it is fitting that God from the beginning should prepare for them a place and abode incomparably more beautiful, loftier, more delightful, and more restful than the earthly paradise. This place is the Heavenly Paradise, the Empyrean Heaven, the Fatherland, the region and dwelling-place of the blessed. It is called the Empyrean Heaven, that is, the fiery Heaven, not because of its heat, but because of its splendour . . . And although incorporeal substances, such as angels, do not need a corporeal place for subsisting, living, and contemplating, still it was fitting that they should be stationed in the highest, loveliest, and most worthy place, since they are joined in beatitude to the Most High Creator of all things, and are filled with all the adornment of the virtues and the light of glory, and are made the heirs of God. Therefore, the Empyrean Heaven is the highest in site, the largest in quantity, the purest in nature, the fullest in light, the most spacious in capacity. Of which Tobias says: 'Happy shall I be if there shall remain of my seed to see the glory of Jerusalem' (Tob. 13: 20). This heaven is the palace of the Most High King, in which the Incomprehensible God Himself manifests Himself most clearly, and in which He operates in a surpassing way. Therefore, He is said to dwell in it in a special way. This heaven is the most beautiful covering of the whole world. In the most seemly way, it is congruous with the location and habitation of glorified bodies and resurrected men, from which also the Empyrean Heaven derives its refulgence. To enter it, he sighed who said: 'I have loved, O Lord, the beauty of thy house, and the place where thy glory dwelleth' (Ps. 25: 8) . . . There, indeed, as St Augustine asserts, we shall truly rest and see, indeed we shall experience and feel how sweet God is (cf. Ps. 33: 9), how great is the multitude of His sweetness (cf. Ps. 30: 20), how infinite is the magnitude of His delight and glory. There we shall see 'the King in His beauty' (Isa. 33: 17), and we shall love Him with a love that is eternally both intense and fervent, delightful and never disagreeable. There we shall praise Him whom the whole host of Heaven praises unceasingly with the greatest harmony, with supreme gladness, with inestimable reverence and fervour. There is our end. For no end is sufficient for us except one of which there is no end. This is the end that does not consume but consummates and perfects. Once it has been attained, nothing more can be desired, since that end fills our desire totally with good things (cf. Ps. 102: 5). This is our end: reaching the kingdom of which the salvation and the glory have no end. Hence St Gregory [the Great] rightly says: 'If we consider what and how great are the things promised us in Heaven, everything possessed on earth becomes worthless in our minds. For earthly substance compared with eternal felicity is a weight, not an aid (*subsidium*); temporal life compared with eternal life is called death rather than life. What tongue can express or what intellect can grasp how great are the joys of the City above, being among the choirs of the angels, assisting the glory of the Creator with the most blessed spirits, beholding the present face of God, seeing the uncircumscribed light, affected by no fear of death, glorified by the gift of perpetual incorruption?[14]

Although it is a place, the Empyrean Heaven is not some place a terrestrial observer could find by using a rocket or a telescope. It is not just one more in the sequence of spherical heavens that, in the ancient and medieval astronomy, enclosed the orb of this earth. By its nature and essential attributes, the Empyrean is 'beyond' the spheres, or, as we might say, 'outside' the observable universe of the galaxies, for, while spheres and galaxies are mobile, the Empyrean, on the traditional understanding, is immobile.[15] This Heaven of heavens is somehow a place beyond all places. As St Thomas says, it cannot be investigated by reason, because it is not subject to motion or to sight.[16] It cannot therefore be the object of observation and mathematical calculation. It is not by natural science that we know of the Empyrean, but by supernatural revelation. That is why it is from Christian theologians such as Basil and Bede, and not from pagan philosophers such as Aristotle and Ptolemy, that we receive the name, and learn so much of the nature, of this shining city of the blessed. As Blessed Denys says, we know of the existence of the Empyrean 'by authority'.[17]

Jerusalem and the Fatherland

The monks of the Middle Ages found figures of the Empyrean Heaven in all the beautiful places on earth and in the heavens that are mentioned by the sacred authors of Scripture. Chief among these types and shadows is the earthly Jerusalem, which, in its so-called anagogical sense, refers to the heavenly Jerusalem. '[Y]ou are come to Mount Sion, and to the city of the living God, the heavenly Jerusalem, and to the company of many thousands of angels, and to the Church of the firstborn, who are written in the heavens, and to God the judge of all, and to the spirits of the just made perfect' (Heb. 12: 22–3). Blessed Denys speaks for the whole Tradition when he says, speaking of the geographical city in his commentary on St Luke's Gospel: '"Jerusalem", [a name] that means "vision of peace", designates the fatherland of the blessed above.'[18]

The monks of the Middle Ages thrilled when they sang the word 'Jerusalem' in the Psalms, for it made their hearts burn with longing for that city which is above, their Mother (cf. Gal. 4: 26). 'As today', says Dom Leclercq, 'people occasionally make the exercise for a good death, then [in the monastic Middle Ages] they used to make the exercise of Jerusalem: they reflected on Heaven, they cultivated the desire to go there one day, and they asked for the grace to do so.'[19] If the monks loved the monastery within which they had vowed stability of place, it was because it was an anticipation of Jerusalem, the vision of peace. And so, throughout the Middle Ages, treatises on Heaven poured out from the pens of monks: *On Celestial Desire, For the Contemplation and Love of the Celestial Homeland, which is accessible only to those who despise the world, Praise of the Celestial Jerusalem, On the Happiness of the Celestial Homeland.*[20]

Another important figure of Heaven is the Promised Land, of which St Bede says: 'The land of Canaan is promised to Abram and his seed, and then, after the long labour of slavery in Egypt, it is restored to the seed of Abram under the leadership of Jesus [Joshua], in order mystically to signify that the heavenly fatherland is to be restored to us, after the affliction of this present exile, by Jesus Christ our Lord.'[21] Here is the biblical origin of the name *patria*: Heaven is our own dear native land, the home of our Father and our fathers. Just as by nature we have the obligation to love and honour the country of our bodily birth, so we have the supernatural duty to love and to seek that land, 'the land of the living' (cf. Ps. 26: 13), the 'sweet and blessed country', which we inherited by our spiritual rebirth in the waters of baptism.[22]

The Church Triumphant

The happiness of Heaven is Catholic, the bliss, not of isolated individuals, but of the interconnected members of the Mystical Body in its glorified state, the Church Triumphant.[23] Christ is the Head of all men, says St Thomas, and first of all of those actually united to Him in the glory of Heaven.[24] Like the precious ointment running from Aaron's brow to his beard and into his garments (cf. Ps. 132: 2–3),[25] supernatural happiness streams from the ascended Christ into His members in Paradise. The incarnate Word is not, strictly speaking, the redeemer of the holy angels, for they never fell and therefore never needed redeeming *from* anything; nonetheless, they, too, receive their heavenly glory from Christ. As God, with the Father and the Holy Spirit, the Son is the object of the angels' bliss, and even as man, according to St Thomas, 'He enlightens and influences [them], as Denys [the Areopagite] proves from the words of Isaiah, "Who is this that cometh from Edom?" (Isa. 63: 1), saying that these are the words of the highest of the angels'.[26]

St John, evangelist and seer, compares the light of 'the holy city Jerusalem coming down out of Heaven from God' to 'a precious stone' (Rev. 21: 11). In his commentary on the Apocalypse, Blessed Denys says that, 'since in Scripture Christ is frequently called a cornerstone and a precious stone (cf. 1 Pet. 2: 6)', this text can be taken to mean that He Himself is 'the light of the Church Triumphant, both light as object, since the Church Triumphant looks on Him without ceasing, and light as efficient cause, since

He happily sheds His light upon her'.[27] And indeed St John also tells us that the Lamb is the lamp of the Holy City (cf. Rev. 21: 23): beatifying light pours out on the heavenly Church from the Holy Trinity through the pierced and risen humanity of the Son.

The Dwelling-place of God

God is said to dwell 'in' the Empyrean Heaven, not as if Heaven circumscribed Him, for we know that the Heaven of heavens cannot contain Him (cf. 1. Kgs. 8: 27), but because it is there that He manifests Himself more magnificently than in any other place. Pure spirits are said to be in a place in so far as they do something in a place. Now what the uncreated and infinite Spirit does in the Empyrean is to communicate the intellectual vision of His essence to angels and the souls of men—the most magnificent thing that can be done to them. As Blessed Denys says, invoking St Thomas's doctrine of the omnipresence of God in the First Part of the *Summa*:

God is not in a place by being circumscribed or bounded by it, but by transcending it. He is indeed everywhere by essence, presence, and power, in Christ as man by the hypostatic union, in the just by grace, in the blessed by glory. Nonetheless He is said to be in the Empyrean Heaven as in a dwelling, inasmuch as there He shows Himself more clearly, and operates more evidently and magnificently, as He testifies through Isaiah, 'Heaven is my throne' (Isa. 66: 1).[28]

As our painting shows, the centre of the Empyrean is God, the Blessed Trinity. Heaven is a God-centred place or state. In the words of St Augustine, '[God] Himself after this life is our place (*locus noster*).'[29] The happiness for which we long is to be found by resting deep within the Trinitarian Godhead. Now this God-centred definition of Heaven is also Christ-centred, for our Lord Jesus Christ, the incarnate Son, is the Second Person of the Blessed Trinity, and no one can go to the Father or reach the Father's house except through Him—His precious blood, saving merits, and sanctifying grace (cf. John 14: 6). It is again St Augustine who grasps the truth: 'Christ as God is the fatherland towards which we go, Christ as man is the way by which we go.'[30] St Augustine's spiritual father, St Ambrose, makes the same point even more succinctly: 'Life is being with Christ, because where Christ is, there is the Kingdom.'[31]

The New Heaven

What of the 'new heaven', which, according to the prophet and the apostle (cf. Isa. 65: 17; 66: 22; Rev. 21: 1), will be manifested on the last day when the dead are raised? According to Blessed Denys, following St Thomas and the Fathers before him, the whole bodily universe will be transfigured when God-made-man comes to conform our lowly bodies to His glorious body. Now 'heaven', in the sense of the 'whole region of the heavenly bodies' (stars and planets), is part of the bodily universe and will therefore, by the power of the risen Christ, be transfigured into a better state. 'For, when the bodies of the elect are glorified, all the celestial orbs, the planets and the stars, will be made new and adorned in a more than usual way.'[32] Denys goes on to argue that these exalted bodies, like all other material things, were created for man, for his use or delight and honour, and so 'they will be conformed to the state of man that the elect will have when the judgement takes place'.[33] The transfiguration of the material universe follows directly from the resurrection of the human body. St Paul pictures the cosmos in its present form 'groaning and travailing in pain', longing for that final 'revelation of the sons of God' and 'redemption of the body' which will at the same time be its own deliverance 'from the servitude of corruption' (cf. Rom. 8: 19–23). When the Apostle speaks of the 'fashion of this world passing away' (cf. 1 Cor. 7: 31), he means that the accidental form, not the substantial form, of the material universe will be changed for the better.[34] God has created nothing in vain, and so He does not, as it were, throw the visible world away. In any case, as St Thomas argues, if the body of man is to be redeemed, the bodily universe of which it is a part must also be renewed, for 'the part is not seen to be perfect without the whole'.[35]

The Nature of Heavenly Beatitude

Our painting comes from Villeneuve-lès-Avignon, the sister-town, or more exactly the daughterly suburb, of Avignon, the city of the popes. On All Saints Day 1331, one of the Avignon popes, Pope John XXII, speaking expressly as private theologian rather than supreme pontiff, made some unfortunate remarks to the effect that the blessed do not enjoy the intellectual vision of the Godhead until the last day, when they receive back their bodies in the resurrection.[36] The saints are 'under the altar' (cf. Rev. 6: 9), protected and consoled by the humanity of Christ, but on the last day they will be raised up on to the altar and enabled to behold the divinity.[37] Pope John's successor, the Cistercian Benedict XII, another resident of Avignon, set the record straight in the constitution *Benedictus Deus*, which remains the definitive statement of the papal Magisterium on the nature of heavenly beatitude. According to Catholic doctrine, as reaffirmed by Pope Benedict, all souls that at the moment of death are altogether free from the guilt of sin and the temporal punishment due to sin enter Heaven immediately, or at least immediately after the particular judgement.

[In Heaven they behold the divine essence] with an intuitive vision and even face to face, without the mediation of any creature by way of object of vision. The divine essence immediately manifests itself to them, plainly, clearly, and openly, and in this vision they enjoy the divine essence. Moreover, by this vision and enjoyment, the souls of those who have already died are truly blessed and have eternal life and rest.[38]

Beatitude in general

As a state, Heaven is supreme beatitude, the final and everlasting happiness of intellectual creatures, both angels and men. St Thomas defines beatitude in general as 'that perfect good which totally satisfies the appetite',[39] that which leaves nothing to be desired.[40] Now the object of the will, the rational appetite of man, is the universal good, just as the object of the intellect is universal truth. But the universal good is found only in God, for in creatures we find only participated goodness. Therefore, in God alone is the beatitude of man to be found.[41] This is the truth that Moses learnt from the mouth of God Himself, when He said, 'I will show thee all good' (Exod. 33: 19), as if to say, 'I will show thee myself, the supreme and sovereign, universal and infinite Good.'

All men ought to be interested in this discussion of happiness, for all men of necessity desire happiness. The trouble is they do not know where true happiness is to be found. Blessed Denys summarizes the arguments of St Thomas:

All desire happiness, because, even though happiness in its substance is unknown, its definition (*ratio*) is known, because all men understand happiness to be a certain most perfect state. But they do not all agree about where you find such a state, say, in bodily goods or spiritual, nor do they agree about when you can possess it, in this life or another.[42]

Like those whose god or supreme good, as the Apostle says, is 'their belly' (cf. Phil. 3: 19), the fallen sons of Adam can easily be diverted from the pursuit of true and final happiness.[43] And yet our very follies in the pursuit of happiness, and the miseries we bring upon ourselves by looking for it in the wrong place, testify—at least to those with the eyes of faith—that perfect happiness must be sought beyond and above all earthly pleasures and contentments. Our poor hearts can find peace only in God, by and for whom we were made.[44] In his conferences on the Apostles' Creed, St Thomas adds his own commentary on the famous words of St Augustine:

No one can in this life fulfil his desire, nor can any created thing satisfy man's yearning. God alone satisfies (*Deus enim solus satiat*) and infinitely surpasses man's desire, and therefore man is never at rest except in God. As St Augustine says: 'Thou hast made us for thyself, O Lord, and our hearts are restless till they rest in thee.' And since in the Fatherland the saints will possess God perfectly, it is evident that their desires will be satisfied, and that their glory will surpass their expectations.[45]

Supernatural Beatitude

By natural reason, without the benefit of supernatural revelation, the greatest of the Greek philosophers discovered that man's highest happiness lay in the contemplation of God. According to Aristotle's definition, happiness (*eudaimonía*) is the best operation (contemplation) of the best power within us (the intellect) directed towards the best of objects (God).[46] The happiness of those who thus dedicate themselves in this life to philosophical contemplation surpasses all the other satisfactions of men. But this natural fulfilment of the intellect, noble though it is, is not 'true and perfect beatitude', which can only be obtained in the life to come.[47] The contemplation that makes us completely happy, without interruption or fear of loss, is the face-to-face vision of God in Heaven. This 'Beatific Vision' is absolutely supernatural and surpasses immeasurably anything that man can know or reach by his unaided powers.[48] As St Thomas says: 'No created intellect can see the essence of God unless God by His grace unites Himself to the created intellect, as an object made intelligible to it.'[49] Heaven's fulfilment of our heart's desire exceeds all our natural powers of striving; it cannot be attained 'except by an endowment from God'.[50] We cannot know that we actually have such an immensely glorious final end except by Divine Revelation,[51] and we cannot attain it without divine grace.[52] None of us can get to the Fatherland unless the Father draws Him (cf. John 6: 44). Even had he not fallen, Adam could not have attained the Beatific Vision without grace, both actual and sanctifying.[53] Moreover, God was not bound to bestow a supernatural final end upon us; the vision of His beauty is His free and loving gift.[54] *Tout est grâce*, says St Thérèse;[55] yes, even Heaven, Heaven above all.

Seeing God

In the altarpiece, each according to his rank in the hierarchy of Heaven, the angels and the saints raise their eyes towards the Godhead. The painter shows by the depiction of bodily posture the doctrine concerning a spiritual act: the angels and saints are enjoying the Beatific Vision, the blissful sight of the Trinity. They contemplate, they *see* the Father, the Son, and the Holy Spirit, the Three Divine Persons in the One Essence, in all Their unutterable beauty. They see, and in seeing they are glorified. As St John says in his first epistle: 'We are now the sons of God, and it hath not yet appeared what we shall be. But we know that, when He shall appear, we shall be like to Him, because we shall *see* Him as He is' (1 John 3: 2). Now at last is King David's longing fulfilled, who prayed: 'O Lord God of hosts, show thy face, and we shall be saved' (Ps. 79: 20).[56]

The face-to-face vision of the divine essence cannot be an act of bodily sight, for it is enjoyed even now by angels, who are pure spirits, and by blessed souls separated from their bodies. Even when we are reunited with our bodies in the resurrection, the Beatific Vision will remain an act of intellectual vision, for God is spirit, not a body, and so, as St Thomas says, 'He cannot be seen by the sense or the imagination, but only by the intellect'.[57] However, our resurrected eyes will be able to see the glorified humanity of the Son and the scars ever glowing in His hands and feet and side.

Sight, not Faith

On earth, according to St Paul, 'we walk by faith, and not by sight' (cf. 2 Cor. 5: 7); faith is 'the substance of things to be hoped for, the evidence of things that appear not' (Heb. 11: 1). But if by God's mercy we reach our heavenly Fatherland, we shall live by sight, not by faith; the greatest of the 'things that appear not', the infinitely magnificent reality of the Three-Personed God, will be manifested clearly to us. Even in the natural order, you cannot always believe something to be so when you can see for yourself that it is so. Hence in Heaven faith gives way to vision, and hope is replaced by possession. As Denys says, here below 'we do not see Him as He is, that is, clearly or face to face, but through created forms, which infinitely fall short of a perfect or facial representation of the divine essence'.[58] By a simple metaphor, the

Apostle teaches the same doctrine: 'We see now through a glass in a dark manner, but then face to face' (1 Cor. 13: 12). As bride of Christ, the soul in Heaven will be enriched by three 'dowries': vision, which succeeds faith, possession, which succeeds hope, and fruition, the enjoyment of beatific love.[59]

Clarity and Immediacy

According to Pope Benedict XII, the Triune God manifests His divine essence to the blessed 'immediately, plainly, clearly, and openly'. In explaining this mystery, Blessed Denys quotes our Lord's words in the Farewell Discourse: '[H]e that loveth me, shall be loved of my Father; and I will love him, and will manifest myself to him' (John 14: 21). He then goes on to say:

> For now we see through a mirror in enigma (cf. 1 Cor. 13: 12), that is, through created forms or species in a certain obscurity, but then Christ will manifest Himself to holy and pious hearts, when we begin to see face to face, that is, clearly and immediately. [We shall not see God] through likenesses representing God obscurely and imperfectly, as all created forms and natures are, for these are infinitely overwhelmed by the divine perfection, and therefore represent Him enigmatically. [No, we shall see God] through the uncreated species, which is the First Truth or divine essence itself. It is utterly necessary for this to be immediately united to every created mind in place of an intelligible form, if the sublime God is to be contemplated, or gazed on, beatifically as He is.[60]

Here our ecstatic Carthusian can be forgiven the language of excess, for what he is describing cannot but dazzle our minds. Like every other revealed truth of our religion, it is not against reason, but it remains far beyond even faith-enlightened reason's capacity fully to grasp. Denys is repeating the doctrine of St Thomas, who says that in the Beatific Vision we do not see the face of God through any created likeness or species. When with our eyes we see a stone, the likeness of the stone, though not the stone itself, is in our eyes. When our mind grasps something outside itself, the thing known is somehow inside the mind, not materially, of course, but, to use the jargon, 'intentionally', in the form of an 'intention' or 'representation' or 'idea' or 'intelligible species'. These are all different names for the same process: we know, whether in sense-knowledge or intellectual knowledge, through the likenesses of things known. Now St Thomas argues that, for three reasons, such icons of the mind cannot represent the divine essence. First, you cannot see a higher created reality (say, the nature of an angel) as it is in itself through the likeness of some lower reality (say, the image of a bird). How much less, then, can we expect to see the Creator as He is in Himself through some created likeness. Secondly, God's essence is His being; He exists of His very nature, but no created likeness, indeed nothing created at all, exists of its very nature; therefore, no created likeness is up to the task of representing Him as He is in Himself. The third argument starts from the fact that every created idea is bounded and circumscribed: an idea of this or that perfection, of some particular aspect of wisdom or virtue or being. But God is boundless and uncircumscribable; not only can you not draw a line round His bodily form, because He doesn't have one, you can't confine Him metaphysically within the boundaries of genus or species. God contains within Himself, in an all-surpassing way, all the perfections we find among His creatures; the truth and goodness and beauty of all things visible and invisible are but a reflection of the truth and goodness and beauty that exist first of all, and most perfectly, in God. Therefore, no created idea, with its sharp contours and essential limits, can adequately represent God in His infinite and super-eminent perfection.[61]

No created species or idea can be the means by which we see the essence of the Trinity. And yet we know, from divine revelation, that we can see the divine essence in Heaven. Therefore, it must be, and indeed it is, by an *uncreated* species that we see God face-to-face, the species by which God sees Himself.

The uncreated species [says Blessed Denys] is none other than the very essence of God, which is the intelligible species of the divine intellect. For in God the known, the knower, and the knowable form, which is the intelligible species, are one and the same. Then we shall be truly like Him, as St John says, when the divine essence will be for us *what* is seen and *that by which* it is seen.[62]

Here Denys speaks with metaphysical sobriety, but in one of his prayers he expresses the same truth in the poetry of praise: 'We shall see thee, O Lord, thyself, for thine essence will be for us the species and the object.'[63]

If the Angelic and Ecstatic Doctors have lost you, don't worry: help is at hand in the person of a twentieth-century German Benedictine with a French-sounding name who lived most of his life in England and developed during his long years at Buckfast something of the allegedly Anglo-Saxon capacity for simplicity and concreteness of expression. Here, then, is Abbot Anscar Vonier's explanation of the high mysteries we have been considering:

In Beatific Vision, according to the profound doctrine of St Thomas, God Himself becomes the idea which is in the mind of the elect. All our cognitions are ideas, of more or less extent and clearness, that come to our mind through a hundred channels. We see clearly that the idea of a thing is not the thing itself; for the thing is outside me, whilst the idea is in my mind, and makes of my mind, from an unknowing mind, a knowing mind. Now, says our great master, in Beatific Vision there is no such idea of God, as distinct from God, to stand for God in my mind. God's very nature is the idea. In fact God has to be the idea, for nothing could ever do duty for God Himself in my mind. If I am to know Him as He is, He must be Himself the idea that makes my mind a knowing mind. We easily see how knowledge, in the words of the Schoolmen, is invariably based on the idea of the thing being in the mind, whilst the thing known has its existence outside the particular mind. I may have a constant thought of a person dear to me, a thought that is representative of many of the attractive qualities of that person; but I see all along that the person is outside me altogether . . . God alone is given by theologians what they call *illapsus*, the power of being personally within a created mind . . . The eternal hills rise higher and higher, and the thoughts of God on their summits are getting purer and purer; but they are mere thoughts of God, they are not yet God. They are mere ideas of God . . .

In Beatific Vision, God Himself is the idea, God Himself is in the mind; and here we have the radical difference between Beatific Vision and every other kind of divine knowledge, however sublime.[64]

No encounter with any human person in this life has the immediacy of the saints' vision of the Three Divine Persons. All human knowing and loving, even of a wife by her husband or of a mother by her child, is surpassed in intimacy by this seeing of God through His very essence.

Lumen gloriae

According to the teaching of the Council of Vienne, the souls of the blessed need a special supernatural illumination, the light of glory, to equip them for seeing the essence of God through the essence of God.[65] This is the light of which David speaks in the Psalm: 'In thy light we shall see light' (Ps. 35: 10).[66] We can only behold the infinite radiance of the Most Holy Trinity if our finite intellects are themselves irradiated by a supernatural quality infused into them by God.

Following the doctrine he finds in St Thomas,[67] Denys begins with the uncontroversial premise that there is no proportion between the created mind and that infinite species (the divine essence) through which it sees the infinite object (the divine essence).[68] From this he concludes: '[I]t is impossible for the divine essence to be united to the created mind as intelligible species, unless it is elevated to a certain Godlike existence through a light that is a likeness of the divine nature, which is called the light of glory.'[69] Before anything is transformed, you have to make sure it is properly disposed, that is, has the capacity to be transformed. For example, if you want a log to burn effectively on your fire, you must make sure it has been thoroughly dried out. Now the capacity or disposition that the soul needs for the Beatific Vision is not something it can acquire by itself, for the Beatific Vision entirely surpasses the natural powers of the soul. Therefore, the soul can only be disposed for the Beatific Vision, for seeing God through His essence, by receiving from Him a supernatural capacity, an infusion of spiritual light for the eyes of the mind: this the Tradition of the Church calls the 'light of glory'.

Once again it is Abbot Vonier who brings this heavenly doctrine a little closer to our earth-bound minds:

[L]umen gloriae, or the light of glory, technically, is not God seen face to face; it is the capability of the created mind to see God . . . The human mind, or even the angelic mind for that matter, is not only infinitely distant from, but is also absolutely incapable of, the vision of God. Therefore, God gives to the mind a new power, a new capacity; He spiritualizes it, so to speak, more completely, to the extent of making it spiritual or immaterial enough to see God, if God offers Himself to the mind as its Idea . . . The doctrine of the light of glory is the noblest and highest instance of that essentially Catholic conviction, that man does, in eternity, not what God through an arbitrary disposition makes him do, but what he has made himself capable of doing through the grace of God in mortal life.[70]

Totum sed non totaliter

In Heaven we see the Triune God face to face, immediately and clearly, and yet we do not comprehend Him: even in Heaven, He remains incomprehensible to us, the ever-greater God. This statement may seem strange, when we consider that Catholic theology calls the blessed comprehensores, 'comprehenders'. The puzzle is resolved when we remember that the Latin verb comprehendere has two meanings. First, it means 'to catch or take hold of' something, as a mother catches hold of her toddler as he tries to run away. In this sense, we do indeed comprehend God in the Beatific Vision: we at last possess the Beloved who hitherto has been the object of our hope and longing. Of this kind of comprehension the Bride speaks in the Song of Songs: 'I held Him, and I will not let Him go' (S. of S. 3: 4). The second meaning of comprehendere is 'to extend round or over, to enclose'. Taken in a spiritual sense, such comprehending would mean knowing something as much as it can be known. Now God is infinitely knowable, and so, applied to God, 'comprehension' would mean knowing God infinitely. But no created intellect, whether by nature or with supernatural assistance, can know God infinitely, perfectly inasmuch as He is knowable. Therefore, neither angels nor men, even when assisted by the *lumen gloriae*, can, in this sense, comprehend God.[71] As Denys says: 'No mind sees the divine essence as fully and as perfectly as it can be seen except the first, divine, and uncreated mind.'[72]

St Thomas says that in the Beatific Vision the angels and saints see God *totum sed non totaliter*, as a whole and yet not wholly, *infinitum sed non infinite*, as the infinite God He is, but not in the infinite way of which He alone is capable.[73] Blessed Denys explains this puzzling assertion by an example from sensory experience:

Someone standing by the shore of the ocean sees the substance of the ocean, in the sense of the water, but he cannot reach by sight the length, breadth, or depth of the ocean; he gazes on the ocean without being able to gauge it by sight . . . Similarly, the blessed in the fatherland see the essence of the Godhead (that is why they are said to be in a certain way 'comprehenders'), but they cannot penetrate its infinity, nor can they understand it as perfectly as it exists in its natural intelligibility . . .[74]

We have the hope of a stupendous intimacy with God, but the condition of its becoming a reality is our acceptance of the truth that He is God, Infinite self-subsistent Being, and that we are His creatures, finite, utterly dependent upon Him for our existence and nature and activity. Our glorification will be our comprehension in one way, by possession and attainment, of the One whom in another way, by confinement and containment, we can never comprehend. And there is no contradiction: the Bride, the Church celestial, reaches the Bridegroom ('I held Him, and I will not let Him go'), but He whom she reaches and gains beyond all loss is a Spouse of inexhaustible richness ('The King hath brought me into His storerooms' (S. of S. 1: 3).

Vision, Love, Joy

In Heaven the blessed see God, love God, and enjoy God. As expounded by St Thomas, beatitude consists formally in an act of the intellect, the vision of God, for even in Heaven we can only love what we know or see.[75] From the blessed vision flows blessed love, and from the love there comes unutterable joy. In the words with which St Augustine concludes *The City of God*: 'We shall rest, and we shall see; we shall see, and we shall love; we shall love, and we shall praise.'[76] Dante follows this doctrine in the *Divine Comedy*,[77] as does Blessed Denys in his many writings on the subject: 'In perceiving, we shall love; in loving, we shall enjoy; in enjoying we shall be truly blessed and in affection totally satisfied and contented.'[78] Our Lord Himself proposes the doctrine to us in St John's Gospel when He says: 'This is eternal life, that they *know* thee, the true God' (John 17: 3).[79] The essence of beatitude is to be found in face-to-face vision, an act of most perfect knowing; the love and the joy are its completion and adornment.[80]

Beatitude and the Physical Body

God wants the whole man, body as well as soul, to be happy with Him in Heaven. This plan will be fulfilled at the resurrection of the dead, when glory flows from the soul into the body.[81] In the glory of the resurrection, the body becomes 'spiritual' (cf. 1 Cor. 15: 44–5), not as if it were now turned into a spirit, but because at last it is fully subject to the spiritual soul.[82] Four 'dowries', new endowments, adorn the flesh: it shines with the beauty of the soul's own clarity, moves with the agility of thought, has the subtlety of a true servant of the soul, can never again suffer or be sundered from the soul. On that last day, when flesh and matter are caught up into incorruption, the good-seeking, God-centred yearnings of the whole cosmos will be fulfilled: '[T]he creation waits with eager longing for the revealing of the sons of God . . . We know that the whole creation has been groaning in travail together until now; and not only the creation, but we ourselves

who have the first fruits of the Spirit groan inwardly as we wait
for adoption as sons, the redemption of our bodies' (Rom. 8:
19–23). For Dom Marmion, thinking about this final flourishing of
our bodies ought to bring home to us the infinite magnitude of
the Father's love for us:

God loves us so much in His Son, Jesus, that He will not separate us
from Him. He wills us to be like to Him, that we may share His glory,
not only as to the soul but also as to the body . . . Well might the Apostle
say that God is rich in mercy, and loves us with an exceeding charity! It
is not enough for God to satisfy our souls with eternal happiness. It is
His will that our bodies, like that of His Son, should share in this endless
beatitude. He wills to adorn them with those glorious prerogatives of
immortality, agility, and spirituality with which the humanity of Jesus
was resplendent on coming forth from the tomb.[83]

It is a truth of the faith, defined by Pope Benedict XII, that fully
purified souls can and do enjoy the Beatific Vision before the resurrection of the last day.[84] At the same time, it is also evident that
the blessed, though glorified in their souls, are not yet glorified
as men, for a man is the possessor of the complete nature of
man, body and soul. Therefore, only with the resurrection is *man*
fully and finally made happy and glorious in conformity to God-
made-man. Dante, following St Augustine, even pictures the
souls of the blessed yearning for their bodies:

And when we put completeness on afresh,
All the more gracious shall our person be,
Reclothèd in the holy and glorious flesh . . .

The lustre which already swathes us round
Shall be outlustred by the flesh, which long
Day after day now moulders underground;

Nor shall that light have power to do us wrong
Since for all joys that shall delight us then
The body's organ will be rendered strong.

So swift they were, so keen to cry Amen,
As made me feel the yearning of those choirs
To welcome their dead bodies back again.[85]

Does the happiness of the blessed increase when they 'welcome their bodies back again'? St Thomas's final answer to this question is that, while the desire of the disembodied soul for an object is fully satisfied by seeing God face to face, it does not possess that object in every way it could wish, and so, when it regains its body in the resurrection, its happiness does not increase in intensity, but it does increase in extent: happiness pervades the body as well as the soul.[86]

Faithful as ever to St Thomas, Dom Vonier of Buckfast confronts us with the corporeality of the truly Catholic hope for blessedness: 'The resurrection of our bodies is the acid test of our orthodoxy; no man is truly Christian in his intellect unless he believes firmly that in the world to come mankind will be, not a multitude of ghosts, however glorious, but a race of distinct personalities, composed of body and soul as here on earth.'[87] The heavenly happiness for which we hope is divine, because it will be happiness in God and from God, but, on the last day, it will also be truly human, happiness for men as men, complete unities of matter and spirit. Why else did the Son of God assume the whole of our nature, body and soul, if not to redeem it as a whole?

Beatitude and the Mystical Body

Quarton's painting of Heaven is a painting of the heavenly Church, the Mystical Body in the state of glory. Now the consummation of the glory of the Mystical Body will take place on the day its members regain their physical bodies. Only then will all parts of the created order be transfigured; only then, as we have seen, will man be redeemed perfectly as *man*, as the unity of body and soul that God created him to be. Then, at last, says Dom Marmion, Christ's 'work as Chief and Head of the Church will be achieved, entirely consummated', and God will be 'all in all' (cf. 1 Cor. 15: 28). Marmion goes on to say:

St Paul, who puts the union of Christ and His Church in such strong relief, could not fail to tell us something of the final glory of the Mystical

Body of Jesus. He tells us (cf. 1 Cor. 15: 24–8) that on the day fixed by the divine decrees, when the Mystical Body will have arrived 'unto a perfect man, unto the measure of the age of the fullness of Christ' (cf. Eph. 4: 13), then will dawn the triumph which is to consecrate forever the union of the Church and of its Head. Associated until then so intimately with the life of Jesus, the Church now completed will be glorified with Him. The resurrection triumphs over death, the last enemy to be overcome; then the elect, being at last united under their Divine Head, Christ, He will present to His Father this society, no longer imperfect, nor militant in the midst of miseries, temptations, and struggles; no longer suffering the fire of expiation, but henceforth transfigured and glorious in all its members.[88]

Superbeata Trinitas

First there must be the form of Paradise, and in this Paradise must be the Holy Trinity, and there must be no difference between the Father and the Son, and the Holy Spirit must be in the form of a dove, and our Lady in front, as will seem best to Maître Enguerrand. The Holy Trinity will put the crown on the head of our Lady.[89]

The centre of the painting is a likeness of the centre of Paradise, the heart of the Empyrean: the Blessed Trinity, or, as Denys likes to say, the *Superbeata Trinitas*. We can imagine him, on some visit to Villeneuve for which we have no evidence whatever, gazing at our altarpiece and singing one of his hymns: 'O fount of perfect happiness, spring of utter loveliness, Superblessed Trinity, Pure goodness in immensity.'[90] The artist depicts an operation of the Triune God: the Father, the Son, and the Holy Spirit are crowning the Blessed Virgin Mary as Queen of Heaven. All three persons are engaged, for, like all the works of God, this action is common to the whole Trinity.[91] God the Father is on the right, God the Son is on *His* right and therefore on our left as we look.

Just as he was commissioned to do, Enguerrand has given the

First and Second Persons of the Blessed Trinity the same features,[^92]
since the Son is the natural and essential Image of the Father,
'the brightness of His glory and the figure of His substance' (Heb.
1: 3). Enguerrand makes the Father resemble the Son in the Son's
glorified humanity, and so Father, like Son, is shown as a young
man. God the Son, in His risen body, as all His members will be
when He makes their bodies like His own on the last day, is for
ever in the full bloom of youth, a young man of thirty. God the
Father has no body, and so His youthfulness, as it appears in the
painting, must have a spiritual sense: it expresses the coeternity of
the Divine Persons. The Father is as young as the Son, while the
Son is as old as the Father, for in the coeternal Trinity there is
no 'before or after'.[^93] In youth a man is in full possession of His
physical strength and vitality. Similarly, the eternity of the Triune
God is, in Boethius' definition, the 'total, simultaneous and perfect possession of unending life'.[^94]

The Holy Spirit appears in the form of a Dove, as He was sent
and seen at our Lord's baptism in the Jordan (cf. Luke 3: 22).
According to St Bede, the dove is a symbol of three things. First,
in relation to the Holy Spirit Himself, the likeness of a simple bird
indicates the simplicity of the Holy Spirit's nature, the divine
nature that is common to Him and the Father and the Son. Secondly, in relation to Christ, upon whom it descends, the dove
signifies the gentleness and mildness of the 'herald and minister
of heavenly mercy'. Thirdly, in relation to Christians, the dove
shows that, by the grace of the Holy Spirit, they must be 'simple
and clean of heart'.[^95] Of all created persons none was more filled
with the grace of the Holy Spirit than our Lady, even from her
conception, and so she more than any other is 'dove-like': gentle
and mild, simple and clean of heart. Indeed, 'dove' is a name that
several of the Church's Doctors give her: for example, St John
Damascene calls her 'the most sacred dove, simple and innocent
of soul, consecrated to the Divine Spirit'.[^96]

The wings of the Dove connect the mouths of the Father and
the Son, because they breathe out ('spirate') the Holy Spirit as

their immanent breath of love. Abbot Marmion speaks thus of
this breathing out within the Godhead:

The Father and the Son are drawn to one another by a common and
mutual love: the Father is of such absolute perfection and beauty, the
Son is so perfect an image of His Father! Thus each gives Himself to the
other, and this mutual love which springs from the Father and the Son
as from one source is, in God, a subsisting love, a Person distinct from
the other two persons, namely, the Holy Ghost.[97]

Our painter makes it seem as if the Spirit-Dove, linking the lips of
the Father and the Son, were a kiss exchanged between Them.
This reflects the interpretation St Bernard gives to the opening
verse of the Canticle, 'Let him kiss me with the kiss of his mouth'
(S. of S. 1: 1).[98] In a hymn in honour of 'the super-praiseworthy
God', Denys takes up Bernard's idea:

> The bond of the Father and the Son
> Thou art, embrace most sweet,
> The Love, the Kiss of both,
> Supremely flawless peace of the Two,
> Infinite communion,
> Full diffusion.[99]

Enguerrand's Spirit-Dove breathed forth by the Father and the
Son, proceeding from Them as Their mutual love, expresses in
image what the Council of Florence just a few years before had
reaffirmed as dogma, thus achieving, albeit briefly, the reunion of
the Byzantine Church with the See of Peter. 'The Holy Spirit is
eternally from the Father and the Son', proclaims the Council,
'He has His nature and subsistence at once from the Father and
the Son; He proceeds eternally from Both as from one principle
and through one spiration.'[100] Our artist includes a detail hinting
at the pleasure that he and indeed the whole Latin Church took in
the reunion of the Greeks: in the streets of Rome he shows a
Carthusian monk stretching out his arms to embrace a priest of
the Greek Church.[101]

Seeing God, One and Triune

The angels and saints see God, the Blessed Trinity, in His inner-most life. The primary object of the Beatific Vision is the Godhead, the Trinity in Unity and the Unity in Trinity. 'They see clearly God Himself,' says the Council of Florence, 'One and Triune, as He is'.[102]

Seeing the One Divine Essence

The blessed look upon the One Divine Essence, and see all its perfections, or rather, as Dom Marmion says, they 'see that all His perfections are but one infinite perfection, which is the Divin-ity'.[103] They perceive in their real identity those divine attributes which we on earth find it hard to harmonize: they see the tender-ness of the divine mercy in the rigour of the divine justice, un-created wisdom in uncreated love and all of its free decrees. On the far left of our painting, just above the souls of the unbaptized infants in Limbo, Moses is receiving the revelation of God in the burning bush, from which he learnt God's most proper name, *Qui est*, 'He Who Is' (cf. Exod. 3: 14), that name which, as Denys says, paraphrasing Aquinas and Damascene, signifies the divine being 'as a kind of immense ocean, includ[ing] in itself all perfec-tion and nobility'.[104] Upon this immense ocean, this all-perfect and most noble sea, the blessed gaze with untiring joy.

From his namesake, the Areopagite, our Denys learnt that the lovable is not only the good but also the lovely. It is therefore the contemplation of the divine beauty to which the Ecstatic Doctor time and again returns when he is discussing the Beatific Vision. Consider these lines from the preface to his treatise *De venustate mundi et pulchritudine Dei*, 'On the Charm of the World and the Beauty of God':

As the great and divine Denys [the Areopagite] asserts in the fourth chapter of *The Divine Names*, the beautiful is what is desirable, lovable, and delectable to all. In short, just as every well-disposed created mind principally and finally loves or seeks to enjoy the First and Supreme

Good, so it longs exceedingly for, or aspires ultimately to see, the First and Supreme Beautiful. Hence the truth of Christian wisdom teaches that the sublime God, who is pure, immense, supremely causal, and fontal goodness, and uncircumscribed, ideal, separate, self-subsistent, and in all respects superperfect beauty, is the fount, object, and cause of all beatitude, for He alone is fit truly and fully to satisfy and quieten the capacity, eagerness, and motion of both His intellect and His power to will.[105]

Seeing the Three Divine Persons

In God, person and essence are really identical, even though the persons are really distinct from each other.[106] Therefore, in beholding the divine essence, the blessed also look upon the Three Divine Persons, the 'adorable Trinity'. As Pope Pius XII says:

In that vision, in an utterly ineffable way, the mind's eyes, enhanced by light from above, will be allowed to contemplate the Father, the Son, and the Divine Spirit, to be close for all eternity to the processions of the Divine Persons, and to enjoy a beatitude very similar to that with which the Most Holy and Undivided Trinity is blessed.[107]

The blessed see the supreme good of the Godhead poured out in the generation of the Son by the Father, and in the spiration of the Holy Spirit by the Father and the Son. They contemplate 'God the Father in God the Son, God the Son in God the Father, and the Holy Spirit in both'.[108]

Sharing the Happiness of the Trinity

We are not made blessed by beholding the Trinity as a merely external object. As our Lady in the painting is enfolded within the copes of the Father and the Son, and sheltered beneath the wings of the Holy Spirit, so she and, at a lower degree, the rest of the blessed are taken up into the blessedness of the Blessed Trinity. We seem to hear the words of the Master of the talents: *Intra in gaudium Domini tui*, 'Enter thou into the joy of thy Lord' (Matt. 25: 21). 'Share, O Mother, share, my brethren and members, in the bliss I enjoy eternally with the Father in the unity and peace

of the Holy Spirit.'[109] Thus speaks the Son, and thus, according to
Abbot Marmion, speaks the Father:

It is as if [God] said: 'I have loved thee so much that I have not willed to
give thee a natural bliss: I have willed to bring thee into my own house,
to adopt thee as my child, that thou mayest partake of my beatitude. It is
my will that thou shouldst live of my very life, that my beatitude should
become thine . . . Here below, I have given thee my Son; become mortal
by His humanity, He delivered Himself up to merit for thee the grace of
being and remaining my child. He has given Himself to thee in the
Eucharist under the veil of faith; now it is I in glory who give myself to
thee to make thee share in my life and to be thy endless beatitude.'[110]

The Father, the Son, and the Holy Spirit, says Denys, contemplate each other 'with super-clarity', and thus they love and enjoy
each other by a 'super-blessed' fruition.[111] Into that enjoyment,
man, by God's infinite generosity and gratuitous decree,[112] is
privileged to enter: 'Thus, when man attains the Beatific Vision
and full enjoyment of the Godhead, his life will be supernaturally
and ineffably like the life and happiness and glory of God.'[113]

Enfolded in the Trinity: Grace and Glory

Despite the surprises God has in store for us when He lifts us
up into the intimacy of His Trinitarian life, there is a wonderful
continuity between all His works, in creation, redemption, and
consummation. Grace perfects nature, and glory is likewise the
perfection of grace. Sanctifying grace, says St Thomas, is 'nothing
other than a beginning of glory in us'.[114] What we are already by
the grace of our Baptism and the other Sacraments—adopted
children of the heavenly Father, living members of Christ, and
temples of the Holy Spirit, partakers of the divine nature, sharers
in the life of the Blessed Trinity—will be brought to its consummation in Heaven. When at last we reach the Fatherland,
our friendship with the Blessed Trinity will be taken out of the
obscurity of faith and plunged into the radiance of face-to-face
sight: we shall know and love the Three Divine Persons as They
know and love Themselves: the Father in the Son, and the Son in

the Father, and the Holy Spirit in Them both. In us the Father will beget the Son, and the Father and the Son will breathe forth the Holy Spirit. Our glorification—first in soul, and on the last day in body—will be the fulfilment of the divinization that began on the day of our Baptism when we were incorporated into Christ and made sharers by grace in His divine sonship as 'sons in the Son'. As the Apostle John says: 'Dearly beloved, we are now the sons of God; and it hath not yet appeared what we shall be. We know that when He shall appear, we shall be like to Him because we shall see Him as He is' (1 John 3: 2). Seeing the natural Son in His glory with the Father and the Holy Spirit will be the perfection of our adoptive sonship. This truth was one of the chief principles of the spiritual doctrine of Dom Marmion, who expresses it most beautifully:

We received the germ [of beatitude] at Baptism. But this germ needs to grow, to develop, to be secured against briars and stones; by penance we have put away from it all that could destroy or diminish its growth; we have maintained it by the Sacrament of life, and by the practice of the virtues. This divine life communicated to us by Christ now remains hidden in us: *Vita vestra abscondita est cum Christo in Deo* ['Your life is hidden with Christ in God'] (Col. 3: 3), but in Heaven it is revealed, its splendour appears, its beauty is manifested.[115]

On the eve of His Passion, Our Lord prays: 'Father, I will that where I am, they also whom thou hast given me may be with me; that they may see my glory which thou hast given me' (John 17: 4, 24). Christ is Head; we His members. Now where the Head is, the members should also be. But the Head is 'in the glory of God the Father' (Phil. 2: 11): in His divinity, essential glory belongs equally to Him with the Father and the Holy Spirit, while His humanity is endowed with a participated glory through the Resurrection and the Ascension.[116] Into this glory our divine Head and Saviour wishes us to enter in the Beatific Vision, the Communion of Saints, the Resurrection of the Body, and the Life Everlasting. 'There', says Dom Marmion, 'is the final term of our predestination, the consummation of our adoption, the supreme condition of our perfection, the plenitude of our life.'[117] 'And whom He predestinated, them He also called. And whom He called, them He also justified. And whom He justified, them He also glorified' (Rom. 8: 30). This, then, is the Trinitarian itinerary of the elect: predestined by the Father's good pleasure, called by the promptings of the Holy Spirit, justified by the grace of the incarnate Son in the Sacraments of His Church, glorified in the sight of the Triune God in Heaven.

Seeing Other Things in God

The secondary object of the Beatific Vision consists in things distinct from God Himself, things that the blessed see in God as their origin.[118] First among these is the human nature of the eternal Son.[119] In his commentary on the First Epistle to the Thessalonians, St Thomas points out that St Paul greets the Church 'in God the Father and in the Lord Jesus Christ' (cf. 1 Thess. 1: 1), 'that is, in faith in the Trinity, and in the divinity and humanity of Christ, for in the knowledge of these our beatitude will be found'.[120] In their intellectual vision of our Lord's Godhead, the saints and angels are enabled also to contemplate the perfections of His manhood: its hypostatic union to His divine person, its infinite fullness of grace, the fire of charity blazing out of His Sacred Heart. They perceive the infinite value of the human acts of the divine person, and of His great gift of the Holy Sacrifice of the Mass. They look upon the loveliness of Blessed Mary Ever-Virgin, His Mother, whom He has given to them to be their Mother; they see the matchless plenitude in her soul of grace, the virtues, and the Gifts of the Holy Spirit.

How much of other things we know in seeing God face to face depends on the degree of perfection in our vision of God, which in turn depends on the measure of our merits.[121] The general knowledge of the blessed is wonderful. They are familiar with 'the choirs and orders of all the angels, the natures and properties of the celestial spheres and all the stars and planets and elements, the forms of mixed things, the natures and powers of all animals, of all precious stones and herbs, and numberless other things unknown to us in this life'.[122] As for individual things, we can say for sure that each of the blessed knows whatever is relevant to him as the person, or before the resurrection the soul of the person, he is.[123] The saints are perfectly happy. Now to be perfectly happy means to possess everything one rightly wants. But everyone rightly wants to know what concerns himself. Therefore, by seeing God, the saints know 'in the Word' everything that concerns themselves.[124] They know each other and all they have known and loved on earth. They know whether their loved ones are still on earth or in Purgatory. Parents know the needs of the children they have left behind, and are eager to help them reach the Fatherland. Moreover, since the blessed, in seeing God, know all that pertains to them, they are also aware of the prayers we address to them.[125] In this way, says St Thomas, they become 'God's co-operators, "than which", as Denys [the Areopagite], says, "nothing is more divine"'.[126]

The vision of God is the primary and essential part of the life of the blessed in Heaven, but it is not the whole of their life. As Jacques Maritain once said 'À propos de l'Église du ciel': 'Just as the Word Incarnate on earth had a life at once divine and human, so the blessed in Heaven, through the Beatific Vision, have entered into the divine life itself, and into the divine joy itself, but, apart from the vision, though penetrated by its radiance, they also live there a glorious and transfigured human life.'[127]

Heaven is not only divine and angelic but also human, a home from home for men. Even before the general resurrection, says Maritain, there are 'human interactions', 'an immense and perpetual conversation', between the separated souls in glory.[128] Later, after their resurrection, the children of Adam will enjoy fellowship with each other as complete persons. Each of the blessed has his own utterly pure and noble thoughts and, in the expansive liberty of those who will only what God wills, is free to share them with others as he chooses. There are none so free as those who in seeing God clearly share in God's own knowledge of Himself, and who in loving God blissfully share in His freedom. 'They love God from the moment they see Him by the necessity of nature without their free will having to be exercised in that respect. But as regards all the rest, the whole universe of creatures, they continue to exercise their free will; they act freely without being able to sin.'[129]

And the saints, in the perfected humanity of Heaven, do not forget the dear earth and the friends they have left behind.

The blessed intervene in this world that they have left in order to dwell where the glorious bodies of Jesus and Mary are (outside and beyond the whole universe and its space). They are still present here by their love and action, and by the inspirations they give us and by the effects of their prayers. And they keep in Heaven the love they had on earth for those they loved; their love is transfigured, not abolished; and if the love was the love of charity, then that love was already on earth what it is now in Heaven. Remember the words of St Thérèse of Lisieux: 'I want to spend my Heaven doing good on earth.' Those words are very profound—they express what one might call the humanism of the saints in Heaven.[130]

Hierarchia beatorum

The Villeneuve altarpiece shows us not only the One who will make us happy in Heaven but also those with whom we hope to share that happiness: the blessed, the angels and saints. Nearest of all to the Blessed Trinity and the Mother of God are the resplendent ranks of the Cherubim and Seraphim, the highest of the orders of the angels,[131] and on either side of them the two archangels, Gabriel and Michael. St Gabriel holds a scroll inscribed with the words he addressed to our Lady at the Annunciation, *Ave gratia plena.* St John the Baptist, the greatest of the prophets, is also close to the throne of God, and behind him, dressed in Jewish costume, are Abraham, Isaac, and Jacob. Abraham, our father, faces us, as if he were looking out on his innumerable offspring.[132] St Peter and St Paul and the beardless Beloved Disciple are at their stations with the other Apostles. St Stephen and St Lawrence are prominent among the martyrs. The confessors include several of monastic interest: St Gregory the Great with his papal tiara, St Jerome in cardinal's kit, and St Hugh of Grenoble wearing a mitre and a Carthusian habit. As requested, the artist supplies representatives of 'all the estates of the world'.[133] There are men but also women, including St Mary Magdalene and the kinsfolk of our Lady, the two Marys (of Clopas and Salome). There are popes and a couple of kings, but also poor men in the smocks of the peasantry. Lowest of all in the hierarchy of the blessed are the souls of the Holy Innocents, their hands lifted up in a gesture that suggests not only prayer and praise but also childlike wonder.

Up Among the Angels

Angels and the blessed souls of men gaze on God together, in a single company. This is fitting, because our Lord says that the saints will be 'like the angels of God' (cf. Matt. 22: 30). The human blessed will not be angel-like in nature, for the separated souls of men are not angels and are destined on the last day to be reunited with their bodies in the resurrection. However, they will resemble the angels in their final end, for, as Denys the Carthusian says, in line with St Thomas, 'all the elect, according to the quality of their merits, are to be assumed into the orders of the angels'.[134] With the angels we hope to be 'immediately joined to God, enjoying a pleasure that is not carnal but spiritual and godlike, a total absorption in God'.[135]

Inequality of Reward

There is a hierarchy of nine ascending orders among the angels, and there is likewise a hierarchy among the saints. Far above all the rest of the blessed, both angels and human souls, is the Queen of Heaven, the Ever-Virgin Mother of God, 'more honourable than the Cherubim and beyond compare more glorious than the Seraphim'.[136] Then, after the angels, comes St John the Baptist, followed by the apostles, martyrs, confessors, and virgins. The Church observes this hierarchical order in the way she arranges the feasts of the saints in the Missal and Breviary and invokes them by name in the litany. The liturgical rule, like the iconographic convention followed by our artist, expresses a dogmatic truth defined by the Council of Florence, namely, that the degree of perfection in the saints' enjoyment of the Beatific Vision is in proportion to their merits.[137] In the words of our Lord in the Gospel: '[The Son of Man] will render to everyone according to his works' (Matt. 16: 27); and: 'In my Father's house are many mansions' (John 14: 2). As star differs from star in their shining in the firmament, so do the blessed in the brilliance of the Empyrean (cf. 1 Cor. 15: 41). The blessed see God to different degrees of perfection and are therefore more or less blessed and glorious.[138]

St Thomas argues as follows for the inequality of heavenly reward. Greater love in this life means greater desire. But desire in your heart makes your heart more open to receive the object of your desire: the more you want to see a football match, the more you enjoy it when you get to the stadium. Therefore, the more the love of God is in our hearts when we die, the more we shall be able to receive of what God has to give us, namely, the light of glory, which makes our souls Godlike and properly disposed for looking upon Him in all His beauty. 'Hence he who possesses the more charity will see God the more perfectly, and will be the more beatified.'[139] When she was a little girl, St Thérèse learnt this point of doctrine with the help of her sister Pauline:

Once I was surprised by the fact that the good Lord does not give an equal glory in Heaven to all the elect, and I was afraid that they were not all happy. Then Pauline told me to go and get 'Papa's big glass', to put it next to my tiny thimble, and to fill both with water. Then she asked me which was fuller. I told her that they were as full as each other, and that it was impossible to put in more water than they could contain. My dearest Mother helped me understand that in Heaven God will grant His elect as much glory as they can take, the last having nothing to envy in the first.[140]

At first the inequalities of Heaven seem shocking, but to a child-like mind such as Thérèse's they manifest the beautiful unity-in-diversity of the Father's house. As Dom Vonier says: 'Equality of state and happiness in Heaven is a thing repugnant to the Catholic mind; and to acknowledge that star differs from star in Heaven is the delight of the humble and generous heart.'[141] Although some of the blessed love God *more* perfectly than others, all love Him perfectly to some degree, all adhere to His will with serenity and delight, and so all, in peace with each other, accept the degree of blessedness they enjoy. As the blessed tell Dante in the *Paradiso*: 'In His will is our peace.'[142] The saints sing 'Alleluia' with voices of varying pitch, but they blend, without dissonance, in the one Catholic symphony of the Empyrean.

Blessed Dom Marmion draws an important moral and ascetical conclusion from the dogmatic premise:

We shall enjoy God according to the same measure of grace to which we have attained at the moment of our going out of the world. Do not let us lose sight of this truth: the degree of our eternal beatitude is, and will remain, fixed forever by the degree of charity we have attained, by the grace of Christ, when God shall call us to Himself. Each moment of our life is then infinitely precious, for it suffices to advance us a degree in the love of God, to raise us higher in the beatitude of eternal life. And let us not say that one degree more or less is a small matter. How can anything be a small matter when it concerns God, and the endless life and beatitude of which He is the source? If, according to the parable spoken by our Lord in person, we have received five talents, it was not that we might bury them, but that we might make them bear increase (cf. Matt. 25: 14–30). And if God measures the reward according to the efforts we have made to live by His grace and increase it in us, do not think it matters little what kind of a harvest we bring to our Father in Heaven.

Jesus Himself has told us that His heavenly Father is glorified in seeing us abound, by His grace, in fruits of holiness, which will be fruits of beatitude in Heaven. *In hoc clarificatus est Pater meus ut fructum plurimum afferatis* (John 15: 8) . . . Can it be that our love for Jesus Christ is so weak that we account it a small thing to be a more or less resplendent member of His Mystical Body in the heavenly Jerusalem?[143]

The Communion of Saints

In our painting, the angels and saints join their hands in intercession. They gaze upon the Triune God, and they praise Him, but, in seeing Him, they also hear us whom they have left behind on earth, and those of their brethren who in Purgatory are preparing to join them. The blessed in the Church Triumphant, the holy souls in the Church Suffering, and the wayfarers in the Church Militant are all members of the one Mystical Body of Christ, making up one Christendom, united together and with God by the Holy Spirit's great gift of charity. 'Neither death nor life . . . shall be able to separate us from the love of God which is in Christ Jesus our Lord' (Rom. 8: 38f), that is, neither death nor life can be a barrier to stop the flow of love among the living members of Christ's Body, the Church. Therefore, between those members, in all their states in Heaven and in Purgatory and on earth, by the working of the Holy Spirit, there is a most wonderful exchange of spiritual goods. St Thomas speaks of this supernatural give-and-take when explaining the phrase 'Communion of Saints' in his conferences on the Apostles' Creed:

Just as in a natural body the operation of one member contributes to the good of the whole body, so is it in the spiritual body, namely, the Church. And since all the faithful are one body, the good of one member is communicated to another; as the Apostle says, 'Everyone members, one of another' (Rom. 12: 5). Therefore, among the things to be believed that the Apostles have handed down is that there is a communion of goods in the Church, and this is what is called the 'Communion of Saints.'[144]

In dependence on the Head of the Body, which is Christ, and on the Soul of the Body, which is the Holy Spirit, there is a flow of supernatural life between the members wherever they may be. The saints in Heaven pray for the pilgrims still on earth and for the poor souls in Purgatory, while we wayfarers pray for each other and for the holy souls, and, as Catholic piety has always held, the holy souls pray for us. Death cannot disrupt this mystical communications system in the Kingdom of God. As Pope Leo XIII said so beautifully in his encyclical on the Holy Eucharist, *Mirae caritatis*:

[T]he Communion of Saints is . . . nothing but the mutual communication of help, expiation, prayers, and benefits among the faithful, who, whether they have already attained to the heavenly fatherland, or are given up to the expiatory fire, or are still pilgrims on earth, all come together in that one city of which Christ is Head, and of which the form is charity.[145]

Conclusion: Up to Heaven, Down to Earth

The monk longs for the life of Heaven, and yet somehow, even on earth in the frailty of his mortal flesh, he already lives the life of Heaven. By his vows he declares his preference for the sovereign and indestructible Good, in which we find our eternal rest in the world to come, to the passing goods of this present world. According to St Gregory the Great, the contemplative life, to which the monk is especially dedicated, 'begins here, so as to be perfected in the heavenly fatherland, because the fire of love, which begins to burn here, blazes with a yet greater love when we see Him whom we love'.[146] Even while walking in the darkness of faith, the monk gives himself up to contemplation, that is, to looking upon Christ with the eyes of faith formed by love, and thereby he has a foretaste of the contemplation that is the Beatific Vision.[147] The perpetual flow of praise in the *opus Dei* is an anticipation of the ceaseless worship of God by the angels and saints in

Heaven. The daily celebration of the Sacrament of the Altar, in which the divine King of Heaven is really present, offered, and received, joins earth to Empyrean, unites wayfarers to those who have already arrived, and pours out from Paradise all the fruits of Christ's Passion. The monastery is indeed a kind of Jerusalem, and with all his heart the monk prays for its peace.

Any Christian, but especially any monk, who hoped only for something in this life, however noble (say, the perfection of some art, such as bee-keeping or book-writing), would be of all men the most to be pitied. Therefore, meditation on man's final super-natural end must be a permanent part of the spiritual life of us all.

I would say to you again [says Dom Marmion], with St Paul: 'Seek the things that are above, where Christ is sitting at the right hand of God. Mind the things that are above, not the things that are upon the earth', such as fortune, honours, pleasures; 'for you are dead' to all these pass-ing things; 'your life', your true life, that of grace, 'is hidden with Christ in God'. But 'when Christ', your Head, 'shall appear', triumphant at the last day, 'you also shall appear with Him in glory', that glory which you will share with Him because you are His members.[148]

By the mysterious workings of God's providence, those men in the history of the Church who have attended most to the things above have done most to transform things here below. During the early Middle Ages, it was the sons of St Benedict, seeking God alone, who achieved more than anyone else for their fellow human beings, laying the foundations of European civilization by the cultivation not only of minds and hearts but also of the soil itself. Take the case of the twelfth century. As Christopher Daw-son points out, to the men who lived in it, such as the monk Bernard of Morlaix in his famous poem *De contemptu mundi*, it seemed like the worst of times, the moment of Antichrist and the last hour of history, but to us who look back, the century of St Anselm and St Bernard seems like the best of times, a golden age, a true renaissance.[149] This paradox of history does not signify a contradiction in thought. The man who purely and humbly loves God and neighbour, and keeps the eyes of his mind set upon the consummation of his charity in Heaven, sees and uses the goods of earth in their proper order; he does not corrupt the goods by abuse, and so he spares the earth from disfigurement. The prospect of Beatitude fills his life with the beatitudes. By contrast, the man without Christian hope for the happiness of Heaven produces Hell on earth—for his neighbour, certainly, but often for himself. As Pope Leo XIII said in his encyclical *Exeunte iam anno*:

[M]ost men, oblivious of where they come from or where they are called to go, fix all their thoughts and cares upon the feeble and fleeting goods of this life; contrary to nature and right reason, they willingly give themselves up to those things of which reason tells man he should be the master. It is a short step from the desire of luxury to the striving after the means to obtain it. Hence arises the unbridled greed for money, which blinds those whom it has mastered, and in the fulfilment of its passion hurries them madly along, often without regard for justice or injustice, and not seldom in contempt for the poverty of their neighbour. Thus many who live in the lap of luxury call themselves brethren of the multitude whom in their heart of hearts they proudly despise . . .[150]

St Thomas likewise argues that hope for the eternal rewards of Heaven inclines political rulers towards justice, while the pursuit of the short-term goods of earth leads princes into tyranny.[151] Thus, to take two examples from the twentieth century, the determination of Pol Pot and Stalin to construct a this-worldly Communist paradise caused the hells-on-earth of the Killing Fields and the Gulag Archipelago.[152]

In the light of these considerations, we can see why the very *being* of the monk as a witness to the 'one thing necessary', even apart from any good works he may do for his neighbour, brings manifold blessings to human society. At the same time it should also become clear why the culture of the West was deeply and almost fatally wounded by the destruction of the institutes of consecrated life during the Protestant revolt of the sixteenth century.

And yet, and yet: the contemplative life in itself remains superior to the active, and God must be sought for His own sake, not just for the temporal benefits that may flow incidentally from the quest of the Fatherland. Monks or seculars, clerics or laymen, we therefore fix our sights on Heaven and pray to our ascended Lord in the words of Dom Marmion:

Draw us after you, great and almighty Victor: *Trahe nos post te*. Grant us to ascend into the heavens with you . . . Grant that we may detach ourselves from all earthly things, which are only passing, so that we may seek the joys that are true and abiding. Grant that in heart we may be where we know that your sacred Humanity has corporally ascended: *Ut illuc sequamur corde, ubi eum corpore ascendisse credimus* ['That we may follow thither in heart where we believe He has ascended in body'].[153]

OPENING HEAVEN'S GATES

The Cross, the Empty Tomb, and the Altars of the Church

Beneath the vault of Heaven stands the Cross of Christ, and at the foot of the Cross kneels a Carthusian monk. The top of the Cross's upright beam touches the lower folds of our Lady's robe of blue, as if to indicate that the immaculate beauty is the fruit of the Tree of Life. Underneath the kneeling Carthusian is the Empty Tomb, the tomb the Son of God Himself emptied when He rose from the dead in the flesh, thereby, as the Easter Sunday Collect says, conquering death and opening up for us an entrance to eternity (*aeternitatis aditum*). On the lower left side of the painting, just below the souls of the Holy Innocents, is an altar at which Pope St Gregory the Great is offering Holy Mass. The artist shows the moment of the consecration, when, according to tradition, the suffering Christ appeared to Gregory, confirming for him and for others the truth of His Real Presence and Eucharistic Sacrifice. The Gothic gable of the church in which the Mass of St Gregory is being celebrated also points to Heaven; indeed it brushes the edge of the cloud on which the Holy Innocents kneel.

The Cross, the Empty Tomb, and the Altars of the Church, each in its own way, open up Heaven's gates. The Cross and the Empty Tomb belong to the so-called 'objective redemption', the Lord's saving work already accomplished, what St Thomas calls the 'universal cause' of man's salvation.[1] The Altars of the Church, by contrast, belong to the 'subjective redemption', each man's assimilation of what Christ has done for Him, something

that still remains to be accomplished. It is by faith and charity |
and the Sacraments of the Church,[2] and above all through the
Sacrament of the Altar, that we make our own what our divine
Saviour has done for us, that the redemption takes hold of our
souls and transforms them.

The chapter that follows is an invitation to come close to the
praying Carthusian by the Cross, and to contemplate with him
the Lord Jesus in the mysteries by which He grants us entry to the
celestial city: dying on the Tree and rising from the Tomb, both
in His proper appearance in glorified flesh at the Father's right
hand and, under the appearance of bread, in that same flesh in the
Holy Sacrament of the Altar.

Arbor alta: Branching into Heaven

Flecte ramos, arbor alta . . .
Bend thy boughs, O tree most lofty!
Thy relaxing sinews bend;
For awhile the ancient rigour
That thy birth bestowed, suspend;
And the King of heavenly beauty
On thy bosom gently tend![3]

In his hymn, St Venantius Fortunatus calls the Cross an *arbor alta*,
a 'tree most lofty'. In Quarton's painting, it seems small in comparison with the Most Holy Trinity in Heaven, and yet, when we
look more closely, we notice it is higher than anything on earth,
even the towers of Rome and the pinnacle of the Temple in
Jerusalem. It is a lofty tree, says Denys, because of its effects.[4] Its
branches stretch into Paradise, for through the Cross the sons of
Adam are given access to the Empyrean. But it is first of all high
and exalted because of the high and exalted Person who is nailed
to it: 'the King of heavenly beauty', the divine person of the
Father's eternal Son. Moreover, according to the Schoolmen,
Christ the King retains a heavenly beauty, not only in His change-

less divinity, but also in His crucified humanity, even in the terrible hour of His agony and abandonment by the Father. In the first part of his chapter, I should like to consider these three ways in which the crucified Christ takes us up into Heaven: by His divine person, in the perfections of His human nature, and in the effects of His human suffering and death.

Crucified King of Heavenly Beauty

Our painter positions the Trinity in Heaven immediately above the Cross on Calvary as if to remind us that the nail-pierced Man of Sorrows is One of the Trinity, the only-begotten Son of the Father. It is in His human nature that He suffers and dies, but He who suffers and dies therein is a divine person, the King of Heaven, *supernus rex*, come down to earth. Now this descent of God the Son is not a change of place, as if, when He went to dwell in the Virgin's womb, He deserted the bosom of the Father. God is incapable of change, and so, in assuming what He was not, He remains what He always was.[5] In coming to be where He has not been before, in the manhood on earth, the Word does not cease to be where He is in His Godhead—in the Empyrean and indeed everywhere. As Pope St Leo the Great says in his *Tome*: 'The Son of God . . . enters this feeble world, descending from His heavenly seat, yet not withdrawing from the Father's glory.'[6] St Thomas Aquinas expresses the same truth in his hymn, *Verbum supernum prodiens*: 'The Word supernal going forth,| Yet leaving not the Father's side.'[7] He descends, from Heaven, says Denys, 'not by losing His divinity, nor by changing place, nor by bringing a body with Him from Heaven, but by assuming a human body and appearing visibly in the world'.[8]

The Son as God does not shift His place or indeed undergo any kind of change when He takes human nature upon Him in the Blessed Virgin's womb. One and the same divine person, the eternal Word, becomes capable of suffering and death in humanity while remaining impassible and immortal in divinity.[9] He

whom we see nailed to the Cross is the 'Lord of glory' (cf. 1 Cor.
2: 8), whose Godhead remains unchanged and unharmed by the
weight of pain that, in manhood, He carries for our salvation.[10]
While pouring out, as God, His splendour on the angels in the
Jerusalem above, the Word as man does combat with the un-
speakable darkness of the demons in the Jerusalem below (cf.
Luke 22: 53).

These dazzling paradoxes of Catholic doctrine concerning the
incarnate Word light up the height, breadth, and depth of His
redemptive work. Since it is a divine person to whom they
belong, Christ's human sufferings and actions have an infinite
saving power. This drama is nothing less than the Passion of God,
One of the Holy Trinity, and so it has a boundless capacity to
make atonement for human sin.

His Passion [says Blessed Denys] was ineffably meritorious, most fruit-
ful, and most efficacious for the redemption of the whole human race.
Indeed, the merit was somehow infinite, since the human nature that
thus suffered was not only most holy, most worthy, and most pleasing
to the eternal Father, above all created things, but also immediately and
hypostatically united to the eternal Word and divine nature, and thus
possessed an efficacy and suitability for redeeming and meriting that
was in a certain way infinite.[11]

Because He is a divine person, 'He that cometh from above' (cf.
John 3: 31), Christ in His human nature has an ability to reach out
to other men that no human person, someone just 'from below',
could ever have. 'He that cometh from Heaven is above all' (John
3: 31), and therefore, from that eminence, He is able to draw all to
Himself as Head (cf. John 12: 32). When a human person is conceived, he contracts Original Sin through his descent from Adam
and therefore joins the long line of men estranged from God and
one another. But when the divine person of the Word is conceived of the Virgin, by the Holy Spirit and without male seed, in
what St Leo calls a 'new order',[12] He breaks the cycle of alienating
birth and sundering death.[13] The scattering of God's children is at
an end; the gathering up has begun (cf. John 11: 52). As man, but

because He is God, Christ is the Head of the Church;[14] indeed, in a certain way He is the Head of all men.[15] As the Word, through and for whom all things were made (cf. John 1: 3; Col. 1: 16–17), He is able in His humanity to 'recapitulate' all things in Heaven and on earth (cf. Eph. 1: 10), that is, to unite all men and the whole cosmos under Himself as Head. According to the Angelic Doctor, Head and members are together 'like one mystical person (*quasi una persona mystica*)', one man, one Christ. Therefore, what the divine Saviour suffers and does on the Cross has a most wonderful power to touch mankind. His satisfaction for sin belongs to us,[16] as does His merit, for through the Sacraments the merit of Christ causes in us the grace that moves us to perform meritorious works.[17]

Jesus died on the Cross for the truth of His divine Sonship, His heavenly and eternal origin in the bosom of the Father. When our Lord says, 'My Father worketh until now, and I work' (cf. John 5: 17), St John the Evangelist adds the comment: 'Hereupon therefore the Jews sought the more to kill Him, because He did not only break the sabbath, but also said God was His Father, making Himself equal to God' (v. 18). In meditating on our Lord's testimonies to His own divinity, Columba Marmion notices that, in the presence of the high priest, He 'speaks only in order to declare that He is the Son of God: "Thou hast said that I am" (cf. Matt. 26: 64)'. The holy Abbot goes on to say: 'This profession is the most solemn that has ever been made to the divinity of Christ: Jesus, King of Martyrs, dies for having confessed His divinity, and all the martyrs were to give their lives for the same cause'.[18] Thus what the protomartyr Stephen once did, all the witnesses to Christ by blood through the ages have repeated. They look up to Heaven, whence the divine person descended, and whither, in His crucified and resurrected humanity, He ascended. 'Behold, I see the heavens opened, and the Son of Man standing on the right hand of God' (Acts 7: 55). The divine person of the Son in His glorified manhood stands ready to welcome His witnesses into the glory of the Father's house.

Heaven in the Mind of the Crucified Christ

Even on earth and as man, Our Lord is in a certain way in Heaven. He is on the road, and yet He has also reached journey's end (*simul viator et comprehensor*).[19] According to St Thomas, Blessed Denys the Carthusian,[20] and the other Schoolmen, from the first moment of the Incarnation, the Son of God enjoys the Beatific Vision at the summit of His human intellect. As God, He has uncreated knowledge, divine omniscience indeed, and as man, He has created knowledge, of which the Beatific Vision is the highest kind. In the womb of the Virgin, in the manger in Bethlehem, and on the Cross on Calvary, Christ, at the fine point of His human mind, gazes clearly and immediately upon the face of the Father, and thus He knows Himself as the eternal Son living and reigning with the Father in the unity of the Holy Spirit. According to the theologians, the beatitude and glory in the higher powers of our Lord's soul should from the beginning have overflowed into the lower powers and into the body, but, by the wise decree of the Trinity, this overflow was delayed till after the Resurrection.[21] Had the glory in the mind of Jesus always been visible in His body, as once it was on the mountain of Transfiguration, men would have been dazzled into discipleship. But that was not the way of revelation and salvation decreed by the Father. The Son of God comes, as man and Messiah, without outward display: 'Behold, thy king cometh to thee, meek and sitting upon an ass' (Matt. 21: 5; cf. Isa. 62: 11; Zech. 9: 9). Before the Resurrection, apart from a few minutes on Mount Tabor, the glory of Christ shines only within.

Nowhere in the New Testament is Jesus said to know God by faith, and yet He knows the Father most perfectly, evidently in a higher way than by faith: 'Neither doth anyone know the Father but the Son' (Matt. 11: 27). Now the only knowledge of God that a human mind can enjoy above and beyond faith is the Beatific Vision, for even the mystic's knowledge is of the order of faith, a faith formed by charity and perfected by the Gifts of the Holy Spirit.[22] Therefore, God-made-man, already on earth, enjoys the

Beatific Vision. The Gospels, especially St John's, testify to this blessed knowledge in our Lord's human mind on several occasions: 'Not that anyone has seen the Father except Him who is from God; He has seen the Father' (John 6: 46).[23] Here is the unique ground of the teaching of Christ, the secret of that authority which astonished the synagogue: 'He was teaching them as one having power, and not as the scribes' (Mark 1: 22). Jesus does not speak of his Father in Heaven as One known by hearsay or through a glass darkly. As God, He knows the Father with complete comprehension, but even as man He sees Him face to face. As the Catechism says: 'Because He "has seen the Father", Jesus Christ is the only One who knows Him and can reveal Him.'[24] In those words, promulgated in the pontificate of John Paul II, we see the restatement of what previous popes have proclaimed. For example, in 1918 Pope Benedict XV condemned the Modernist denial of the Saviour's enjoyment on earth of 'the knowledge that the blessed . . . possess'.[25] Pope Pius XII set forth the doctrine, in words of great beauty, in the encyclical Mystici corporis: '[T]hrough the Beatific Vision, which He enjoyed from the very moment He was received into the womb of the Mother of God, He has all the members of His Mystical Body continually and perpetually present to Him, and embraces them with His salvific love.'[26]

St Thomas presents several arguments for Christ's Beatific Vision. The first looks towards the final cause, the purpose for which our Lord became man and died on the Cross. The incarnate Word, so the argument runs, brings us to enjoy the Beatific Vision in Heaven (cf. Heb. 2: 10). Now the cause must always be better than the thing caused. 'Therefore, that knowledge of God which consists in the vision of God had to belong to Christ as man in a most excellent way.'[27] The second argument is a reply to an objection according to which Christ does not need to share in the divine light in His human soul, because He has the whole fullness of the Godhead dwelling in Him bodily (cf. Col. 2: 9). To this argument, which comes close to the heresy of Apollinaris, who thought that the Logos, being Logos, needed no human intellect, Thomas replies that in Christ the distinction of the two natures remains alongside the unity of person. As distinct from His divine nature, His human nature does not, of itself, possess the light of the Godhead. It must therefore be perfected 'by a light participated from the divine nature, so that it can enjoy beatific knowledge, by which God is seen by essence'.[28] Thus, far from being a doctrine that would confuse the two natures, the Beatific Vision of Christ presupposes and confirms their distinction. Christ as God has the essential light of the Godhead by which to see the Father, but, as man and as the Saviour of men, He also needs a participated light in His manhood for the vision of the Father's face.

In addition to His supernatural human knowledge, beatific and infused, Christ as man on earth also had that natural human knowledge which every man has, the kind we acquire through the experience of our senses and the abstracting of ideas. It was in this experimental knowledge that, as St Luke says, 'Jesus increased in wisdom' (cf. Luke 2: 52).[29] However, in the human mind of Christ, underlying the ordinary way of experiencing and understanding the world, are deeper levels of knowing, by which, as the Catechism says, the eternal Son made man has 'intimate and immediate knowledge . . . of His Father' and 'divine penetration . . . into the secret thoughts of human hearts'.[30]

The Schoolmen teach us that, even in the depths of His agony in the Garden or in His dereliction on Golgotha, our Lord continues to gaze upon the face of His Father in Heaven. In one respect, the soul of Jesus is entirely plunged into the unimaginable pain of the Father's absence, and yet, seen from another angle, it continues to rest in the peace of the Father's presence.[31] Adhering closely to the explanations of St Thomas, Pope John Paul II presents the same doctrine. Here is what he said in one of his catechetical addresses in 1986:

Dominant in His mind Jesus has the clear vision of God and the certainty of His union with the Father. But in the sphere bordering the senses, and therefore more subject to the impressions, emotions, and influences of the internal and external experiences of pain, Jesus' human soul is reduced to a wasteland, and He no longer feels the 'presence' of the Father, but He undergoes the tragic experience of the most complete desolation . . . In the sphere of feelings and affection this sense of the absence and abandonment by God was the most acute pain for the soul of Jesus, who drew His strength and joy from union with the Father. This pain rendered more intense all the other sufferings. That lack of interior consolation was His greatest agony.[32]

In other words, while storms rage on its lower slopes, the summit of our Lord's human mind bathes in the radiance streaming from the face of the Father.

In a document of higher authority, his encyclical on the third millennium of Christianity, the Holy Father again reaffirms Christ's enjoyment of the Beatific Vision as well as the paradoxical union in Him of grief and bliss.

Jesus' cry on the Cross ['My God, my God, why hast thou forsaken me?'] . . . is not the cry of anguish of a man without hope, but the prayer of the Son who offers His life to the Father in love, for the salvation of all. At the very moment when He identifies with our sin, 'abandoned' by the Father, He 'abandons' Himself into the hands of the Father. His eyes remain fixed on the Father. Precisely because of the knowledge and experience of the Father that He alone has, even at this moment of darkness He sees clearly the gravity of sin and suffers because of it. He alone, who sees the Father and rejoices fully in Him, can understand completely what it means to resist the Father's love by sin. More than an experience of physical pain, His Passion is an agonizing suffering of the soul. Theological tradition has not failed to ask how Jesus could possibly experience at one and the same time His profound unity with the Father, by its very nature a source of joy and happiness, and an agony that goes all the way to His final cry of abandonment. The simultaneous presence of these two seemingly irreconcilable aspects is rooted in the fathomless depths of the hypostatic union.[33]

'He alone, who sees the Father and rejoices fully in Him, can understand completely what it means to resist the Father's love by sin.' This statement does indeed plunge us into 'fathomless depths'. The Pope seems to be saying that, not despite but some-how because of our Lord's blissful seeing of the Father, He experiences 'an agonizing suffering of the soul' in reaction to sin. In contemplating the Godhead, the human intellect of Christ also views all reality, past, present, and future, including the thoughts of every member of the race of which He is Saviour and judge.[34] He therefore sees all the acts by which the sons of Adam have turned away from God and offended His infinite goodness.[35] While rejoicing as man to share in the happiness that belongs to Him as God with the Father and the Holy Spirit, He is also sorrowful as man because of the misery that the children of Adam bring upon themselves by their sin. Moreover, by His beatific knowledge His human mind is able to know every single human being who has ever existed or will ever be, and with the charity that burns in His human heart, He loves every single human being and offers His Sacrifice for them. This is the teaching of the Catechism, which here invokes the authority of the Apostle Paul and Pope Pius XII:

Jesus knew and loved us each and all during His life, His agony, and His Passion, and gave Himself up for each one of us: 'The Son of God . . . loved me and gave Himself for me' (Gal. 2: 20). He has loved us all with a human heart. For this reason, the Sacred Heart of Jesus, pierced by our sins and for our salvation, 'is quite rightly considered the chief sign and symbol of that . . . love with which the divine Redeemer continually loves the eternal Father and all human beings' without exception.[36]

The last words in that quotation come from Pope Pius XII's encyclical on the Sacred Heart, *Haurietis aquas*. In a footnote, the Catechism also refers to the already quoted paragraph in *Mystici corporis* in which the Pope tells us that, through His enjoyment of the Beatific Vision, Christ on earth always has the members of His Mystical Body present to His mind.

Christ's self-oblation on the Cross is an act at once priestly and spousal: He offers Himself to the glory of the Father as priest, but He also offers Himself for the good of the Church as Bridegroom.

'Husbands, love your wives, as Christ also loved the Church, and delivered Himself up for it . . . that He might present her to Himself a glorious Church, not having spot or wrinkle or any such thing, but that she should be holy and without blemish' (Eph. 5: 27). Now, if He is to love His Bride in all her members, He must also somehow know both her and them, the Bride in the members and the members in the Bride. But, by natural means, no human mind can have such extensive knowledge, spanning all times and places. The Son as man must therefore have supreme supernatural knowledge, the kind we call beatific. By this blissful contemplation, He sees the Godhead, His own divine person and that of the Father in the unity of the Holy Spirit, and, in seeing the Godhead, He also sees His Mystical Body and Bride and all the members in every age that compose her.

The doctrine of Christ's beatific knowledge, especially in its relation to the Passion, may seem technical and abstract, but, as Pope John Paul points out, it has been readily grasped by the simplest and least educated of the saints.

In the presence of this mystery, we are greatly helped not only by theological investigation but also by the patrimony that is the theology lived by the saints. The saints offer us precious evidences enabling us to understand more easily the intuition of faith, thanks to the special enlightenment some of them received from the Holy Spirit, or even through their personal experience of those terrible states of trial which the mystical tradition describes as the 'dark night'. Very often the saints underwent something akin to Jesus' experience on the Cross in a wonderful blending of bliss and pain. In the *Dialogue of Divine Providence*, God the Father shows Catherine of Siena how joy and suffering can be present together in holy souls: 'Thus the soul is blissful and afflicted: afflicted on account of the sins of its neighbour, blissful on account of the union and the affection of charity which it has inwardly received. These souls imitate the immaculate Lamb, my Only-begotten Son, who on the Cross was both joyful and afflicted'. Similarly, St Thérèse of Lisieux lived out her torment in communion with the suffering of Jesus, 'experiencing' in herself the paradox of Jesus' own bliss and anguish: 'In the Garden of Olives our Lord was blessed with all the joys of the Trinity, yet His dying was no less harsh. It is a mystery, but I assure you that, on the basis of what I myself am feeling, I can understand something of it.' What an illuminating testimony! Moreover, the narrative of the Evangelists confirms and supports this insight in the Church into Christ's consciousness, when it teaches us that, even in the depths of His pain, He died imploring forgiveness for His executioners (cf. Luke 23: 34), while at the same time professing His ultimate self-surrender, as Son, to the Father: 'Father, into your hands I commend my spirit' (Luke 23: 46).[37]

In the midst of pains of body and mind, the one who loves Christ, and who offers up his sufferings in union with Christ for the glory of the Father and the good of the Church, can attain, beyond all feeling, an objective peace, a foretaste of the Sabbath rest of Paradise. Such is the beatitude (with a lower-case 'b') that is a promise and beginning of Beatitude (with a capital 'b'). 'Blessed are they that suffer persecution for justice' sake, for theirs is the Kingdom of Heaven' (Matt. 5: 10).

'The Beatitudes', says the Catechism, 'depict the countenance of Jesus Christ and portray His charity . . . they are the paradoxical promises that sustain hope in the midst of tribulations; they proclaim the blessings and rewards already secured, however, dimly, for Christ's disciples; they have begun in the lives of the Virgin Mary and the saints.'[38]

The Cross and the Opening of Heaven's Gates

According to St Thomas, Christ in His Passion saves us in four ways: by merit, satisfaction, sacrifice, and redemption.[39] Now the final goal of each of these four modes of salvation is the same: the glorification of God and the attainment by human beings of their happiness with Him in Heaven. By suffering in loving obedience to the Father, the Head of all men merits for His members the reward of everlasting life.[40] He makes satisfaction for the sin by which we offend the God in whom alone we can be fully and finally happy.[41] He offers sacrifice, that great work of religion, by which, as St Augustine says, 'we cling to God in holy fellowship' and attain that end 'by which, in all truth, we can be blessed'.[42] Finally, He redeems us *from* enslavement to the devil and *for* the liberty of the children of God in glory.[43] In all these ways, the crucified God-man removes the obstacle blocking entry into Heaven: human sin, both the sin of nature we contract through descent from Adam and the personal sins we commit by the free exercise of our will.

The closure of the gate is the obstacle preventing men from entering. But it is on account of sin that men were prevented from entering the Kingdom of Heaven, since, according to Isaiah, 'It shall be called the holy way, and the unclean shall not pass over it' (Isa. 35: 8). Now there is a twofold sin hindering men from entering the Kingdom of Heaven. The first is common to the whole of human nature, for it is the sin of the First Parent. By this sin access to the Kingdom of Heaven is blocked off for man. Hence we read in Gen. 3: 24 that after the sin of the First Man, God 'placed . . . cherubim and a flaming sword, turning every way, to keep the way of the tree of life'. The other sin is the special sin of each person committed by the proper act of each man. Now by Christ's Passion we have been delivered not only from the common sin of the whole human race, as to both guilt and the liability to punishment, when He Himself paid the price for us, but also from the personal sins of individuals, who share in His Passion by faith and charity and the Sacraments of faith. Therefore, the gate of the Kingdom of Heaven is opened for us through Christ's Passion. This is what the Apostle says: 'Christ being come a high priest of the good things to come . . . by His own blood entered once into the Holy of Holies, having obtained eternal redemption' (Heb. 9: 11–12).[44]

'The gate of the Kingdom of Heaven is opened for us through Christ's Passion.' Those words of Thomas Aquinas sum up the message that Enguerrand Quarton strove by his painting to convey. Only through the Cross, by the Precious Blood and saving merits of the Crucified Christ, can we join the angels and saints in the blessed vision of the Trinity. The way to the sweet and blessed country is the road of the Rood.

Post transitum maris rubri:
Passing over into Paradise

> At the Lamb's high feast we sing
> Praise to our victorious King.
> The Red Sea crossing now is past (*Post transitum maris rubri*),
> And robed in white we rest at last.[45]

In the contract for the altarpiece, the painter was instructed to place the Empty Tomb of our Lord just below the Cross and the kneeling Carthusian. One of the angels of the Resurrection was supposed to be standing nearby, saying: *Surrexit, non est hic, ecce locus ubi posuerunt eum*, 'He is risen, He is not here, behold the place where they laid Him' (Mark 16: 6).[46] The Tomb is empty, because the body once laid there lifeless is not there any more and is no longer lifeless. This is the faith the Church confesses in the Roman Canon on Easter Sunday, the Son of God has risen from the dead *secundum carnem*, 'in the flesh'. The body He assumed from the Virgin's pure blood, the body in which He suffered and died, has been reunited to His soul and enriched with glorious new properties. The body of Easter Sunday is the same as the body of Good Friday, in both essence and number. It is full and complete with everything that belongs to a true human body, but its condition has changed in a most wonderful way.

On the day of His Resurrection [says Abbot Marmion], Christ Jesus left in the tomb the linen cloths, which are the symbols of our infirmities, of our weaknesses, of our imperfections; He comes forth triumphant from the sepulchre; His liberty is entire, He is animated with intense, perfect life with which all the fibres of His being vibrate. In Him, all that is mortal is absorbed by Life.[47]

The risen body of Jesus is so perfectly subject to His soul that soul and body can never again be sundered in death or undergo any kind of suffering. 'Death shall no more have dominion over Him' (cf. Rom. 6: 9).[48] The glorious body can pass through any material barrier, whether it be the seal on the tomb or the bolted doors of the Upper Room (cf. John 20: 19, 26).[49] It obeys the soul with sublime ease and can thus travel at the speed of thought; that is how the risen Christ suddenly comes to be with His disciples and just as rapidly takes His leave (cf. John 20: 19, 26).[50] The risen body of Jesus is also most beautiful and full of brightness, though, when He meets the disciples during the forty days of Easter, He hides the radiance, lest they doubt the reality and solidity of His flesh.

In His great conquest of corruption, the incarnate Word acts as Head of the Mystical Body, sharing with His members what He Himself has achieved: we draw upon His glory in and through the Church. In the words of Pope St Gregory:

He promised us the Resurrection that He showed in Himself, because the members strive after the glory of their Head. Our Redeemer, there-fore, took upon Him death, lest we should be afraid to die. He mani-fested the Resurrection, so that we might be confident about rising again. That is why He did not want to be dead for longer than three days, lest, if the Resurrection were delayed in Him, we should utterly despair of it . . . When, therefore, He rose again on the third day, He showed what is to follow in His Body, the Church.[51]

According to St Gregory, and indeed many other Fathers and Doctors of the Church, the social character of the resurrection of the dead was manifested already on the first Easter Sunday. When our Lord rose from the grave, He did not come forth alone. St Matthew in his Gospel tells us that, at the Saviour's death on Good Friday afternoon, 'the graves were opened, and many bodies of the saints that had slept arose, and coming out of the tombs after His resurrection, came into the holy city, and appeared to many' (Matt 27: 52–3). St Gregory comments: 'At that time He died alone, but by no means did He rise alone.'[52] Accord-ing to Denys the Carthusian, after our Lord's descent into the Limbo of the Fathers, He not only took the souls of the Patriarchs and Prophets into Heaven, He also reunited the souls of many of them to their bodies, giving them a share in His own risen glory.

The purpose of this anticipated resurrection was, says Denys, to bear witness to the truth that 'Jesus was the Messiah, and had truly risen, and harrowed Hell'.[53] The Fathers and Doctors give us no certain knowledge of who exactly was raised with Christ from the dead. Denys mentions Adam and Eve, the patriarchs Abraham, Isaac, and Jacob, and King David, whose sepulchre, says St Peter, 'is with us to this present day' (Acts 2: 29). Notice, Denys points out, that the Apostle says 'sepulchre', not 'body and bones'.[54]

The Patristic and medieval interpretation of the 'bodies of the saints' in Matt. 27: 52 provides us with an argument of fittingness for our Lady's Assumption. If the remote forefathers of Christ are deemed worthy of an anticipated resurrection of the body, how much more so is the Virgin Mother from whom the eternal Word took His human body. The traditional exegesis of this mysterious episode also explains why the Byzantine Church calls the icon of Christ's Descent into Hell the Resurrection icon. We see our Lord there delivering Adam and Eve from the pit of darkness, so that with Him, even in their flesh, they might exult in the Paradise of light. As we look at our icon of Heaven, the Villeneuve altarpiece, we should recall that, though all are *portrayed* in visible bodily form, only some of the blessed—the Mother of God and the greatest of her ancestors—dwell in Heaven in glorified bodies. The rest of the saints must wait till the last day before receiving back their bodies in the resurrection.

Aditus aeternitatis: The Empty Tomb and the Opened Gates of Heaven

In the Collect of Easter Sunday, the Church tells us that our Lord's Resurrection opens up an entry into eternity (*aeternitatis aditus*). Again, in the *Te Deum*, she sings: 'When thou hadst overcome the sharpness of death, thou didst open the Kingdom of Heaven to all believers.' Now we have seen that the opening up of Paradise is an effect of Christ's Passion. How, then, do these two Heaven-opening mysteries, the Passion and the Resurrection, differ from each other? In what distinct ways do they unblock the road to the Fatherland?

First, the Passion and Resurrection differ in the way they cause eternal life. By suffering in obedience to the Father and charity for us, our Lord is the meritorious cause of eternal life for both our souls and our bodies: He earns heavenly glory for us.[55] His rising from the tomb is an instrumental and exemplary cause, the means and model of the resurrection of our souls and bodies.[56] In this world, in the Sacrament of Baptism, Christ delivers our souls from the spiritual death of sin by infusing His justifying grace, which is the beginning of heavenly glory in us: He 'rose again for our justification' (cf. Rom. 4: 25). In the world to come, on the last day of human history, He will resurrect our bodies. His own glorified body will then be the instrument through which He as God, with the Father and the Holy Spirit, raises up the dead, but it will also be the model for our glorification: 'He will re-shape our lowly bodies on the model of His glorious body' (Phil. 3: 21).[57]

The second way in which the Passion and Resurrection differ in relation to the attainment of Heaven concerns the Sacrifice of Christ. On Good Friday, the incarnate Son, in consummate docility to the Holy Spirit, offered His Father the sacrifice that, in principle, opened up the heavenly house of the Father to men. On Easter Sunday, the Father accepted the sacrifice, 'giving,' as Pope John Paul says, 'in return for this total self-giving by His Son, who "became obedient unto death" (cf. Phil. 2: 8), His own fatherly gift, that is, the granting of new immortal life in the Resurrection'.[58] Thereafter, the doors of the Father's house stand perpetually open.

The third contrast between Passion and Resurrection is in relation to the divinity of Christ, which we hope to contemplate in Heaven. In suffering and dying, our Lord confesses that He is true God and Son of God. Now, in rising again, He confirms this same most glorious truth. As St Thomas teaches, referring to Psalm 29 and the Gloss:

The Psalmist asks: 'What profit is there in my blood?' In other words, [what profit is there] in the shedding of my blood, 'whilst I go down to corruption' (cf. Ps. 29: 10), as if descending through certain degrees of evil? The answer of the Gloss [the medieval commentary on Scripture] is: 'No profit at all, for if I do not immediately rise again, and if my body is corrupted, I shall proclaim nothing to anyone; I shall be of no use whatever.'[59]

A merely 'spiritual' resurrection is no resurrection at all, and of no use to anyone for anything. Were the risen Christ no more than a soul separated from His body, He would be a dead man,[60] not a living man, and therefore indistinguishable from John Brown and all those other mere men whose poor bodies lie a-mouldering in the grave. His claim to be the only-begotten Son of the Father would be, as Scottish law has it, 'not proven'.[61] The prayer on the Cross, 'Father, into thy hands I commend my spirit' (cf. Luke 23: 46), would have received no response from Heaven. 'Resurrection' means the rising again of what has fallen, that is, of the body in death. Now God the Father did not abandon the human soul of His Son in Sheol, nor did He suffer the body of His Holy One to see corruption (cf. Acts 2: 27); He thereby endorsed all the claims of Jesus concerning His divine person. God the Son, from the first moment of the Incarnation to His last breath on the Cross, glorified the Father with every fibre of His human soul and body, and then, in the Resurrection, the Father glorified Him by reuniting His soul to His body (cf. John 17: 4–5). Moreover, the Resurrection reveals not only the divine person of the Son, by which He is distinct from the Father, but also the divine nature, in which He is one and the same with the Father, for, as St Thomas says, 'by the power of the divinity united to it, the body took up again the soul it had laid down, and the soul took up again the body it had left. This is what is said of Christ in 2 Corinthians: "[A]lthough He was crucified through weakness, yet He liveth by the power of God" (13: 4).'[62]

Victricis carnis gloriam: The Ascension of the Head, the Hope of the Body

> O King triumphant in the fray,
> Conqueror of the world's false prince,
> To the Father's gaze displaying
> The glory of victorious flesh (*Victricis carnis gloriam*).[63]

When our Lord rises bodily from the tomb, He promises the glory that will beautify our own bodies on the last day, but when He ascends bodily into Heaven, He prepares the very place—the Empyrean, the mansions and homeland of the Father—in which our glorified bodies are to dwell.[64] Here is the high ground of Christian hope, expressed so well by St Ambrose in his Ascensiontide hymn just quoted: our complete humanity, including the body, has pride of place in Heaven, in the person of the Son at the Father's right hand. Or, as another Christian hymn-writer put it: *Regnat Deus Dei caro*, 'God, the flesh of God, hath reigned'.[65] The human body, which hedonists adore and Manichees despise, has not only a noble origin, through its creation by the Word, but also a magnificent destiny, through its assumption by the same Word and His victory in it over death and corruption.

The ascended Christ, the Head of the Mystical Body, 'lives to make intercession' for His members (cf. Heb. 7: 25), so that where He is, they too may be. Now, according to some of the Church's theologians, especially those of the Benedictine tradition, our Lord does not make intercession by offering petitions in words. No, says St Gregory the Great, 'His prayer is His continual presentation, in the sight of God the eternal Father, of the humanity that He assumed for our salvation.'[66] St Bede teaches the same doctrine, as does Blessed Columba Marmion twelve centuries later:

He is there before His Father unceasingly presenting to Him His Sacrifice, recalled by the marks of His wounds which He has willed to retain . . . He is the beloved Son in whom the Father is well pleased; how can He fail to be heard, after having manifested by His Sacrifice such love to His Father *Exauditus est pro sua reverentia* ['He was heard for His reverence'] (Heb. 5: 7).[67]

Thus the glorified body of the Son of God, still bearing the marks of the nails and lance, is both a plea and a pledge for mankind's entry into Paradise.

Denys the Carthusian accepts the monastic Doctors' positive arguments about the objective intercessory power of our Lord's glorified humanity, but he is reluctant to follow those theologians who proceed to a negative conclusion about the divine Mediator's use of words:

Since Christ desires our salvation, and on that account presents to the Father His side and His wounds, so that the Father may have mercy on us, why should He not make that will explicit by praying for us with His voice? And since He longs for our salvation more than does any of the blessed, why should He not pray vocally in the way in which the Virgin Mary and the other saints do?[68]

The glorified Christ lives to make intercession for us not only by presenting His crucified and resurrected humanity to the Father, but also by uttering vocal prayers that express the desires of His Sacred Heart.

Fons vivus, ignis, caritas: The Heavenly Flame

In our painting, we see Heaven bidding welcome to earth. No sword-wielding angel guards the entrance of this Paradise. Thanks to the death and resurrection of Christ, the gates of the celestial city stand permanently open. The gesture of blessing used by the Father and the Son, when they crown our Lady, looks like an invitation. The Father and the Son seem almost to be beckoning us to follow where our Blessed Mother has gone before, for she, as Blessed Denys says, quoting the words of a hymn, is the *Felix caeli porta*, that is, 'the way and means of entering the Kingdom'.[69] But how do we respond to the invitation? What gives the prayers of the Virgin their force? The answer is in the painting. We rise up to Heaven on the wings of the Dove; it is the *fons vivus*, the living fount, whose waters flow through the Virgin's prayers. Only in the Holy Spirit, by His grace and seven-fold Gifts and the virtues He pours into our faculties, can we reach the place that the glorified Christ has prepared for us in the house and heart of the Father.[70] In the words of St Thomas, the Holy Spirit is *amor in caelestia rapiens*,[71] the Love that bears us away into Heaven.

By the invisible mission of the Holy Spirit, by the grace of the virtues and Gifts He pours out in the Sacraments of the Church, we take hold of the Heaven-opening achievement of the Son in His visible mission. No one ends up in the heavenly kingdom of charity without some participation in that uncreated charity which is the Holy Spirit, the 'person-love', as the Holy Father calls Him,[72] to whom all the Trinity's works of love outside the Godhead are appropriated. As Abbot Marmion explains with his wonted lucidity:

What is [the Holy Ghost] in the Holy Trinity? He is the ultimate term of the divine operations, of the life of God in Himself; He closes, so to speak, the cycle of the intimate divine life: it is His personal property to proceed from both the Father and the Son by way of love. This is why all that is a work of achievement, of perfection, all that is a work of love, of union and consequently of holiness—for our holiness is measured by our degree of union with God—is attributed to the Holy Ghost. Is it because He sanctifies more than the Father and the Son? No, the work of our sanctification is common to the Three Divine Persons; but, once again, as the work of sanctification in the soul is a work of perfecting, of achievement and union, it is attributed to the Holy Ghost because in this way we more easily remember what are His personal properties so as to honour and adore Him in that which distinguishes Him from the Father and the Son.[73]

The Holy Spirit is the Spirit of the Father and the Son, the Spirit of God and the Spirit of Jesus. Within the Godhead, He proceeds from the Son, as from the Father, as from one principle, and within the assumed manhood, as a consequence of the hypostatic union,[74] He fills the soul of the Son with a plenitude beyond measure (cf. John 3: 34) of His grace and Gifts.[75] The soul of Jesus, says Marmion, was 'infinitely docile to the promptings of the Spirit of Love who inspired and ruled all [His] movements, all [His] acts, and made them pleasing to [His] Father'.[76] When, therefore, our Lord offered Himself to the Father as an unspotted victim on the Cross, He did so, as the Apostle says, 'through the Holy Ghost' (cf. Heb. 9: 14), words that St Thomas interprets to mean, 'by the movement and inspiration of the Holy Spirit, that is, by charity for God and neighbour'.[77] Thus the Holy Spirit, through the grace of the virtues and the Gifts, enabled the acts of our Lord's sacred humanity to be worthy of the One whose acts they were, the eternal Word of God.[78] Having come down from the Father in Heaven, the incarnate Son makes the return journey— throughout His earthly life as *viator et compehensor*, but above all in the final 'passover' of His Passion—in perfect docility to the Holy Spirit. 'Full of the Holy Spirit' and 'led by the Spirit' (cf. Luke 3: 1), the divine person of the Son directs all His human actions, with exquisite exactness, towards Heaven—towards the heavenly Father, whom He lives and dies as man to glorify, and towards the attainment of the heavenly kingdom by men, for whose salvation the Father has sent Him. In Christ the Head, as in the members of His Mystical Body, the impulses of the Holy Spirit are always heavenward. Material fire has a natural tendency to rise upwards; so does the immaterial and uncreated fire that is the Holy Spirit when, by His created gifts, He sanctifies the soul of Jesus and the souls of His members.

The Holy Spirit's perfections of the sacred humanity are not a mere private possession for our Lord. The soul of Jesus is filled with the grace of the Holy Spirit, so that, as St Thomas says, 'it could be poured out from Him into us'.[79] The incarnate Word is the Head of the Mystical Body, and from Him have we all received, grace upon grace, one blessing after another from the Comforter (cf. John 1: 16). However, as St John the Evangelist says, the Holy Spirit was not given, or at least was not given abundantly and by visible signs,[80] until Jesus had been glorified (cf. John 7: 39).[81] Only after our Lord has died on the Cross and risen from the dead does He breathe the Holy Spirit upon the Apostles to give them the priestly power of absolution (cf. John 20: 22–3); not until He has ascended into Heaven does He send the 'Power from on High' (cf. Luke 24: 49) to equip them for preaching the Gospel to the nations. As the Holy Father says so beautifully, Jesus gives His disciples the Holy Spirit, as it were, 'through the wounds of [the] Crucifixion' in His risen body.[82]

Why could the Holy Spirit not be given fully until Jesus had been glorified in His Resurrection and Ascension? St Augustine's opinion, as reported by St Thomas, is:

[T]he Holy Spirit is given to us to raise up our hearts from love of the world to spiritual resurrection, that they we may wholeheartedly hasten unto God. Therefore, [our Lord] promised those who are fervent in the charity of the Holy Spirit that they would have eternal life, where we shall not die or know any fear. That is why He did not want to give the Holy Spirit Himself until He had been glorified: He wanted to show in His body the life we hope for in the resurrection.[83]

We might simplify the argument as follows. It is the Holy Spirit who moves us towards the enjoyment of eternal glory. But the members only have a hope of eternal glory when Christ their Head has Himself been glorified in His Resurrection and Ascension. Therefore, only when Christ has been glorified can the Holy Spirit be given.

Thus, in all of His working, the Holy Spirit brings us nearer to Heaven, to the final completion of our incorporation into Christ, and of our adoption by the Father, in the glory of soul and body. As the Apostle says: '[O]urselves also, who have the first fruits of the Spirit, even we ourselves groan within ourselves, waiting for the adoption of the sons of God, the redemption of our body' (Rom. 8: 23). Actual graces, the inspirations of the Holy Spirit, are intended to get us onto the royal highway that leads to the sweet and blessed country. They turn the heart of the unbeliever towards Christ and His true Church, and they stir the heart of the believer in the state of mortal sin towards repentance and recourse to the Sacrament of Penance. And, if we are already in the state of grace, the seven Gifts of the Holy Spirit makes us docile to those actual graces of the Spirit by which He steers us towards greater charity and so brings us closer to the Kingdom of charity above. As St Bede says: 'The Holy Spirit is rightly called "Comforter" (*paraclitus*), because He encourages and refreshes the hearts of the faithful with the desires of heavenly life, lest they faint amidst the adversities of this world.'[84] By sanctifying grace itself, accompanied by the infused virtues and the seven Gifts, the Holy Spirit, with the Father and the Son, dwells deep within our souls; this intimate presence is the first-fruits of the eternal communion with the Trinity that we hope for in Heaven. As Pope Leo XIII says in his encyclical on the Holy Spirit:

This marvellous union, which is called by its special name of 'indwelling', differs only by reason of condition or state from that union in which God embraces and beatifies the citizens of Heaven. Although it is most truly brought about by the presence of the whole Trinity ('We will come to him, and will make our abode with him', John 14: 23), it is nevertheless ascribed in a special way to the Holy Spirit. While traces of divine power and wisdom appear even in the bad man, only the just man partakes of charity, which is, as it were, the Holy Spirit's proper token.[85]

The mission of the Third Divine Person is inseparable from that of the Second.[86] The Holy Spirit leads us always to the incarnate Word and only thus to the Father. He is at work in all the Sacraments of the Church, in order to plunge men into the saving mysteries of Christ.[87] Such is the message of the beloved disciple when he says that there are three that together give testimony to Christ on earth: 'the Spirit and the water and the blood' (1 John 5: 8). Or, as the Catechism puts it: '"Sacramental grace" is the grace of the Holy Spirit, given by Christ and proper to each sacrament. The Spirit heals and transforms those who receive Him by conforming them to the Son of God. The fruit of the sacramental life is that the Spirit of adoption makes the faithful partakers in the divine nature by uniting them in a living union with the only Son, the Saviour.'[88] This living union, which is intended by God to be a kind of spiritual marriage, begins on earth and is consummated in Heaven. 'And the Spirit and the Bride say: Come . . . Come, Lord Jesus' (Rev. 22: 17, 20).

Pignus futurae gloriae: Heaven and the Mystery of the Holy Eucharist

The Villeneuve 'Coronation of our Lady' is an *altar*-piece, an image for meditation by monks who celebrate or assist at Holy Mass. It contains several references to the Eucharistic mystery. On the left, it shows the Mass of St Gregory the Great being celebrated in the church of Santa Croce in Rome. Bishops and deacons are clothed in the heavenly sanctuary in the vestments they once wore when officiating on earth. The depiction of the Cross on Calvary is so placed that it can serve as the crucifix of the altar. By painting such a radiant Heaven as the background to the celebration of Holy Mass, Enguerrand seems to be expressing by colour and shape what Pope John Paul expressed in words:

The Eucharist is a straining towards the ultimate goal, a foretaste of the fulness of joy promised by Christ (cf. John 15: 11); in a certain sense, it is the anticipation of Paradise, the 'pledge of future glory' . . . The Eucharist is truly a glimpse of Heaven opening up on earth. It is a ray of the glory of the heavenly Jerusalem piercing the clouds of our history and lighting up our journey.[89]

In the Holy Eucharist, under the sacramental species, Christ, the King of heavenly beauty, is really present, offered, and received. In all these aspects, as the Blessed Sacrament in which He is really present, as the Holy Sacrifice of the Mass in which He is offered, and as the Holy Communion in which He is received, the Eucharist makes Heaven accessible to men. It is in truth the 'pledge of future glory'. If we want to reach the sweet and blessed country, the City whose lamp is the Lamb of God (cf. Rev. 21: 23), then with increasing fervour we must adore that same radiant Lamb humbly hidden beneath the form of bread, join ourselves to His offering of Himself to the Father, and eat His Body and drink His Blood as the food and drink of immortal life.

Gloriosi corporis mysterium: Heaven and the Real Presence

In the altarpiece, we see Christ in Heaven—on our left but on the Father's right—in what St Thomas calls *propria specie*, the proper appearance of His resurrected flesh. On the Villeneuve altar, above which the painting once hung, that same resurrected flesh, the *gloriosum corpus*, was truly, really, and substantially present *in specie sacramentali*, under the appearance of bread. When the Carthusian priest-monk said the words of consecration, the true body of Christ did not leave the right hand of the Father and arrive by local movement in the chapel of Innocent VI.[90] The monks of the Charterhouse, well schooled in the doctrine of St Thomas, knew that the only way the true body of Christ can come to be present in the Sacrament, in truth and reality, is by the change of the whole substance of the bread into the substance of that body.[91] The Church's Magisterium—from the Fourth Lateran Council in the thirteenth century[92] and the Council of Trent in the sixteenth[93] to Pope John Paul's Eucharistic encyclical promulgated in 2003[94]—fittingly and properly calls this change 'transubstantiation'.

Moreover, according to the same Magisterium, the *whole* Christ—Body, Blood, Soul, and Divinity—is substantially present under each species. The Body is present under the species of bread in virtue of the Sacrament, that is, by the instrumental power of the words of consecration and the transubstantiation. The Blood is with the Body under the species of the bread, the Body with the Blood under the species of wine, and the Soul with both Body and Blood under both species, in virtue of what the Council of Trent calls, following St Thomas, 'that natural connection and concomitance, by which the parts of Christ our Lord, who has risen from the dead, never to die again (cf. Rom. 6: 9), are united with each other'.[95] Moreover, the divinity is present with the Body, Blood, and Soul, because of the hypostatic union of divinity and humanity in the divine person of the Word. What God takes, He keeps; the hypostatic union is perpetual and 'without separation'.[96] Thus the whole risen and ascended Christ, true God and true man in one person, is substantially present in the Blessed Sacrament. The King of Heaven, together with all those accidents of His glorified humanity that enrapture the saints, lies hidden beneath the humble accidents of bread.

Transubstantiation in a certain way breaks down the barriers of space. The wondrous change enables wayfarers to enjoy, under the sacramental species on the altar of the Church Militant, what the blessed enjoy under its proper species on the altar of the Church Triumphant: the bodily presence of the Lamb standing as though slain (cf. Rev. 5: 6). Even after His Ascension, the Word incarnate remains bodily, though not visibly, present among us. As the Christian mind ponders this truth, it begins to see why, as St Thomas argues, our Lord's bestowal of His real presence in the Blessed Sacrament is an act of stupendous love, a gift from His infinitely generous Heart.

This goes with Christ's charity, out of which, for our salvation, He assumed a true body of our nature. Since it is the special property of friendship for friends to live together (as the Philosopher says), He promises us His bodily presence as a reward: 'Where the body is, there shall the eagles be gathered together' (Matt. 24: 28). Meanwhile, however, He does not deprive us of His bodily presence on this pilgrimage of ours; but unites us with Himself in this Sacrament through the truth of His Body and Blood. Hence He says: 'He that eateth My flesh, and drinketh My blood, abideth in Me, and I in him' (John 6: 57). Thus this Sacrament, because it joins Christ so intimately to us, is the sign of supreme charity, and lifts up our hope.[97]

Blessed Denys presents the same argument more briefly, when He makes our Lord say: '[W]hat I give in the Fatherland in revealed reality, I have given here [in the Eucharist] in veiled reality.'[98]

Through the mystery of the real presence, the Eucharistic Sacrifice brings Heaven down to earth, takes earth up to Heaven. The Church Triumphant's glorious Head is really present in the Sacrament, and, in a kind of extension of the principle of concomitance, alongside Him come also the angels and saints, escorting Him with their praise: 'Joining in communion with (*communicantes*), and venerating the memory, before all others, of the glorious Ever-Virgin Mary, Mother of our God and Lord Jesus Christ, and of thy blessed apostles and martyrs.'[99] We do not participate in the Holy Sacrifice as isolated individuals, but as members knit together in the one Mystical Body, the undivided Communion of Saints, on earth, in Purgatory, and in Heaven. Spiritual goods are therefore exchanged, by the working of the Holy Spirit, between these various states of the Church, above all in the divine and heavenly liturgy of the Eucharist. In his *Expositio missae*, Blessed Denys writes thus of the *communicantes* section of the Roman Canon:

Communicantes, that is, applying to ourselves the prayers and merits of the saints and those who please thee. For all the elect are one Mystical Body, the Head of which is Christ; and so the prayers and merits of one are of benefit to another inasmuch as they are united in Christ. Now this union takes place through charity and grace. Therefore, whoever has charity and grace communicates with all the saints, that is, is helped by and partakes of their merits, as Scripture says: 'I am a partaker with all them that fear thee' (Ps. 118: 63).[100]

The opening up of earth to Heaven can also be seen in the prayer *Supplices te rogamus* in the Roman Canon:

Humbly we beg thee, almighty God: bid these gifts be borne by the hands of thy holy angel to thine altar on high, into the presence of thy divine majesty, so that all we who receive the most sacred Body and Blood of thy Son by partaking at this altar may be filled with every heavenly blessing and grace.

This prayer, dense with meaning but difficult to unfold, is explained by St Thomas with wonderful clarity. When the priest prays, 'Bid these gifts be borne', he is not asking for the sacramental species to be transferred to Heaven, nor that the true Body of Christ be moved there, because since the Ascension the true Body of Christ has never ceased to be at the Father's right hand.[101] From these considerations we may conclude that the priest says *Supplices te rogamus* on behalf of the Church, the Mystical Body, 'so that the prayers of both people and priest, with the assistance of the angels, be presented to God'. What, then, is the 'altar on high', the *sublime altare*? St Thomas says that it is either the Church Triumphant, into which we, the members of the Mystical Body on earth, ask God to take us, or it is the Triune God Himself, in whom we ask to partake. But why should God be called 'the altar on high'? St Thomas quotes a text from the book of Exodus: 'Thou shalt not go up by steps to the altar' (Exod. 20: 29), together with the commentary in the Gloss, 'Thou shalt not make steps in the Trinity'. There are no 'steps' in the Trinity, that is, no person is greater or less than the others; the Three are coequal. The Triune God is, therefore, fittingly represented by a stepless altar in Exodus and fittingly referred to as a 'sublime altar' in the Roman Canon. St Thomas suggests that the angel may be Christ Himself, 'the Angel of the Great Counsel', who joins His earthly Mystical Body to God the Father and the Church Triumphant. This prayer also helps to explain why the Eucharistic Sacrifice is called 'Mass', *missa*, the late Latin form of *missio*, 'sending'. Holy Mass is a sending because Christ is the Victim sent us by the Father, and in Him, through the priest and the angels, we send our prayers to God.[102]

O salutaris hostia: Heaven and the Sacrifice of the Mass

> O saving Victim, opening wide
> The gates of Heaven to man below,
> Our foes press on from every side,
> Thine aid supply, thy strength bestow.[103]

On the lower left side of the altarpiece, we see the 'Mass of St Gregory the Great', in which the saving Victim appears in visible form in place of the sacramental species, in order to confirm faith in the reality of His Eucharistic Presence and Sacrifice.[104] The image brings home the truth that the Sacrifice of the Cross and the Sacrifice of the Mass are, as the Catechism says, 'one single sacrifice'.[105] On Golgotha and on the altars of the Church, one and the same Victim is offered: Jesus Christ, the Lamb of God. The Priest who offers is the same, for Christ is the principal priest of the Mass, the ministerial priest being His representative and instrument. The ends, the sacrificial fruits of Calvary and the Mass, are also the same: adoration, thanksgiving, propitiation, supplication.[106] The only difference is the manner of offering: 'In this divine sacrifice enacted in the Mass, that same Christ is contained and immolated in an unbloody manner who "once offered Himself in a bloody manner" (cf. Heb. 9: 14) on the altar of the Cross.'[107]

The essential sacrificial action of the Mass takes place at the consecration, because at that moment Christ's Body and Blood are mystically sundered. Being glorious and incorruptible, Christ's resurrected body at the right hand of the Father can suffer no harm or hurt, and so there can be no separation of Body and Blood in the *physical* order. However, separation is possible in the *sacramental* order, as regards the real presence of Christ's Body and Blood under the sacramental species. In virtue of what the words of consecration themselves effect, *only* the Body becomes present under the species of bread, and *only* the Blood becomes present under the species of wine; as noted already, all those other parts that make up the 'whole Christ' are present in the Blessed Sacrament for other reasons (concomitance and the hypostatic union). Thus, in the sacramental order, Christ is shown forth by the twofold consecration in the state of Victim, while remaining, in the physical order, unchanged and invulnerable.[108] By this mystical immolation, the Sacrifice of the Cross is, as the Council of Trent says, 're-presented', that is, 'made present ever anew, sacramentally perpetuated'.[109] Moreover, in and through the Mass, all the fruits of the Cross are poured out, and its saving power 'applied' to the needs of the living and the dead.

The Sacrifice of the Cross is 'made present ever anew' in the Sacrifice of the Mass. Now the Sacrifice of the Cross opens up the gates of Heaven; as the Apostle says: 'He is the Mediator of the New Testament, that by means of His death . . . they that are called may receive the promise of eternal inheritance' (Heb. 9: 15). Therefore, the Sacrifice of the Mass, making present the Sacrifice of the Cross, also throws open the gates of Heaven; one of its fruits is the attainment of eternal life, as is evident in the very words of consecration: 'This is the chalice of My blood, of the New and Eternal Testament.'[110] The merits of the Sacrifice of Calvary, says Pope Pius XII, are 'boundless and immeasurable', for this is a sacrifice offered by a God-Man, the Head of the human race; its purchase of the world's salvation is made with the precious blood of the Father's only Son. However, the Pope adds, the 'purchase does not immediately have its full effect'. What the universal cause achieved in the objective redemption must be applied to individual men in the subjective redemption.

Christ, having redeemed the world at the lavish cost of His own blood, still has to come into actual possession of the souls of men. Therefore, so that the redemption and salvation of each person and of all subsequent generations to the end of the age may be effectively accomplished, and be acceptable to God, it is absolutely necessary that men should individually come into vital contact with the Sacrifice of the Cross, so that the merits flowing from it should be imparted to them.[111]

It is in the Sacrifice of the Mass that men come individually into contact with the Sacrifice of the Cross and partake of its fruits, including the attainment of eternal life. Consider, for example, the fruit of atonement for human sin, the sin that is the great obstacle blocking the entrance into Heaven. In the Mass the propitiation achieved by our Lord on the Cross is applied to the living and the dead. More exactly, in the case of the holy souls, the Sacrifice of the Mass infallibly remits at least part of the temporal punishment still outstanding for their sins; the suffrage, the intercession, of the Mass speeds them on their way from the pains of Purgatory into the sweet bliss of the Fatherland. Thus in the Roman Canon the priest prays for 'all those who rest in Christ', 'that is', explains Blessed Denys, 'those who have died in the grace of God', that they may have 'a place of refreshment, light, and peace' in 'the celestial Paradise'.[112]

Viaticum: Heaven and Holy Communion

The attainment of eternal life is one of the effects of Holy Communion when it is worthily received, that is, when the communicant is in the state of grace and properly disposed and thus in a position to 'discern' the Lord's true Body and Blood in the Sacrament (cf. 1 Cor. 11: 29). The Eucharist, as St Thomas says, 'really contains that by which the gate of Heaven is opened to us, namely, the blood of Christ; that is why it is called "viaticum"',[113] that which opens the way to the Fatherland.[114] The Blessed Sacrament is sustenance for the heavenward journey, like the food that kept Elijah going on his march to the mount of God.[115] In his prayers before and after Holy Communion, St Thomas asks directly for this most wonderful fruit of the Eucharist:

O most loving Father, grant to me, who now purpose in my pilgrimage to receive beneath a veil thy beloved Son, to behold Him unveiled face to face for ever . . . I pray thee that thou wouldst vouchsafe to bring me, a sinner, unto that ineffable banquet where thou with thy Son and the Holy Spirit art to thy saints true light, full satisfaction, everlasting joy, delight fulfilled, and perfect felicity.[116]

Christ is eternal life in Himself, in both His divinity and His humanity: the sight of His divinity is eternal bliss for our souls, and from His body comes the glory that will be extended to our own bodies on the last day. Now when we eat Christ's Body and drink His Blood worthily, we are, in St Thomas's words, 'transformed into [Christ]', and our incorporation into Him is perfected.[117] Therefore, eternal life for both body and soul comes to us as a fruit of Eucharistic Communion that is both sacramental and spiritual. As the Fathers teach us, the Holy Eucharist is in truth the 'medicine of immortality'.[118] 'He that eateth my flesh and drinketh my blood', says our Lord, 'hath everlasting life, and I will raise him in the last day' (John 6: 55).

Dom Marmion argues that even in this life the Body of Christ in the Eucharist has a transforming effect on our bodies in preparation for the resurrection. He quotes a postcommunion from the Missal: 'Grant, O Lord, that the operation of thy heavenly gift may possess both our minds and bodies, that its effect, and not our senses, may ever have dominion within us.' He then makes this comment:

This prayer of the Church leads us to understand that the Eucharistic action overflows from the soul upon the body itself. It is true that it is to the soul that Christ immediately unites Himself; it is to the soul that He comes first of all, to assure and confirm its deification . . . But the union of body and soul is so close that in increasing the life of the soul, in powerfully drawing it towards heavenly delights, the Eucharist tempers the heat of the passions, and brings peace to all our being.[119]

Conclusion: The Open Gates of the Monastery

The Carthusian kneels at the foot of the Cross, and with him kneels every monk, every Christian. The monk knows he cannot join our Lady in the bliss of her union with Christ in Heaven if he does not stand by her in the sorrows of her union with Christ on Calvary. Neither monk nor Christian in the world can know the power of Christ's Resurrection without first sharing in the infirmity of Christ's Passion. That is the teaching of the Apostles (cf. Rom. 8: 17; 2 Cor. 1: 5; Phil. 3: 10; Col. 1: 24; 1 Pet. 4: 13), and indeed of our Lord Himself: we must take up our cross and follow Him if we want to achieve our final goal (cf. Matt. 16: 24). St Benedict states the doctrine in the last lines of the prologue of the Holy Rule, where he speaks of the monks 'partaking by patience in the Passion of Christ, that [they] may also merit a share in His Kingdom'.[120] Abbot Marmion, likewise, returns to the theme in many places: 'Upon the Cross,' he says, 'Christ Jesus represented us all; but although He suffered for all, He applies the fruit of His immolation to us only if we associate ourselves with His Sacrifice.'[121]

But how do we share in the sufferings of Christ Jesus? The first way mentioned by Marmion is *contemplation* of those sufferings in faith and love: that is exactly what we see our Carthusian doing in the painting. Year by year in the liturgy of Holy Week, every Friday through the sorrowful mysteries of the Rosary or the Way of the Cross, we draw near to the Mother of Sorrows and ask for access to her heart, a share in the compassion with which she looked upon her crucified Son. According to Denys the Carthusian, such consideration of the Passion of Christ is indispensable for ascending to the 'contemplation of the superlatively blessed Trinity and incomprehensible Deity'.[122] Meditation on the self-abasement of the Son of God helps to detach us from our fallen tendency to self-aggrandizement, and opens up that mystery of uncreated charity by which the Father and the Son love each other in the Holy Spirit. To gaze upon the crucifix, as the Carthusian gazes, disposes us for receiving the graces proper to the purgative way, by which we are freed from 'passions and sins, negligences, inconstancy and sloth', and begin to advance in the moral virtues, especially 'patience, meekness, humility, fortitude, [and] obedience'.[123] There is no other way to transforming union with the Trinity, whether on earth in the spiritual marriage or in Heaven in the Beatific Vision, than searing purgation and dazzling illumination, which is only another way of saying what Enguerrand expresses in his painting, namely, that we can only reach the sweet and blessed country through conformity to Christ in the bitter pain of Calvary.

The second way of sharing in the Passion of Christ, according to Abbot Marmion, is through the Sacraments, and especially the Sacrament of Sacraments, the Holy Eucharist, which we have just been considering, in which the Passion of Christ is represented and its fruits poured out.

We sometimes say: Oh! If I could have been at Golgotha with the Blessed Virgin, St John and Magdalen! But faith brings us face to face with Jesus immolated upon the altar; He there renews His Sacrifice, in a mystical manner, in order to give us a share in His merits and satisfactions. We do not see Him with our bodily eyes, but faith tells us that He is there, for the same ends for which He offered Himself upon the Cross. If we have a living faith, it will make us cast ourselves down at the feet of Jesus, who immolates Himself. It will unite us to Him in His love for His Father and for mankind and in His hatred of sin. It will make us say with Him: Father, behold I come to do thy will . . . We shall enter especially into these sentiments if, after offering ourselves with Jesus, we unite ourselves to Him by sacramental communion. Christ then gives Himself to us, as the one who comes to expiate and destroy sin within us.[124]

The third way of sharing Christ's Passion is, as Marmion says, 'by bearing, for the love of the Christ, the sufferings and adversities which, in the designs of His providence, He permits us to undergo'.[125] The Word incarnate, the Head of the Mystical Body, suffered beyond measure for our redemption, but He wants His members to make that gift of redemption their own by enduring the sufferings of life in loving union with Himself. He wants us, in faith and charity, to suffer with the same intentions with which He suffered, namely, the glory of the Father and our own and our brethren's salvation. Only so are the members made fully conformed to the Head; only so are they fully transformed in Him. To be with Him where He is, in the glory of the Father and the Fatherland, we must tread the path He Himself has taken.

Christ has opened His suffering to man, [says Pope John Paul], because He Himself in His redemptive suffering has become, in a certain way, a sharer in all human sufferings. When man through faith discovers the redemptive Passion of Christ, he also discovers in it his own sufferings; he perceives them, through faith, enriched with new content and new meaning.[126]

Contemplation, Holy Mass, bearing the afflictions of life with the help of the infused theological and moral virtues: these three ways of 'sharing the sufferings of Christ' are connected causally, for it is through the Eucharistic Sacrifice, and especially through worthily receiving the sacrificed Lamb in Holy Communion, that, together with sanctifying grace, the Holy Spirit increases the infused virtues within us—the very virtues we need if suffering is to be transformed into an opportunity for surrendering ourselves in love to Christ and, with Him, to the Father. Such is the pattern of every Christian life, but especially of the Christian life of the monk. By solemn profession and holy rule, he shares the sufferings of Christ: he contemplates the Cross, and he also, in the words of St Benedict, 'denies himself in order to follow Christ, chastises his body, does not grasp at pleasure, loves fasting, relieves the poor, clothes the naked, visits the sick, buries the dead, helps the afflicted, consoles the sorrowful, avoids worldly conduct, prefers nothing to the love of Christ'.[127] What makes these *instrumenta bonorum operum* into, so to speak, 'power tools' for the quest of Heaven? There is only one answer: the grace of the Holy Spirit flowing from the Eucharistic Heart of Christ. Regarded thus, the offering of the Eucharistic Sacrifice is the radiating centre—the source and summit—of every other act of the monastic day.

The gates of a Benedictine monastery stand open, as do the gates of Heaven, and by the same causes: the Cross, the Resurrection, and the Holy Sacrament of the Altar. In the power of His Resurrection, Christ continues to suffer, not in Himself and His true body in impassible glory at the right hand of the Father, but in the least of His brethren (cf. Matt. 25: 40), the suffering members of His Mystical Body. That is why, till the last day, the sons of St Benedict will welcome and worship the divine Master in the persons of the poor: 'Let all guests that come be received like

Christ, for He will say: "I was a stranger, and you took me in" (cf. Matt. 25: 35) . . . Let the head be bowed, or the whole body be prostrate on the ground, and so let Christ be worshipped in them (*in eis adoretur*), for indeed He is welcomed in their persons.'[128] In one of his homilies, St Gregory the Great tells the story of Martyrius, whose fidelity to this injunction had a miraculous effect. He found a leper collapsed on the side of the road. Covering him with his cloak, and putting him on his shoulders, he carried the poor man to the monastery. There the leper manifested Himself as 'the Redeemer of the human race, God and man, Christ Jesus', who, before disappearing, blessed the monk and said: 'Martyrius, you were not ashamed of me on earth; I shall not be ashamed of you in Heaven.'[129]

In its hospitality, too, the monastery is meant to be an anticipation of Heaven. That is why the biographer of St Aelred was able to apply to Rievaulx as a refuge for the infirm a text that the Fathers generally use of the celestial Jerusalem as the destination of the elect: '"Whither the tribes go up, the tribes of the Lord, unto the testimony of Israel, to give thanks unto the name of the Lord" (Ps. 121: 4). There are tribes of the strong and tribes of the weak. The house that withholds toleration from the weak is not to be regarded as a house of religion.'[130] When we look at the altarpiece, we likewise see tribes of the strong and weak, princes and prelates but also peasants; all have a place in Heaven, for all, in their immense human diversity, were called by the Trinity to the perfection of love, and all responded with a generous heart. Moreover, just as in the guesthouse of the abbey those who know Christ by faith find and venerate Him in His members still suffering and seeking, so in the hospice of Heaven those who see the face of Christ in all its beauty recognize and revere reflections of that beauty in His members now blessed and fulfilled.

The mystical presence of Christ in our brethren must not be confused with the true and substantial presence of Christ, 'whole and entire', under the sacramental species in the Eucharist, which, as the Holy Father reminds us in *Ecclesia de Eucharistia*, is

His presence *par excellence*, surpassing all.[131] The two modes of presence must not be confused, and yet they ought not to be separated either. By giving them His Body, Blood, Soul, and Divinity in Holy Communion, Christ unites His members more closely to Himself. According to St Thomas, the Eucharistic Jesus not only increases sanctifying grace and the *habit* of charity within us, He also stirs our charity into act: He moves our hearts to love Him and our neighbour with a new fervour.[132] Those who allow their hearts to be enlarged by the Holy Eucharist will not only apprehend our Lord's substantial presence beneath the sacramental species with a more perceptive faith and worship Him with a more reverent love, they will also find Him more easily beneath the features of the poor and serve Him there with renewed devotion. That is why, in every age of the Church's history, the most zealous saints of Eucharistic adoration—St Francis of Assisi, St Vincent de Paul, Blessed Teresa of Calcutta—have also been the most generous apostles of the poor. They loved the King of heavenly beauty in all of His hidden modes of presence, and by their devotion they made this our exile more like the sweet and blessed country for which we yearn.

·3·

HEAVEN LOST AND HEAVEN LONGED FOR

As monks have always done, the Carthusians of fifteenth-century Villeneuve made a habit of meditating on the last things of man: on death and judgement, on Heaven already attained, but also on 'Heaven lost', which is Hell, and 'Heaven Longed For', which is Purgatory. When they knelt before the *Coronation* altarpiece, they could see, at the bottom on the right, the pit of Hell, which Quarton, like Dante, places immediately underneath Jerusalem at the centre of the earth. On the left of the painting, underneath the city of Rome, is Purgatory. A good angel is helping one of the poor souls out of the purging flames: soon, as Dante would say, he will be 'leaping up into joy celestial'.[1] By contrast, there is no door leading out of Hell, no chance of an upward leap: the souls are imprisoned there for ever, and the bad angels torment them without ceasing. In both places, as requested in the contract, Quarton has represented the souls of all sorts and conditions of men: Popes and bishops, clergy and laity, regulars and seculars, princes and paupers, males and females. The message is evident: eternal punishment is a terrible possibility for any of us, whatever our state of life, and it is already an actuality for many who have died. Purgatory is likewise available for any holy soul that needs to be purged and thus prepared for the bliss of Heaven.

Next to Quarton's Purgatory, on the far left side, is the *limbus puerorum*, Limbo, where the souls of infants who have died without baptism are detained. Quarton shows them turning their heads upwards but with their eyes closed, as if to imply what St Thomas taught, namely, that such souls, though they do not enjoy the Beatific Vision, nonetheless know God by a natural contemplation and are blessed with a proportionate natural happiness. They do not suffer any pain of the sense, nor do they experience even the pain of loss as an affliction, because they do not know that they were created for supernatural beatitude.[2] Neither in the fifteenth century nor in the twenty-first has the Church made the Limbo of the infants a matter of divine faith. In the Catechism she speaks beautifully of the hope that the Christian may have, despite the lack of revealed light on the subject, that, by God's mercy, 'there is a way of salvation for children who have died without Baptism'.[3] Nevertheless, while exercising this hope, as the Church encourages us to do, we should not disregard the doctrine of Limbo, particularly as expounded so compassionately by St Thomas. It affords us a precious minimum of consolation. At the very least, infants departing this life without baptism enjoy a natural joy in God and are spared any pain of the sense. We hope they have much more, but this much is guaranteed.

Having so far accentuated the positive, by contemplating Heaven, I want now to consider the Church's teaching on the eternal suffering of the wicked souls in Hell, and on the temporary and purifying sufferings of the holy souls in Purgatory. In their writing on both doctrines, our monastic theologians shed light on our minds and stir our hearts with a new zeal for holiness and the conquest of sin.

Hell: Heaven Lost

For all Christians, one of the traditional ways of keeping oneself on the road to the sweet and blessed country, the land of the living, is soberly to ponder the destiny of those who take the road that leads in the opposite direction, towards the empire of death. In our painting, on one of the turrets on the walls of Jerusalem, we see the figure of Satan. He is not so much prowling like a lion (cf. 1 Pet. 5: 8) as poised like a vulture. In any case, he is hunting for souls he can seduce into his own rebellion against God and thence into the fires reserved for him and his angels (cf. Matt. 25: 41). For all its magnificent, God-given goodness and beauty, this earth on which we live is not only a vale of tears but a battleground. To our last breath, we are engaged in a battle against the enemies of our souls, the world, the flesh, and the devil, and if we die unrepentant, having knowingly and freely surrendered to them in some grave matter, then we shall suffer everlasting torment, the pain of loss and the pain of sense.

The Names and Definition of Hell

The Latin words *infernus* and *inferi* can be used in a generic as well as a specific sense. Generically, they denote 'that which is below' and 'those who are below', that is, the underworld or place of the dead, and the souls that dwell there, deprived of the Beatific Vision, whether for a time or for ever. Specifically, the terms can be used to describe the essentially different states in which souls that have not entered Heaven find themselves: the Limbo of the Fathers, the Limbo of the Children, Purgatory, and the Hell of the damned. Thus, when, in the Apostles' Creed, the Church says, *descendit ad inferna* (or *inferos*), she is referring to the descent of Christ's soul, on Holy Saturday, into the Limbo of the Fathers. The saints of the Old Testament were detained in this underworld until the long-expected Messiah came to take them into glory. Similarly, in the Roman Canon, the priest commemorates our Lord's Resurrection *ab inferis*, since, until it was reunited to His body on Easter Sunday morning, His soul was in that hell or underworld which we call the Limbo of the Fathers.[4] Sometimes, in her liturgy, the Church even refers to Purgatory as an underworld, when, for example, she prays in the *Offertorium* of the Requiem Mass: *Libera animas fidelium defunctorum de poenis inferni*, 'Deliver the souls of the faithful departed from the pains of Hell'. Now no departed soul can be delivered from the Hell of the damned. Therefore, it must be from some other state or place— namely, from Purgatory—that the Church begs for the souls to be delivered. The Doctors of the Church likewise call the Limbo of the Children a 'hell', an underworld, the state or place in which this particular group of departed souls resides.[5] St Thomas says that, while 'in essence' the soul of Christ descended only to the Limbo of the Fathers, He descended 'in effect' into all the underworlds.[6] Satan has a certain dominion over death, even death of the body. It was through succumbing to his temptation that our first father sinned and therefore became liable to bodily death: 'Sin came into the world through one man, and through sin death' (Rom. 5: 12). Thus, when the glorious soul of Christ descends into the Limbo of the Fathers, He breaks down the doors of Satan's 'culture of death' and opens up a way, through death, into the civilization of beatific love and eternal life.

The modern English word 'Hell' comes from the Anglo-Saxon *Hel*, which is related to the modern German *Hölle*. The root meaning seems to be covering or concealment, being placed underneath something. In the ancient pagan mythology of the Germanic peoples, it was the name of the underworld and of the goddess who presided over it. In English translations of the Bible, 'Hell' translates two Hebrew words: *Sheol*, which corresponds to the Limbo of the Fathers, the place where the souls of the righteous of the Old Testament await the coming of Christ; and *Gehenna*, which in the teaching of our Lord is the place of eternal punishment, the Hell of the damned. The Greek word *Hades*, used by pagan authors for both the underworld and its god, appears in the New Testament as a translation of *Sheol*.

Gehenna is the New Testament's name for the Hell of the damned. It is a Greek adaptation of a Hebrew place-name, *ge'hinnom*, the valley of Hinnom, an area to the south-west of the city of Jerusalem used for burning rubbish. It was also the place where in the past the Canaanites had offered human sacrifice to Moloch. As Jeremiah says: 'And they have built the high places of Topheth, which is in the valley of the son of Ennom, to burn their sons and their daughters in the fire' (Jer. 7: 31). King Ahaz burnt his son there as an offering to the idols of Canaan (cf. 2 Kgs. 16: 3).

As a place, then, of fire and of foulness, both physical and moral, 'black Gehenna', in Milton's words, became 'the Type of Hell', a suitable earthly symbol of the Hell of the damned.[7] This is a striking and sobering fact: for the Jews of our Lord's time and indeed for the God-made-man Himself, the most hellish place on earth was the valley in which children were offered as a holocaust to false gods, a sin of unutterable depravity. It should not therefore surprise us that the holy anger of the Sacred Heart should be directed above all against the man who sins against little ones: '[I]t were better for him that a millstone should be hanged about his neck, and that he should be drowned in the depth of the sea' (Matt. 18: 6). Such a man repeats the sin of the votaries of Moloch.

Since the geographical Gehenna is but a short distance from Jerusalem, it is no surprise to find Christian theologians, as well as Christian poets and painters, locating Hell underneath the city of Jerusalem, at the centre of the earth. Even if we must abandon this idea in its literal meaning, we can reclaim it in its spiritual sense. It is fitting that the place of eternal punishment should be placed beneath the historical Jerusalem, for it was there that the incarnate Son of God suffered, died, and rose again in order to save us from the fires of Hell.

The Hell of the damned—which is the subject of the first part of this chapter—can, therefore, be defined as the state or place of eternal punishment reserved for the fallen angels and the souls of those human beings who die unrepentant in the condition of actual mortal sin. As the Catechism says: 'To die in mortal sin without repenting and accepting God's merciful love means remaining separated from him for ever by our own free choice. This state of definitive self-exclusion from communion with God and the blessed is called "Hell".'[8]

The Existence of Hell

'Truth Himself speaks truly or there's nothing true.'[9] Our Lord Jesus Christ is eternal Truth incarnate. Therefore, whenever He speaks, He speaks truly. But among the things of which He speaks in the Gospels is the existence of the Hell of the damned. For example, He describes how the angels will cast the wicked into the furnace of fire, where 'there shall be weeping and gnashing of teeth' (cf. Matt. 13: 50), and how the goats on His left hand will go off into the 'everlasting fire' prepared for the devil and his angels (cf. Matt. 25: 41). From statements such as these, we conclude, with the certainty of faith, that there truly is such a place or state as the Hell of the damned. Of course, Catholics do not draw that conclusion about the existence of Hell on the basis of Scripture alone, but on Scripture as read within the Church's Tradition and as expounded by her Magisterium, the proximate rule of faith. In the Athanasian Creed, in the decrees of ecumenical councils from Lateran IV to Vatican II, and in the teachings of the popes, not least Benedict XII, the existence of Hell is affirmed from age to age with vigour and clarity. *The Catechism of the Catholic Church* sums up the traditional doctrine: 'The teaching of the Church affirms the existence of Hell and its eternity. Immediately after death the souls of those who die in a state of mortal sin descend into Hell, where they suffer the punishments of Hell, "eternal fire".'[10]

Notice that the Catechism presents Hell as having 'existence', that is, as an actuality for an indeterminate number of human souls. This statement excludes the theory of those who claim that, in order to call us to conversion, our Lord presented Hell only as a possibility for any man still living rather than as an actuality for any souls already departed.[11] The gravest objection we can bring against this theory is that it seems to imply that, in His teaching on Hell, our Lord systematically said 'is' or 'will be' when He meant 'may be'. Now if you say that something is an actuality, when you know full well that it is only a possibility, you are guilty of deception. Therefore, this theory seems to make our Lord guilty of deception. But our Lord is true God from true God, the Father's incarnate Wisdom and Truth, who can neither deceive nor be deceived. Therefore, the theory is false and, whatever its intentions, a kind of blasphemy. The divine Saviour's teaching on Hell is indeed a 'call to conversion',[12] but what concentrates the mind about this teaching is the thought that even now a vast number of the souls of our fellow men are eternally lost, and that we may join them.

The denial of the existence of Hell is a heresy that offends not only divinely revealed truth but also divinely manifested love. For the Father of mercies so loves the race of Adam that He does not abandon us to the power of eternal death, and instead sends His Son in human nature, conceived by the Holy Spirit and born of the Virgin Mary, so that, by His Passion and Death, He may save us from the fires of Hell. Why did One of the Trinity descend so deeply into our human condition on earth, if not to save us from falling into the foul depths of perdition in Hell? In the words of our Holy Father, Pope John Paul:

> God gives His Only-begotten, so that man 'may not perish', and the meaning of that phrase, 'may not perish' is defined more exactly in the words that follow, 'but have eternal life'. For man 'perishes' when he loses 'eternal life'. The opposite of salvation is not, therefore, just temporal suffering, just any kind of suffering, but certain and definitive suffering: the loss of eternal life, being rejected by God, damnation. The only-begotten Son has been given to humanity first of all to protect man against this definitive evil and against definitive suffering.[13]

Confutatis maledictis: The Nature of Eternal Punishment—The Principal Pain

Confutatis maledictis . . . 'While the cursed are confounded, | Doom'd to flames of woe unbounded, | Call me with thy saints surrounded.'[14] The author of the *Dies irae* calls the damned *maledicti*, 'cursed', because that is what the Son of Man Himself calls them: 'Depart from me, you cursed' (Matt. 25: 41). In his *Catena aurea* on St Matthew's Gospel, St Thomas quotes some wise words of Origen, who points out that, though our Lord calls the saints 'ye blessed of my Father', He does not call the wicked 'ye cursed of my Father', 'because of all blessing the Father is the author, but each man is the origin of his own curse when he does things that deserve a curse'.[15] The cursed have made themselves accursed by the abuse of their freedom when they sinned mortally and refused, to their last breath, to accept the mercy of the heavenly Father. The damned have, therefore, placed themselves in Hell. In the splendid words of the Catechism, the state of the damned is one of 'definitive *self*-exclusion from communion with God and the blessed'. The Catechism goes on to say, with equal clarity and robustness: 'God predestines no one to go to Hell; for this, a wilful turning away from God (a mortal sin) is necessary, and persistence in it until the end'.[16] Thus, once again in the twentieth century, the Church repeats her condemnation of the Calvinist and Jansenist heresy of double predestination: there is no divine 'hit list', as if God willed in advance the eternal punishment of the wicked in exactly the same way in which He willed the salvation of the elect. There can be no strict parallel between good works and evil, and therefore none between predestination and reprobation. 'God is the first cause', says the Catechism, 'who operates in and through secondary causes.'[17] It is He, as the Apostle says, who 'worketh in [us], both to will and to accomplish, according to His good will' (Phil. 2: 13). Our good works, whether natural or supernatural, are therefore truly His before they are ours.[18] But our morally evil works come about in a quite different way. As a positive reality, something that has being, the physical action is from God, but the sinfulness of the action, its moral deficiency, comes entirely from the free will of the creature.[19] Of our sins alone can we say: '*All* my own work'.[20] Therefore, if a man sins mortally and remains obstinate in his sin to his last breath, he has no one but himself to blame when he ends up in Hell. Almighty God willed the sin and the final impenitence neither directly nor indirectly; He only permitted them, and He only permitted them, because out of their evil He is able to bring some good.

The principal pain of the damned, of both the fallen angels and the souls of wicked men, is the loss of the Beatific Vision. Our Lord refers to this loss, when He says to the foolish virgins: 'I know you not' (Matt. 25: 12). The loss is not of actual possession, for the Beatific Vision, once attained, can never be lost, but of potential possession: the damned are for ever deprived of the possibility of being admitted to eternal glory. The only souls that suffer this most dreadful pain are the souls of men who have died unrepentant in the state of mortal sin. By their last free act they insisted on being turned away from God, and in that state they spend eternity. As a faithful disciple of St Thomas,[21] Denys the Carthusian says that in every mortal sin there are two movements: a turning away from God, the 'supreme and unchangeable good', and a turning towards some 'empty and ephemeral created good'. Now the pain of loss corresponds to the turning away from God, while the pain of sense is linked to the turning towards the creature. Of the two pains, the loss is by far the greater.[22] As Blessed Abbot Marmion says:

What is it to feel oneself eternally drawn with all the natural energy of one's being towards the enjoyment of God, and to see oneself eternally thrust back? The essence of Hell is this inextinguishable thirst of God which tortures the soul created by Him, for Him . . . To hunger and thirst for infinite beatitude, and never to possess it![23]

St Thomas says that 'God turns away from someone only to the degree that the man turns away from him'.[24] Thus, Dom Marmion concludes, '[w]hen man, at the hour of death, in spite of all the divine invitations to repentance, remains obstinate in his voluntary opposition to the Lord, He, in His turn, abandons [the man]'.[25] Then indeed is the soul lost, and for ever. 'Eye hath not seen nor ear heard', says St Paul, 'what things God hath prepared for them that love Him' (1 Cor. 2: 9). Alas, says Dom Marmion, we have to recognize that the torment of Hell, especially the chief torment, the loss of God, is likewise, in its horrors, beyond all conceiving.

God has destined man for supernatural fulfilment in the sight and enjoyment of His truth, goodness, and beauty, but the damned have chosen irrevocably against Him. By their last free act, they chose something else, instead of God, as their final end. They preferred a lie to the First Truth (cf. Rom. 1: 25), and by that preference they suffer the agony of an unending contradiction. They departed this life rejecting the Sovereign Good, who contains eminently in Himself all goods, and so in the life to come they forfeit all the goods that God had in store for them. To the very end, they fixed themselves on some created beauty to the point of spurning the Uncreated Beauty, and so, to the ages of ages, they endure the hideousness of Hell.[26] God created us for Himself, and our hearts are restless till they rest in Him. As King David so often says in the Psalms, we hunger and thirst for the living God: 'For thee my soul hath thirsted; for thee my flesh, O how many ways' (Ps. 62: 2). Now if I finally and obstinately reject the sustenance provided by the Father of mercies, if I refuse to my last breath the Word of truth, who is the very bread of the angels, and the Spirit of love, who is living water, then I condemn myself to unending thirst and hunger with Tantalus in Tartarus. 'The soul is tortured by an insatiable hunger for happiness; its whole nature craves desperately for the joy which it has lost for ever.'[27]

Abbot Marmion enables us to hear the words of the heavenly Father as He speaks to the damned:

I called you to share my glory and beatitude. I wished to fill you with all 'spiritual blessings' (cf. Eph. 1: 1–3). Therefore, I gave you my Son and filled Him [in His sacred humanity] with the fullness of grace that it might overflow to you. He was the Way destined to lead you to Truth and Life. He accepted to die for you, He gave you His merits and satisfactions. He gave you the Church, He gave you His Spirit; with Him, what have I not given you, so that you might one day take part in the eternal banquet which I have prepared for the glory of this well-beloved Son? You have had years to make yourself ready for it, and you would not. You insolently despised my merciful advances, you rejected light and life. Now the time has gone by: depart from me, ye cursed, I know you not, for you do not bear the likeness of my Son. There is only place in my kingdom for His brethren, who, by grace, are like unto Him. Depart to the eternal fire prepared for the devil and his angels. Because you chose sin, 'you are of your father the devil' (cf. John 8: 44; 1 John 3: 8) and bear his image. *Nescio vos* [I do not know you].[28]

Flammis acribus addictis: The Nature of Eternal Punishment—The Secondary Pain

Flammis acribus addictis, says Thomas of Celano in the *Dies irae*, 'Doom'd to flames of woe unbounded'. The secondary pain of Hell, corresponding to the turning to the creature in the act of mortal sin, is the pain of sense. Sacred Scripture most commonly describes this as an effect of *fire*. Hell is a 'furnace' (cf. Matt. 13: 42), a 'pool burning with fire and brimstone' (cf. Rev. 21: 8). Commenting on the words of St John the Baptist, when he says of Christ that 'the chaff He will burn with unquenchable fire' (Matt. 3: 12), Blessed Denys the Carthusian adds a gloss: '*unquenchable fire*, that is, with the unceasing flame and punishment of Hell'.[29] He goes on to quote the Apocalypse: '[T]hey shall have their portion in the pool burning with fire and brimstone . . . and the smoke of their torments shall ascend up for ever and ever' (Rev. 21: 8; 14: 11). He then concludes: 'If only the soul would wisely ponder these terrifying words, and listen to them with the ears of the heart! Then indeed nothing carnal or passing would delight it, but it would say with holy Job: "I have always feared God as waves swelling over me" (Job 31: 23).'[30]

According to the Schoolmen, following some of the Fathers, the fire of Hell is a material one,[31] essentially the same as the fire we have on earth, differing from it only accidentally, since it needs no fuel.[32] Now, how can something material cause pain in a spiritual soul separated from its body[33] or in a pure spirit such as a demon? The answer of the Schoolmen is by means of an analogy with the Sacraments. In the Sacraments, matter—for example, the water of Baptism—becomes an instrument by which God produces a spiritual effect in the soul.[34] Similarly, in the pain of sense, a material fire, as an instrument of the divine justice, produces a mysterious effect in spiritual entities. St Thomas says that the effect is of being tied down or restricted, the fire 'retarding [the soul] from carrying out its own will, so that it cannot operate where and as it wants'.[35] 'Material elements detain the reprobate spirit,' says Abbot Vonier, 'and circumscribe his activities.'[36] Hell-fire is the inflammation of eternal frustration.[37] In sinning mortally and without repentance, the damned turned away from God and turned instead towards some created thing, usually some bodily thing. One can readily see the terrible appropriateness of the punishment: those who prefer the creature to the infinitely superior Creator, thereby inverting the order of justice, are afflicted with things that are inferior to them.[38] By their own disordered act of the will, sustained obstinately to the end, the damned tie themselves up in the fiery knot of sensory pain.

Voca me cum benedictis: The Purpose of Meditation on Hell

Voca me cum benedictis, 'Call me, with thy saints surrounded'. The author of the *Dies irae*, having glanced fearfully at Hell, looks hopefully towards Heaven. It is for the sake of reaching the Fatherland of truth that we meditate on the wasteland of lies. If we want to be with the blessed in the beauty of their love, then we cannot fail, at least sometimes, to think about the damned in the ugliness of their hate. The observance of God's commandments, says Denys, becomes easier in our thoughts and in our actions, when we remember that by being faithful to the commandments we can escape 'the intolerable and perpetual damnation of Hell',[39] and instead attain the everlasting joys of Heaven. It is for positive reasons, for the sake of their eternal happiness, that Christians, whether or not they are monks, should contemplate that most negative of subjects and that most unhappy of places which is Hell.

In quoting Denys with approval on the subject of Hell, I am not trying to preach an asceticism of gloom and foreboding, the kind of spirituality that, through Calvinism and Jansenism, has blighted entire cultures. To ensure a properly Catholic balance, let me quote one of our guides on this journey to Heaven, that most positive and cheerful of men, Columba Marmion. 'Far be it from me', he writes in *Christ the Life of the Soul*, 'to wish to establish our spiritual life on the fear of everlasting punishment. For, says St Paul, we have not received the spirit of servile fear, the spirit of the slave who fears chastisement, but the spirit of divine adoption.'[40] However, the holy abbot goes on to say that, far from being an ugly embarrassment, the supernatural fear of Hell is a beautiful encouragement from Christ, a salutary instrument that our dear Lord bestows upon us for the perfection of our union with Him by charity.

[D]o not forget that our Lord, whose words, as He Himself says, are principles of life for our souls (cf. John 6: 64), tells us to fear not chastisement but the Almighty who has power to cast our body and soul for ever 'into Gehenna'. And note that when our Lord makes this admonition of the fear of God to His disciples, He does so, because they are His friends: *Dico autem vobis amicis meis* (Luke 12: 4). It is a testimony of love He gives them in thus instilling in them this salutary fear.[41]

A true friend wants us to share his own happiness and to avoid the unhappiness into which he knows we may fall. Now Jesus is our most perfect friend, and so He wants us to share the best happiness there is, the divine happiness He enjoys with the Father and the Holy Spirit in Heaven. What is more, He wants us to be spared the misery of the souls that have plunged into the pit with Satan and his demons. It is for this reason that in His Passion Christ our Lord offers up to the Father the sacrifice that makes atonement for the sins that merit Hell, and that in His public ministry He brings down from the Father the doctrine that reveals the very real danger of Hell. In fidelity to the Master, St Paul likewise displays a tough friendship towards us. He praises

the richness of the divine mercy, of which he himself was a bene-
ficiary; but he also insists that '"it is a fearful thing" for the soul,
after having obstinately resisted the divine law, "to fall into the
hands of the living God" (Heb. 10: 31)'.[42] Dom Marmion quotes
the Apostle's words and then adds a prayer from the heart: 'O
Father in Heaven, deliver us from evil!'[43] The great beauty of the
divinely revealed Catholic religion is that the fear of Hell, moving
us to imperfect contrition, is sufficient disposition for receiving
the absolution of our mortal sins, however many and terrible
they may be, and thus for being restored to the divinizing life of
grace and charity and intimate communion with the Trinity.
Moreover, even when we make progress in the spiritual life, the
fear of Hell protects us from the sin of presumption and impels us
to pray for the gift of perseverance in the true faith and the state
of grace even unto our last breath. 'We must not deceive ourselves', says Marmion, '[r]eprobation is a possibility for each one
of us, and for every soul committed to our care.' He points out
the places in the rite of Holy Mass in which the Church brings this
terrible possibility before the eyes of our mind. In the Roman
Canon, in words added by St Gregory the Great, the priest
implores of God the grace of being 'snatched from eternal
damnation', and, in the prayer he says before Holy Communion,
the priest asks Christ never to let him be separated from Him.
The Church, Christ's beloved Bride and our dear Mother, never
allows her children to lean back in the soul-destroying luxury of
presumption. As Abbot Marmion says, even 'the soul in the state
of union cannot say: "I don't need to think about Hell or practise
mortification any more"'.[44] In his book on the priesthood, he
adds these personal reflections, the thoughts of a true father and
shepherd in Christ:

Sometimes, in the silence of the cloister when I am alone with God and
face to face with eternity, I think of this separation from the absolute
Good and of this overwhelming malediction which men, and even
priests, can call down upon themselves: 'Depart from me, you cursed'
(Matt. 25: 41), and I feel that one should accept all the suffering, all the

contempt of this world rather than risk incurring such a torment, and that in our capacity as apostles of Christ we should consecrate all our talents, all our strength and all our zeal, to save these poor blind souls who are rushing into the abyss of eternal misery.[45]

Purgatory: Heaven Longed For

Purgatory is the state or place in which human souls, separated from their bodies, are purified and made ready for entry into Heaven. These are the souls of human beings who have left this world in the state of grace, and therefore in charity with God, but who bear upon them some blemish, which must be removed before they can look upon the face of the thrice-holy God in the Empyrean of perfect bliss.[46] 'There shall not enter into it', says the seer of the Apocalypse, 'anything defiled' (Rev. 21: 27). Heaven is for the pure alone, as Blessed Denys explains:

No one can enter the heavenly Jerusalem unless they are utterly free from all spot and liability to punishment. For who can say how pure must the heart be that will be united immediately and beatifically to the divine and uncreated Light? There could be not the slightest stain in it. If, then, we do not want to be held back too long from glory after this present life, nor undergo the very grave pains of Purgatory, let us strive here and now unceasingly to direct ourselves towards God with a pure mind, and serve Him with a vigilant heart, obeying Him with all reverence, advancing in the fervour of charity, guarding our hearts with care, and raising up our minds at all times to God, praying without ceasing with the sweat of our brow, lamenting, correcting, and avoiding our defects, and mortifying and offering ourselves to God in this daily martyrdom.[47]

I have described Purgatory as Heaven 'longed for'. Those words need careful explanation. The holy souls are assured of their salvation and confirmed in grace: God has revealed their heavenly destination to them in the particular judgement. Their Christian hope, their longing for Heaven, therefore, has a different quality to ours in the wayfaring state. It is like the yearning in the heart of a soldier returning home from war as he walks the last mile, compared with the yearning he felt when he was still on the battlefield. The hope of the holy soul has the certitude of one who is arriving, whereas the hope of the wayfarer has the certitude of tending in the right direction.[48]

The Existence of Purgatory

Quarton places Purgatory directly under the foundations of the city of Rome. This feature of his design has a sound basis in Church history and indeed in Church doctrine, for it is the Church whose visible head on earth is the Roman Pontiff, the one true Church of Jesus Christ, that, for a large part of the last millennium, has defended the divinely revealed truth concerning Purgatory against those who deny it. The Eastern Orthodox pray for the souls of the faithful departed and offer the Eucharistic Sacrifice for them, but they misunderstand the nature of the state in which the righteous dead find themselves before entering Heaven. By contrast, Protestants reject the very existence of Purgatory and refuse to pray or do good works for those who have departed this life. For example, despite the magnificence of its English prose, Cranmer's Protestant Burial Service in *The Book of Common Prayer* is bleak in its doctrine: the dead would seem to be exclusively either in Hell or in Heaven, in any case beyond the reach of the prayers and love of those they have left behind.

At the Council of Florence, in its decree for the reunion of the Greek Orthodox, promulgated just fifteen years before the altar-piece was painted, the Church asserts the existence, and defines the nature, of Purgatory.

[I]f they are truly penitent and have died in the charity of God, before they have made satisfaction by worthy fruits of penance for their sins of commission and omission, their souls are cleansed after death by purgatorial punishments (*poenis purgatoriis*). In order that they be relieved of punishments of this kind, the suffrages of the faithful who are still alive are of benefit to them, namely, the sacrifices of Masses, prayers, alms, and other works of piety which the faithful are accustomed to do for the other faithful according to the Church's practice.[49]

A century later, in response to Protestant denials, the Council of Trent would restate this teaching on the existence of Purgatory and the help given to the holy souls by the suffrages of the faithful. The Council Fathers also instructed the bishops to make sure their priests preached nothing but the 'sound doctrine of Purgatory (*sanam de purgatorio doctrinam*)', to exclude 'the more subtle and difficult questions' from popular sermons, and to forbid doubtful and erroneous opinions, as well as anything smacking of superstition or 'dishonourable gain'.[50]

Less than twenty-five years after the painting of our altarpiece for the Villeneuve Charterhouse, a child was born in England who would later consider a vocation at the London Charterhouse, decide instead on the state of Christian marriage, be appointed Chancellor of England by the king of England, and finally die as a martyr for the King of Heaven. His name was Thomas More, and, in addition to his other claims to glory, he gave the Church one of the most eloquent defences ever made of the existence and nature of Purgatory.

In October 1529 More completed a little book, *The Supplication of Souls*, composed in response to a pamphlet written by the Protestant agitator, Simon Fish, under the title of *Supplication for the Beggars*. Fish argued for the confiscation of Church property and endowments, apparently for the benefit of 'the needy, impotent, blind, lame, and sick',[51] but, as More perceived, by a more zealous intention, for the destruction of the pious practices associated with Purgatory. In medieval England many institutions—chantry chapels, of course, but also colleges—were endowed with the specific goal of providing prayers, especially of Masses, for the souls of the dead. In his pamphlet, with his customary satirical flair, More allows the poor souls in Purgatory to plead for the continuation of 'the daily Masses and other ghostly suffrages of priests, religious, and folk of Holy Church' offered up for their intention. He exposes the cruelty of Protestant individualism, which cuts off the faithful departed from solidarity with their kinsmen and fellow Christians on earth. '[N]ature and Christendom', they plead, 'bindeth you to remember us . . . [We . . . are] your late acquaintances, kindred, spouses, companions, play-fellows, and friends.'[52] Both by charity and the character of their baptism, the holy souls remain united with us as members of the Mystical Body. Indeed, because of their confirmation in grace and charity, the virtuous dead in Purgatory are more perfectly incorporated into Christ than we are. '[N]one is there yet living that is more very member of Christ's Mystical Body that is His Church than we be nor no man living that hath more need of help than we.'[53] Nothing, not even death, can separate us from the love God has for us, nor from the love that we have for each other 'in Christ Jesus our Lord', as His living members (cf. Rom. 8: 38–9). Now the members of Christ are called to express their love by praying for each other. Therefore, we are called to express our undying love of the holy souls by means of unfailing prayers for them. In so doing, we help them, but we also help ourselves by a meritorious act.

For as he that lighteth another the candle hath never the less light himself, and he that bloweth the fire for another to warm him doth warm himself also therewith, so surely, good friends, the good that ye send hither before you both greatly refresheth us, and yet is wholly reserved here for you with our prayers added thereto for your further advantage.[54]

Shakespeare reveals his Catholic mind by making the same point, when Horatio cries out to the ghost of Hamlet's father: 'If there be any good thing to be done, | That may to thee do ease and grace to me, | Speak to me'.[55]

One of St Thomas More's arguments for the existence of Purgatory is, as far as I know, original to him. It concerns the incident recorded in the second book of Maccabees, according to which Judas Maccabeus, 'the great good and godly valiant captain of

God's people', ordered prayer, almsgiving, and sacrifice to be offered for the remission of the sins of Jews who, though they died fighting for the liberty of Israel, were found to have been wearing pagan amulets (cf. 2 Macc. 12: 42 46). Protestants refuse to accept this text as proof of Purgatory, because they exclude the books of the Maccabees from the canon of inspired and inerrant Scripture. More responds by proving the canonicity of Maccabees from the text of the Gospel of St John.[56] The argument runs as follows. To accept any one of the religious reforms of Judas Maccabeus is, at least implicitly, to affirm the divinely inspired character of the books in which those reforms are recounted. Now, according to St John, our Lord celebrated the midwinter feast of the Dedication of the Temple (cf. John 10: 22), *Hanukkah*, which was introduced by Judas Maccabeus in order to commemorate the cleansing of the Temple after its pagan defilement. Therefore, in More's own words, 'the books of that noble history [of the Maccabees], . . . continually kept and reserved so long after and honoured by Christ's own precious person and testified by His holy Evangelist in the book of his holy Gospel, cannot be but endowed with undoubted truth and of divine authority'.[57]

Pie Jesu Domine: The Nature of Purgatory

In the Villeneuve altarpiece, the angel helping the purified souls out of Purgatory is standing on the rocky approach to Golgotha, as if to imply that Purgatory is an effect of the Passion. It is by the atoning sacrifice of God-made-man, by His precious blood and saving merits, that the poor souls are made ready for the sight of His glory in Heaven. *Pie Jesu Domine, | Dona eis requiem . . .* 'Lord Jesus, in thy merciful kindness and by the power of thy holy Cross, grant the faithful departed a speedy entry into the eternal Sabbath rest of Heaven.' What purges us in Purgatory is the fire of love that pours out from the pierced Heart of Jesus.

But *what* is purged in Purgatory? The answer of Catholic theology is that the holy souls are cleansed of venial sins, the temporal punishment due to sins, and the relics of sin (*reliquiae peccatorum*). It is these last two that require most comment.

Paying off the Debt

'Amen I say to thee, thou shalt not go out from thence till thou repay the last farthing' (Matt. 5: 26). There is an eternal punishment, one that goes on for ever in Hell, but there is also a temporal punishment, which lasts just for a time, whether on earth or in Purgatory. It is a divinely revealed truth that, even when our mortal sins have been forgiven and the liability to eternal punishment removed, we still have to pay off a debt of temporal punishment.[58] Sacred Scripture gives us many examples of this taxation of pain. Consider, for example, King David's sin and repentance. He committed a mortal sin when he contrived the death of Uriah the Hittite in order to take Uriah's wife as his own. When the prophet Nathan confronts him with his wickedness, he confesses with noble simplicity: 'I have sinned against the Lord' (2 Sam. 12: 13). In the Psalm, too, we hear his acts of contrition and confession: 'Against thee alone have I sinned' (Ps. 50: 6). God forgives David; the king is restored to friendship with the Lord. However, he still has to undergo a temporal chastisement: the child born of the union with Uriah's wife dies (cf. 2 Sam. 12: 19).

All the sufferings we endure in this world have the characteristic of punishment or pain.[59] As St Thomas says, 'every involuntary suffering is a punishment'.[60] He does not mean that there is an exact correspondence between the amount we suffer in this life and the sins we commit, because, as we learn from the example of Job, a holy man may suffer grievously as a test or as a vocation of vicarious reparation; moreover, flagrant sinners may live long lives without any apparent troubles. St Thomas is making a different point. First, he recognizes that by our personal sins we bring many pains of soul and body both upon ourselves and upon our fellow men. Secondly, he is reminding us that, without the 'sin of nature', that is, without Original Sin, the deprived state of our human nature that we contract at our conception, men would not suffer at all. When Adam sinned by disobeying the divine commandment, he brought death and suffering upon himself and his descendants: 'Sin came into the world through one man, and through sin death' (Rom. 5: 12). God placed our first parents in the beautiful Garden with multiple blessings, both natural and supernatural. In particular, he freely bestowed upon them the so-called preternatural gift of freedom from the necessity of bodily death and from the disease and pain that precede it. Thus, for us fallen sons of Adam, suffering and death are the consequences, indeed the penalty, of Original Sin. As the Angelic Doctor puts it: '[T]he tradition of faith holds it as certain that the rational creature could have incurred no evil, either in the soul or in the body, had there not been a preceding sin, whether of the person or of nature.'[61]

But why should sin and suffering be co-ordinated in this way? Why must the infliction of pain follow the commission of fault? The Catechism gives this wise answer: 'These two punishments [eternal and temporal] must not be conceived of as a kind of vengeance inflicted by God from without, but as following from the very nature of sin.'[62] St Thomas, in turn, offers us the metaphysical understanding that lies behind the Catechism's simple assertion. A man commits sin, says Thomas, 'according to his will' (*secundum voluntatem*), but he suffers pain or punishment 'against his will' (*contra voluntatem*). When I sin, I cosset myself by doing just what I like. I insist on doing what I want, even though it is not what God, who knows what is best for me, wants for me. By contrast, when I suffer punishment, something happens to me that I don't like. Through this balancing of indulgence by injury, the order of divine justice is to some extent restored, and, if lawful authority inflicts the punishment, the disruption of human justice is also made good. The trouble is that, though punishment helps to restore the order of the world, by itself it does not address the disorder within *me*: punishment alone doesn't turn my soul from a bombsite into a garden. However, if I accept the punishment freely with my will, it will have the power of *satisfaction*. I begin to make up, to atone, for what I have done wrong, and the transformation of my soul is set in train.[63]

Here we reach a deep mystery. According to human law, and for the purposes of restoring friendship with my fellows, I may be able to make up for what I have done, but how can I ever hope to make adequate satisfaction to the thrice-holy God, since my sins, which are first of all against Him (cf. Ps. 50: 6), are in a way infinite in their offensiveness? 'Since . . . God surpasses the creature to infinity, the offence of the man who sins mortally against God will be infinite.'[64] Now no man, by his natural powers, can remove such an infinite offence.[65] Only God-made-man, the divine person of the eternal Son in His human nature, can make, and has made, satisfaction for the immense mass of human wickedness. So rich is the Father in His mercy that He sent His only-begotten Son as man to do what we mere men could never do. In obedience to the Father, and out of love for us, the sinless Son took the burden of our sins upon Himself, and, by His Passion and death, He made not merely adequate but superabundant satisfaction.[66] 'He was wounded for our iniquities, He was bruised for our sins; the chastisement of our peace was upon Him, and by His bruises we are healed' (Isa. 53: 5).

'But, surely,' we may protest, 'we human persons are the sinners, the ones who need to make atonement; how can the human suffering of a sinless divine person be of benefit to us?' St Thomas considers this objection and offers the following resolution of the difficulty. Christ is the Head of the Mystical Body, we His members, and together we, with Him, are 'like one mystical person'. Now what belongs to the Head belongs also to the members. Therefore, the satisfaction of Christ belongs to us as His members.[67] As the Fathers of the Council of Trent explain in their decree on the Sacrament of Penance, when we make satisfaction for our sins, we do so only as members of Christ, as those who by His grace live in Him and act through Him:

The satisfaction that we make for our sins is not ours in such a way that it be not through Christ Jesus, for, though we can do nothing of ourselves as of ourselves, 'we can do everything' with the co-operation of 'Him who strengthens us' (cf. Phil. 4: 13). Thus man has nothing in which to glory; all our glorying is in Christ (cf. 1 Cor. 1: 31; 2 Cor. 10: 17; Gal. 6: 14), in whom we live (cf. Acts 17: 28), in whom we merit, in whom we make satisfaction, 'bringing forth worthy fruits of penance' (cf. Luke 3: 8), fruits that derive their power from Him, are offered by Him to the Father, and through Him are accepted by the Father.[68]

It is through, with, and in Christ that we make satisfaction, pay off the debt of temporal punishment due to our sins. But *how*, practically speaking, do we make satisfaction? The Council, summarizing the teaching of the Fathers, gives us three examples. First, there are the penances that we voluntarily take upon ourselves (for example, during Lent or on Fridays). Secondly, there is the penance imposed upon us by the priest when we go to confession. Thirdly, there are 'the temporal afflictions imposed on us by God, if we bear them with patience'; these, says the Council of Trent, are 'the greatest proof of love'.[69] Here the Council Fathers anticipate the doctrine of the 'little way' of St Thérèse: the simplest way of doing penance, the way that is sweetest in the sight of God, is bearing and offering up the pains, great or small, that come to us in the course of our daily lives. If we offer up our sufferings in loving union with Christ, then they can be 'satisfactory', help to make up for all that we have done wrong in our lives, heal the world, and restore us to true loving.

Since we are members of one another in the one Mystical Body of Christ, we can make satisfaction not only for our own sins but also for those of our brethren, thereby 'bearing one another's burdens' (cf. Gal. 6: 2). As St Thomas explains: 'Insofar as two men are one by charity, one can make satisfaction for the other.'[70] St Paul speaks of this apostolate of vicarious suffering in many places in his epistles. For example, writing to the Colossians, he says that he 'fills up those things that are wanting of the sufferings of Christ, in my flesh, for His Body, which is the Church' (Col. 1:

24). St Augustine points out that nothing is 'wanting' in the sufferings of Christ the Head: on earth He suffered more in body and soul than any man has ever suffered or will ever suffer in this life, and now, in Heaven, glorified at the right hand of the Father, death and suffering no more have dominion over Him. However, much is still wanting to the sufferings of Christ's members, for, till the end of the age, they are called to unite their sufferings to Christ's in order to make reparation for their own and their brethren's sins, for the good of 'His Body, which is the Church'.[71] '[O]ur Saviour', says Pope Pius XII in *Mystici corporis*, 'wants to be helped by the members of His Mystical Body in carrying out the work of redemption, not because of any need or weakness in Him, but because He has arranged it for the greater honour of His immaculate Bride'. Thus, concludes Pope Pius, 'the salvation of many depends on the prayers and voluntary mortifications undertaken to this end by the members of the Mystical Body of Jesus Christ'.[72] Pius's successor-but-one, Pope Paul VI, speaking of the same mystery, sums it up as follows:

This is the ancient dogma of the Communion of Saints, according to which the life of each of the sons of God is joined, in Christ and through Christ, to the lives of all his brother Christians by a wonderful link in the supernatural oneness of the Mystical Body of Christ, in the mystical person, as it were.[73]

The Pope goes on to show how, through the Communion of Saints, the Church administers indulgences, that is, the remission of temporal punishment through an application of the great treasury of satisfaction of Christ and His saints.[74] Here, then, is a fourth way by which the debt of temporal punishment can be reduced, either in part or as a whole: we can acquire *indulgences* for ourselves or for the faithful departed.

The Church's doctrine of temporal punishment may seem severe, but behind the unprepossessing façade lies an interior of radiant and consoling truth. St Thomas, followed later by the Council of Trent, insists that, by attaching the requirement of temporal punishment and satisfaction to forgiven sin, God acts not only out of justice but also out of mercy. First, temporal punishment and satisfaction bring home to us the gravity of sin, and they help to restrain us from committing sin in the future: those lessons of Providence are a great kindness.[75] Secondly, by inviting us to make satisfaction through the merits of Christ and by the grace of the Holy Spirit, God the Father does us the courtesy of involving us, as co-operators, in the mystery of our own salvation.[76] He wants us to be, not spectators, but partners in the new and everlasting covenant. In the words of St Augustine, treasured by St Catherine of Siena, 'He who created us without us will not save us without us.'[77] Thirdly, temporal afflictions, when patiently endured, are a gift of our provident Father in Heaven, for, with the help of His grace, they can serve to train us back into the ways of self-giving love. When we sin we pamper our wills and turn more and more inward upon ourselves; when we suffer, or at least when we try to bear our suffering in Christian patience, our wills, which do not like the suffering, are, so to speak, bent outwards and away from self: we have a new, God-sent opportunity for growing in charity.[78]

Let us apply this general doctrine of temporal punishment to the mystery of Purgatory. If we depart this life, having made insufficient satisfaction for our sins, then we have to pay off the outstanding debt by enduring purifying pains in Purgatory. The Church's Doctors explain that in Purgatory we do not pay by meriting or satisfying, for the time of obtaining merit and actively working out our salvation by fear and trembling is restricted to this life; no, the holy souls settle their account by 'satispassion', by suffering enough.[79]

But how do souls suffer in Purgatory? It is once again a Benedictine of an English monastery, Dom Vonier, who offers, to my mind, the clearest explanation of this mystery. He points out that the separated soul of the just man really 'ought to see God, in virtue of its grace and of its spirit-state'. If it is held back from entry into full beatitude because it needs purification, it finds

itself, in St Thomas's phrase, *in statu violento*, 'a violent, an unnatural state; the soul is still deprived of what, by the very laws of its
charity and its spiritualness, it ought to have, and this deprivation
constitutes its suffering'.[80] The delay in reaching the Fatherland is *1) Delay*
the holy soul's chief pain: so near and yet, how piercingly, so far.
As Cardinal Newman says in *The Dream of Gerontius*:

> The longing for Him,when thou seest Him not;
> The shame of self at thought of seeing Him,
> Will be thy veriest, sharpest purgatory.[81]

There is a secondary pain in Purgatory, the pain of sense, of *11) Sense*
which the instrumental cause, according to most Scholastic theo- *Fire?.*
logians, is a material fire. The Catechism mentions this fire,[82] but
the Magisterium of the Church does not insist upon its acceptance (for example, by the separated Greek Orthodox);[83] it is at
best a probable opinion. The important truth to grasp is that,
whether or not the poor souls are purged by means of material
fire, the principal cause is the immaterial fire of the Triune Godhead. 'Our God is a consuming fire' (cf. Deut. 4: 24). Now, says
Blessed Denys, 'as fire consumes and devours and inflames, so
God consumes sins and enkindles hearts. In fire, too, are brightness and heat, through which the light of wisdom and the fervour
of charity are made known.'[84] Before we are made blessed within
this enlightening and warming fire of the Godhead, the furnace of
the Father's Wisdom and Love, the same uncreated Fire must
first rid us of anything left of the shadows of ignorance or the
coldness of unlove. The living flame of love burns in order to
transform.

The holy souls accept their suffering with their wills; indeed, *Acceptance* *D* *Key*
they offer it up, with the most generous charity, as an act of worship of the thrice-holy God. For them in their pain, as for the
saints in their bliss, peace is found in conformity to God's most
loving will, and from the peace comes a joy that, according to St
Catherine of Genoa (who was a child when our altarpiece was
painted), surpasses anything we can know in this life.[85] The pain

of Purgatory is unimaginable, but so, too, is the joy of those poor souls who are certain of finally attaining the Fatherland and looking upon the long-sought face of the heavenly Father Himself.

Getting Rid of the Rust

Some of the saints—for example, St Catherine of Genoa—compare the relics of sin to rust.[86] The repeated performance of sin leaves its mark on the soul of the penitent even after the guilt of sin has been remitted, just as a ship builds up rust on its hull from exposure to the salt of the sea. Preferring metaphysics to metaphor, St Thomas defines the relics of sin as 'dispositions caused by previous acts of sin, the result being that the penitent finds difficulty in doing deeds of virtue'.[87] The habitually angry man, even after sincere repentance and valid absolution and the restoration to him of the grace of virtues and the gifts, is going to find it hard to be meek in the face of frustration and annoyance. If he dies in the state of grace without having made further spiritual progress, he will be in friendship with God, but the unfortunate tendencies will remain, and he will lack the purity and totality of self-surrender necessary for immediate entry into Heaven. To achieve this purification, and to complete the gift of self, God provides for all converted souls who need it the precious gift of Purgatory. As St Catherine of Genoa teaches us:

A thing that is covered cannot respond to the sun's rays, not because of any defect in the sun, which is shining all the time, but because the cover is an obstacle; if the cover be burnt away, this thing is open to the sun; more and more as the cover is consumed does it respond to the rays of the sun. It is in this way that rust, which is sin, covers souls, and in Purgatory is burnt away by fire; the more it is consumed, the more do the souls respond to God, the true sun.[88]

Helping the Holy Souls

As we have seen, one of the innovations of the Protestants that most shocked St Thomas More was their refusal of Christian charity towards the souls of the faithful departed: the beloved dead were cut off from Christendom, unconnected with their fellows by prayer or any other practical instrument of love. By contrast, our painting shows the living communion of the different states of the Mystical Body, on earth, in Purgatory, and in Heaven. The Carthusian on Calvary is worshipping his crucified Lord and God, but he doubtless also offers up his supplications on behalf of his fellow Christians on earth and in Purgatory. The angel helping the bishop (or pope) out of the cleansing fires shows the friendship of Heaven and Purgatory, while the Mass of St Gregory the Great demonstrates the solidarity of Church Militant with Church Suffering. The artist's intention in placing the celebration of Holy Mass so close to Purgatory is evident: the saving power of Christ's Sacrifice on the Cross, which is re-presented in the Eucharistic Sacrifice, is being applied to the needs of the poor souls. As the Council of Trent teaches, the souls detained in Purgatory are helped by the 'suffrages' (acts of intercession) of the faithful, 'and especially by the acceptable Sacrifice of the Altar'.[89] The same Council teaches that the Sacrifice of the Altar is 'truly propitiatory' and is 'rightly offered, according to apostolic tradition, not only for the sins, punishments, satisfaction, and other necessities of the living faithful, but also for those who have died in Christ but are not yet fully purified'.[90] In the Sacrifice of the Mass, the Sacrifice of the Cross is re-presented, and its saving fruits poured out. Now one of the fruits of Calvary is propitiation, that is, superabundant satisfaction for the sins of the world. Therefore, when Holy Mass is offered, in virtue of the activity of Christ the Priest and the presence of Christ the Victim, the satisfactory power of the Precious Blood is applied to the holy souls (either all of them or one of them in particular), and at least part of their outstanding debt of temporal punishment is removed.[91]

Conclusion: The Monastic and Christian Life—The Fight against Hell and the Purgation of Love

In its dedication to the contemplation of God and the love of the brethren, a monastery is a kind of Jerusalem, an anticipation of Heaven. However, it is situated in a world of ceaseless struggle and pilgrimage, and so it is also a bulwark against Hell and a sort of earthly Purgatory, a place and a society in which men can defend themselves against the deadly fire of demonic envy and dispose themselves to be transformed by the Living Flame of divine love.

The monastery is a bulwark against Hell in two senses: first, because the sons of St Benedict are obliged by the Holy Rule to meditate upon Hell in order to avoid being condemned to it in the particular judgement; and secondly, because by their spiritual battles against the powers of Hell, they help to fortify and encourage the rest of their brethren in the Church Militant on earth. Among the 'instruments of good works', that is, among the means by which the monk can make progress in the love of Christ, St Benedict includes the following practices: '[T]o fear the Day of Judgement. To dread Hell.'[92] One of the motives of obedience mentioned in the Holy Rule is 'the fear of Hell'.[93] Benedict warns his sons of the danger of eternal punishment for those who culpably neglect or abuse the gifts they have been given by God: 'We must at all time so serve Him with those gifts of His that are in us that He may never as a wrathful father disinherit his sons, nor yet as a fearful master be so enraged by our evils as to cast into everlasting punishment the wicked servants who would not follow Him into glory.'[94] At the same time, the last word of the Holy Rule is not 'fear' or 'Hell' but 'Christ' and 'love' and 'Heaven'. Once he has climbed the rungs of the ladder of humility, says Benedict, 'the monk will presently come to that perfect love of God which casts out fear; whereby he will begin to observe

without labour, as though naturally and by habit, all those pre-
cepts which formerly he did not observe without fear: no longer
for fear of Hell, but for love of Christ and through good habit
and delight in the virtues'.[95] As he perseveres in the search for
God, for the ever more wholehearted gift of himself to Christ in
charity, the monk finds, as Benedict puts it, that he is able to 'run
the course of God's commandments with broadened heart and
ineffable sweetness of love'.[96] Monks like this have hearts conformed to the Heart of Jesus and therefore full of gratitude and
humility. They are not presumptuous, and so they still dread
Hell; but now the dread is of offending or ever being thankless to
Him whose love they so sweetly know, the Son of God who
loved them and gave Himself up for them (cf. Gal. 2: 20), that
they might not be cast into everlasting fire.

The monastery is also a bulwark against Hell in the sense that
it is a special kind of battleground for struggle against the fallen
created pure spirits, the first denizens of Hell, the devil and his
demons: 'For our wrestling is not against flesh and blood; but
against principalities and powers, against the rulers of the world
of this darkness, against the spirits of wickedness in the high
places' (Eph. 6: 12). St Benedict sets forth this part of the monastic
vocation in the opening lines of the Holy Rule: 'To thee is my
discourse now addressed, whosoever thou mayest be, that,
renouncing thine own will to fight for Christ, the true King, dost
take up the very strong and glorious weapons of obedience.'[97] It
is a consolation for us who fight the same battle in the world to
know that, in the solidarity of the Mystical Body, we receive re-
inforcement from the example, prayers, and merits of those of
our fellow soldiers of Christ who have taken up the strong
weapons of the counsels according to the Holy Rule. Nothing is
suffered or done in vain in the Communion of Saints, if it is
suffered or done to God's greater glory. When a monk, for the
love of Christ, renders his will in holy obedience to his abbot,
when by the grace of the Holy Spirit, he resists the blandishments
of the demonic prince of pride and disobedience, then—to adapt

Blessed Mother Teresa's famous words—he does 'something beautiful for God' and indeed for the whole people of God.

Every monastery has a special closeness to Purgatory. Others may forget the poor souls, but monks do not. The departed brethren are remembered daily in the refectory. Traditionally, Carthusians recite the Office of the Dead in addition to the monastic office and the Office of our Lady. Moreover, by committing themselves to the quest of God and the perfection of charity, monks declare themselves to be ready for the earthly purgatory of the nights, active and passive, of sense and spirit, by which charity is made more pure, the gift of self to God more generous.[98] As Dom John Chapman says in a letter to a nun: 'God calls people in various ways, and some feel their love of Him in a different way . . . But whatever the exact way in which people tend to God, they get into the "Night of the Spirit", if they are to make real progress.' Of course, the monk, the ordinary Christian indeed, should not waste time plotting his precise position on the ascent of Mount Carmel. Dom Chapman makes the point with a bluntness at once British and Benedictine: 'The less we look into ourselves the better.'[99] All we need to know is that, if we are serious about being more nearly united in charity with Christ and the Father, we must be ready for a purgation by the Spirit of Love so searching that, if it is completed, no further cleansing after death will be needed.[100] For the fallen sons of Adam, purgation, in this life or the next, is the only way to union with the Trinity.

AVE REGINA CAELORUM

Heaven's Sweet Queen

The Three Divine Persons crown our Lady as Queen of Heaven. God the Father and God the Son breathe forth God the Holy Spirit, the Dove of Love, and as a gift of Their Love, under the wings of the Dove, They place the crown on the Blessed Virgin's head. The angels are in the background, and the saints kneel or stand at a certain distance from the throne of God, but our Lady is entirely enfolded in the crimson copes of the Father and the Son, and the gold of her dress matches the panels on the copes. By these details, the artist is suggesting a tremendous truth: no created person, not even the highest of the Cherubim and Seraphim, has a more intimate communion with the Trinity than does the Mother of the Only-begotten Son. And yet Mary is placed at a lower level than the divine persons: she remains only a creature, and, though exalted above all other created persons, she is infinitely less than God. Our Lady herself bears witness to this truth by her posture: she kneels, and her hands are crossed in an attitude of perfect docility and adoration, as if to say again, as she is crowned by the Holy Spirit, what she said once when she conceived by the Holy Spirit, *Fiat mihi secundum verbum*, 'Be it done unto me, according to thy word' (Luke 1: 38). Three of Mary's fingers are joined, symbolizing the Persons of the Godhead, whom she worships. *Gloria Patri et Filio et Spiritui Sancto*, she says, 'Glory be to the Father, who from all eternity predestined me; glory be to the Son, whom in the flesh I conceived as a virgin, and to whom in the flesh I gave birth as a virgin, and for whom in the flesh I remained for ever a virgin; glory be to the Holy Spirit, my

Spouse, by whose operation I conceived, and with whose grace my soul was filled from the beginning of my existence. Blessed be the Holy and Undivided Trinity!'

The geometrical plan of the altarpiece is made up of two triangles, one equilateral, and the other isosceles.[1] The triangle with three equal sides, which has the higher position, represents the coequal Trinity, while the one with just two equal sides is a sign that creatures reflect the Trinity by way of trace or image, but that, however like their Creator they may be, the unlikeness is always greater. The outstretched wings of the Dove form the base of the equilateral, while the apex points towards the centre of our Lady's body, towards her womb and her heart. Now, if you draw a line along the perpendicular axis of this first triangle, beginning with the upright of the cross above the head of the Dove, it will lead you to the Blessed Virgin's mouth and heart, and from there downwards to the upright beam of the Cross of Christ on Calvary. The isosceles has as its base the bottom line of Heaven, and its two equal angles rest on the gable of the church of Santa Croce in Rome and on the pinnacle of the Temple in Jerusalem; the apex of the isosceles is also at the heart of the Virgin.

The Trinitarian equilateral points down towards earth, while the creaturely isosceles reaches up to Heaven, the two apexes meeting at the Immaculate Heart. The meaning of this Euclidian symbolism is not hard to uncover: the Blessed Trinity, by the power of Christ's Cross, pours out grace upon men through the loving intercession of Blessed Mary Ever-Virgin, the Mother of God and Queen of Heaven. As one commentator on our painting has said, Quarton depicts, with consummate artistry, 'Mary's radiating influence upon the whole earth'.[2] The Villeneuve altarpiece is an image of our Lady's spiritual motherhood and her mediation of all graces.

This painting, which displays to our gaze all the chief doctrines of our religion, has its centre in the heart of the Immaculate. That is most fitting, because, as the Gospel tells us, Mary keeps all of God's words, 'pondering them in her heart' (Luke 2: 19). All the mysteries of the divinity of the Trinity and the humanity of the Son, of creation, redemption, and consummation, were contemplated by the Mother of God on earth in perfect faith, and are now contemplated by her in Heaven in the perfection of immediate vision. Our Lady contemplates the mysteries in her own mind, and somehow she brings them all together in ours. Mariology is the recapitulation of all theology. As the Fathers of the Second Vatican Council say: 'Mary, who entered intimately into the history of salvation, in a certain way unites and re-echoes in herself the greatest teachings of the faith, and when she is preached and venerated, she calls believers to her Son and His Sacrifice, and to the love of the Father.'[3]

The Council's statement might almost be a summary of the lesson that the monks of the Villeneuve Charterhouse wanted to impart through the altarpiece of Enguerrand Quarton. It is also the argument of this final chapter: *the Queen of Heaven is the most perfect embodiment of Heaven.* In her glorified body as well as in her soul, she contains all that the Triune God has in store for us in Paradise, those good things of which ear has never heard nor eye seen nor the earthly mind of man conceived. After God Himself and the sacred humanity of Christ, she herself is the best of all the good things we hope to see and enjoy. If you want to reach the Heart of Jesus in Heaven, then fly to the Heart of Mary, His Mother and yours. If you want to know what Heaven will mean for our souls and eventually also our bodies, then think of Mary in the beauty of her glorified person. If anything in Catholic doctrine, including Heaven, seems abstract or remote to you, then consider it in relation to the Virgin in whose womb and by whose faith the eternal Word was made flesh. Our Lady makes the abstract to be concrete, makes the distant seem close. The Queen of Heaven brings everything, including Heaven, down to earth.

In this final chapter, listening to the words of the antiphon *Ave regina caelorum*,[4] and gazing on the figures in our altarpiece, I shall consider the four great Marian dogmas, Our Lady's divine motherhood, perpetual virginity, Immaculate Conception, and bodily Assumption, and show how each of these mysteries proceed from and return to the Blessed Trinity, the vision of which is the very essence of heavenly beatitude. But, first of all, I shall consider our Lady's Queenship of Heaven, which, both in the Villeneuve altarpiece and in reality, is the effect of an operation of the Holy Trinity.

Regina caelorum, Domina angelorum: The Queenship of Our Lady

The Father, the Son, and the Holy Spirit place a crown on the head of the Blessed Virgin. Everything about her speaks of royalty. The gold of her dress would have reminded the Carthusians of Villeneuve of the forty-fourth Psalm, so often sung in the Office and at Mass in praise of the Incarnate Word and His Blessed Mother: *Astitit regina a dextris tuis*, 'The queen stood at thy right in gilded clothing, surrounded with variety' (Ps. 44: 9). In the Jerusalem below, that is, in the historical Judah, the queen or Great Lady (*g'bîrah*) was the *mother* of the king,[5] and so it is in the Jerusalem above. It is the Mother of Heaven's King who is Heaven's Queen, 'the Queen of Queens', says Denys, 'empress and incomparable lady'.[6] Around her, to right and left, we see her many subjects. The nine orders of the blessed pure spirits are in attendance, for she is the *Domina angelorum*. The saints of the Old Testament look upon her with eyes at once fatherly and filial, for this daughter of Abraham and David, the fairest lily of Israel, is the Queen of Patriarchs and Prophets, the Queen of the Jews. The Apostles, Martyrs, and Confessors are there, for she is regent of them all. The virgins have a small delegation, for Mary of Nazareth is their Queen and Mother and supreme exemplar, as David says in the Psalm: 'After her shall virgins be brought to the king' (Ps. 44: 14). 'All virgins', comments Denys, 'coming to Christ on the way by faith, and into the Fatherland by hope, follow Mary as the first and highest [of virgins], and submit to Christ by her example.'[7] As we can see in paintings of the mystical espousal of St Catherine of Siena,[8] it is through our Lady's mediation that virgins are united to Christ the Bridegroom.

The most important document of the Magisterium on the Queenship of our Lady is Pope Pius XII's encyclical *Ad caeli reginam*, promulgated during the Marian year of 1954, which instituted for the whole Latin Church the liturgical feast of the Queenship of our Lady. The venerable Pope shows that, just as Christ is King not only as God, but also as man and redeemer, so our Lady is Queen not only as Mother of God but also as the co-operator of the divine Redeemer. As prophesied in Genesis, the Mother of the Messiah helped her Son in the crushing of the Serpent (cf. Gen. 3: 15), that is, in the rescue of men from the dark dominion of Satan and in their transfer to the luminous Kingdom of Christ (cf. Col. 1: 13). Pope Pius goes on to say:

[I]n the full, proper, and absolute meaning of the term, only Jesus Christ, God and man, is King; but Mary, too, as Mother of Christ our God, as His associate in the work of redemption, in his struggle with His enemies and His final victory over them all, participates, albeit in a limited and analogous way, in His royal dignity. For from her union with Christ the King she attains a glory and eminence surpassing that of any other creature; from her union with Christ she receives the regal power to distribute the treasures of the Divine Redeemer's Kingdom; finally, from her union with Christ is derived the inexhaustible efficacy of her motherly intercession with the Son and His Father.[9]

Quarton shows the Blessed Trinity crowning the Mother of God as Queen of Heaven. From her conception, she has enjoyed an incomparable intimacy with the Three Divine Persons by grace, and now that intimacy is consummated in glory in the bestowal of regal dignity. On earth and in Heaven, our Lady is—as the medievals like to say, quoting the hymn of Adam of St Victor— *totius trinitatis nobile triclinium*, 'noble resting-place of the whole Trinity'.[10] In his commentary on the 'Hail Mary', leaning on St Thomas's conferences on the same prayer, Blessed Denys interprets the angel's words, 'The Lord is with thee', in a Trinitarian sense, in order to show how the Mother of the Son enjoys a familiarity with the Father and the Holy Spirit:

The Lord of Lords, the most high, true and only Lord God Himself, I say, is 'with thee', O [Mary] our Mother, as He has been with no other creature. For God the Father is with thee as with His only daughter, overshadowing thee by His power. God the Son is with thee as with His true Mother, remaining in thee by His wisdom. God the Holy Spirit is also with thee, as with His dearest friend and spouse, coming upon thee by the fire of His divine love. The whole of the most glorious Trinity and undivided Unity is with thee to accomplish in thee the glorious mystery of our restoration and this sacred mystery of the divine Incarnation.[11]

Such was our Lady's communion with the Trinity at the first moment of the Incarnation. However, already from the beginning of her existence, the predestined Mother of the Son was by grace the Father's adopted 'dearest daughter'[12] and the Holy Spirit's most perfect 'temple and sanctuary'.[13] Now, as we have seen, the degree of perfection in one's enjoyment of the Beatific Vision corresponds to one's closeness to God by the friendship of charity when one departs this life.[14] But our Lady, says Denys, is 'more familiar with, dearer and closer to, the super-blessed Trinity' than is any other created person. Therefore, she 'sees [the Trinity] more clearly, loves [the Trinity] more warmly, and rests in [the Trinity] more sweetly'[15] than does any other. 'O Queen of Gladness, the Holy Trinity now gladly embraces thee, endows thee with superlucent splendour, fills thee with glory, and exalts thee with incomparable honour.'[16] To be related so closely to the Triune God, to be so full of His grace and glory, is to have a rank and dignity beyond all human and angelic hierarchies, to be Queen of the Universe. That is what our Lady is already in principle on earth, and that is what she becomes in practice, by the operation of the Trinity, in Heaven: '[The] woman clothed with the sun, and the moon under her feet, and on her head a crown of twelve stars' (Rev. 12: 1).

But let us gaze more attentively at the star-crowned Queen of Heaven, lest we miss the true splendour of her queenship. She is Queen, but she is more Mother and Handmaid than Queen.[17] Her hands carry no orb or sceptre, but are folded gently on her breast. Her eyes look down in gratitude towards God for the great things He has done for her, and in charity for her subjects, that is, her children, on earth and in Purgatory. Everything about her speaks of royalty, but even more so of humility, of the exaltation of the lowly: the last become first. As we look at the Spirit of Love above her head, we hear the words of the heavenly Father asking through the prophet, 'Upon whom shall my Spirit rest, if not upon the quiet and humble?' (cf. Isa. 57: 15; 66: 2), and the Incarnate Son declaring in His own person: 'Blessed are the poor in spirit, for theirs is the Kingdom of Heaven' (Matt. 5: 3). And we hear the Blessed Virgin herself: 'He hath regarded the humility of His Handmaid' (Luke 1: 48).

St Thomas and all the masters of the Tradition teach us that humility is based on truth, on the perception of the reality of our littleness in relation to God in His infinitude and omnipotence.[18] Now, as Blessed Denys argues, the sinless Mother of God does not have the kind of perception of truth we sinners need to have, that is, the recognition of our woundedness and inclination to sin. However, she does have, and, most perfectly, the humility every creature ought to own, namely, an exact sense of her dependence upon God, both in the natural order and in the supernatural.[19] 'I who am full of grace', she says, 'know that all is grace, that I was elected and predestined to be the Mother of God, conceived immaculate and preserved from all sin, enabled to serve the Son of God as His most perfect disciple, and now crowned with glory as Queen of Heaven, as a stupendous free and loving gift from the Father rich in mercy. Like every other creature, I depend upon Him for my coming to be and continuing to be, and in my every action. Blessed be God for ever!' These are the words that our dear Mother Mary speaks to every monk and every Christian as he seeks God and Heaven by climbing the ladder of humility.

But she does not just impart a doctrine or furnish an example; she also pours out her motherly prayers, so that her divine Son may give us the graces to move and sustain and perfect us in the pursuit of humility. 'All is grace' she says of herself, and all grace is what she is for us, the Mother of Divine Grace.

Salve porta: The Divine Motherhood—The Chief Reason for the Queenship

Salve radix, salve porta, ex qua mundo lux est orta, 'Root of Jesse! Gate of morn! | Whence the world's true light was born'. Here we hear the chief reason for the Queenship of our Lady and indeed for all her other privileges: her divine motherhood. She is more Mother than Queen, Queen only because first of all she is Mother, Mother of God. The Blessed Virgin is *Regina caelorum*, Queen of the realm of the created light of glory, because she is the *porta, ex qua mundo lux est orta*, the Mother, according to the flesh, of the uncreated Light from Light, the Father's eternal Word and brilliant Wisdom, who is the lamp of the celestial city.

By being Mother of God, the Blessed Virgin has a dignity and therefore a claim to reign above that of all other creatures. Indeed, there is something almost infinite about the divine motherhood, as Blessed Denys argues, citing the authority of the Angelic Doctor:

Alhough no mere creature is of infinite dignity, yet, according to St Thomas, there are three created things that are somehow of infinite dignity. The first is the humanity of Christ, because it has been assumed into union with the personal and uncreated being of the eternal Word, that is, the only-begotten Son of God . . . *The second is the Most Blessed Virgin Mary, since she has been made the Mother of the true God, which is a dignity almost immense.* The third is the beatitude of the saints, since, as we say, it is the immediate enjoyment of the infinite good.[20]

To say that Mary is the Mother of God means that she conceived, carried in her womb, and gave birth to God the Son, not in the divine nature, of course, but in the human nature that He took upon Him for our salvation. According to St John Damascene, this greatest of all of our Lady's titles—*Theotokos, Deipara, Mater Dei*—in a certain way sums up the whole mystery of the Incarnation: as *Mother* of God, Mary is proof that her Son is true man; as Mother of *God*, she demonstrates that He is true God, and therefore also that, without ceasing to be true God, one and the same person has been made true man. Now the divine motherhood, like every other mystery of our faith, has a Trinitarian dimension, that is, opens up a perspective in faith on the Three-Personed God whom we hope to know one day by vision. The person whom the Mother of God conceives and gives birth to in the flesh is Himself One of the Trinity, the Second Divine Person, God the Son. And by thus giving Him human birth, Mary is given a unique relation to God the Father: as Blessed Denys says, she is '"co-parental" with God, since she has the same Son that He has'.[21] And finally, in becoming Mother of God, our Lady is related to God the Holy Spirit, for she conceives her Son in the flesh by the overshadowing of the Holy Spirit (cf. Luke 1: 35).

As we ponder Mary's glory as Mother of God, we must not forget what a gift of loving condescension it was for God to have a Mother. As Blessed Columba Marmion points out, the eternal Word could have made for Himself, as He did for Adam, a human nature 'already formed in the perfection of its organism', but He did not. 'In uniting Himself to humanity, the Word willed to pass through all the stages of human growth in order to sanctify them; He willed to be born of a woman.'[22] God the Son chose to be, so to speak, 'mothered' into human nature. And the condescension does not end with the physical fact of motherhood. '[W]hat is so wonderful in this birth is that the Word made it subject, so to speak, to the consent of this woman.'[23] Blessed Marmion goes on to quote the words of St Thomas, who said that, in saying Yes to the Incarnation of the Son of God, the

ᜃ ᜃ Blessed Virgin represented the whole of the human race. The uniting of human nature to the divine person of the Son is a kind of 'spiritual marriage', says St Thomas: the Son weds human nature to Himself, and through His concrete human nature He reaches out with spousal love to the whole human race. Now where there is a marriage, there must be consent. The Son gives His consent, for, with the Father and the Holy Spirit, He freely wills His Incarnation. But how does human nature, the nature of our race, give its consent to be assumed? St Thomas answers: *Per annuntiationem exspectabatur consensus virginis loco totius humanae naturae*, 'Through the Annunciation the consent of the Virgin was sought in place of the whole of human nature.'[24] So courteous is our God that He does not force Himself upon us when He comes in the flesh: He wants to be freely welcomed by the woman who, on behalf of us all, is to give Him our flesh.

In Heaven, high among the truths that the blessed see in God is our Lady's motherhood of God. With their beatified intellects they enter into the secret recesses of this mystery, by which a mere creature, a humble Jewish maiden, in faith and love gave her very blood to be the matter from which God made a body for Himself, carried Him in the womb for nine months, brought Him forth in a stable, fed Him from her breast, and, like every other Jewish mother, taught Him His prayers, the very words that He as God had already given to her fathers by supernatural revelation. And this exalted, almost infinite dignity of being Mother of God is the object of the veneration, says Blessed Denys, of 'the whole host of the heavenly court', and 'the more abundantly they praise the excellence [of the Mother of God], the more fervently they love her, and the greater the mercy that any of the blessed has obtained from God by [Mary] and through her, the more heartily do they cherish and honour her'.[25]

Our Lady's divine motherhood can never be taken for granted. Here below the confession that Mary is Theotokos protects and supports that orthodox faith in Christ without which no man can be pleasing to God.[26] High above, after the Blessed Trinity and the sacred humanity of the Son, the very person of God's Mother is the chief object of the vision and delight of the saints. Without the Mother of God, there is no Heaven for the children of Adam. It was through the divine motherhood of the Blessed Virgin, in her flesh and through faith, that the Incarnation of the Son of God took place. But, without the Incarnation, without the Son of God's Death and Resurrection in the flesh He took from Mary, human beings cannot attain the happiness of Heaven. Therefore, even if we consider only this first great truth about our Lady, leaving aside for a moment her actual intervention by intercession on our behalf, we have to say that the Mother of God is the joy of all the saints, *causa laetitiae*. Her divine Motherhood is an instrumental cause of their blessedness. In the liturgy named after him, St Basil the Great joins Heaven and earth in Marian jubilation: 'In thee rejoiceth, O thou who art full of grace, every created being, the hierarchy of the angels, and all mankind, O consecrated temple and supersensual paradise, glory of virgins, of whom God, who is our God before all the ages, was incarnate and became a little child.'[27] Denys the Carthusian is also certain that 'all the joys of this world gathered up in one cannot compare with the joy that each one of the blessed has in the presence and sight of the Most Blessed Virgin Mary'.[28] He adds a qualification, which, far from detracting from Mary's glory, reveals that glory's ultimate ground, the infinite majesty of her Son, who is of one substance with the Father and the Holy Spirit in the Godhead: 'And yet all these joys pertain to the accidental reward of the blessed, which, taken as a whole, is incomparably less than the joy of the essential reward, namely, the blessed enjoyment, by which they enjoy the Most Excellent Trinity and the one most simple Godhead of the Trinity.'[29]

In the conclusion to his book on *The Divine Motherhood*, Abbot Vonier argues that '[t]rue civilization is easily tested by its attitude towards motherhood',[30] or, as Catholics of the twenty-first century have learnt from Pope John Paul II to say, there can only be a civilization of love if it is built on the culture of life, on respect for human life from conception to the last breath. Abbot Vonier goes on to claim that 'Christianity is the religion of birth': the eternal birth of the Son of God from the Father, His temporal birth from Mary the Virgin, the spiritual birth of Christians in Holy Baptism, and the Church's moral teaching governing the natural birth of every man, which, he says, constitutes 'Christianity's moral power, Christianity's social contribution to the life of mankind'.[31] He then mentions the shrine in Rome of the *Madonna del Parto*, the Madonna of Childbirth, and adds this comment: 'Rome's instinct and language are always true; they reveal a comprehension of divine things which has the characteristic of universality. The direct simplicity of such a title proves that in it the Christian man and woman have come very near to the Fountains of Life.'[32]

Gaude, virgo gloriosa: The Perpetual Virginity of Heaven's Sweet Queen

Gaude, virgo gloriosa, 'Glorious Virgin, joy to thee'. The sky blue of her robe is the symbol of Our Lady's glorious virginity. A glorious day is one in which the sun shines in a blue and cloudless sky, untroubled by clouds. Likewise, in the sky of the Blessed Virgin Mary, the eternal Day, the Sun of Righteousness, shines forth without any clouding of her maidenly integrity: she conceives Him as a virgin without seed, gives birth to Him as a virgin without corruption, and remains for Him a virgin without ceasing. The Burning Bush, shown to the left of our painting, teaches the same lesson. For the Fathers, it is a type of the Virgin Birth of Christ, and indeed of the hypostatic union itself: fire without destruction, birth without corruption, human nature assumed, not absorbed.

In her virginity at its every stage, the Blessed Virgin gives glory to the Blessed Trinity, the glory we hope to gaze on in Heaven.

By conceiving Jesus without seed and by the direct operation of the Holy Spirit, she glorifies God the Father, or, as St Thomas puts it, she 'preserves the dignity of the Father who sent Him [into the world]'. Jesus is 'the true and natural Son of God'. It was therefore 'not fitting that He should have another father apart from God, lest the dignity of God be transferred to another'.[33] Who is God the Father? The One who eternally begets the Son; His relation to the Son constitutes Him as the person He is. In other words, fatherhood is not so much what God the Father does as who He is.[34] Now had there been someone else who generated the Son of God, albeit a human person begetting Him as man, the unique dignity of God the Father would have been obscured. It is to prevent such obscurity, to ensure clear knowledge of the Father, whom she loves and praises, that Mary conceives Jesus in a virginal way. Now to ensure clear knowledge of a person, along with love and praise, is to glorify that person,[35] to show forth his identity with sufficient light for the mind. Therefore, by conceiving His Son in a virginal way, our Lady glorifies the Father. Indeed, the Doctors of the Church see a beautiful correspondence between the Son's eternal generation by the Father and His temporal generation by the Virgin. As Pope St Gregory the Great says: 'One and the same is before the ages of the Father without a mother and at the end of the ages of a mother without a father.'[36] Thus, by the very fact of the Virginal Conception, Mary points us towards Heaven and the Father in Heaven, and invites us to worship Him with the Son and the Holy Spirit, as if to say: 'Jesus' only Father is God, for Jesus is God's only Son.' It is for this reason, too, that our Lady is for ever a virgin: it is fitting, says St Thomas, that the only-begotten of the heavenly Father should be the only-begotten of the human Mother.[37]

The preservation of our Lady's virginity in the very act of giving birth is likewise an objective testimony to the Triune God, who is blessed and in Heaven makes saints and angels blessed. In this second aspect of her maidenhood, the undefiled Mother reveals the identity of her Son as the Word of God, the eternal Idea of the Father. When we conceive an idea in our minds, the act of conceiving does not of itself corrupt our minds, nor does the utterance, when the idea in the mind comes to birth on our lips.[38] So it is with the eternal Word: when, in His human nature, He comes forth from His Mother's womb, He does not harm its virginal integrity. As He entered, so He leaves, with infinite delicacy. This is fitting, as St Thomas says, because He has not come into this world to hurt, to be a source of corruption, but to rid the world of its corruption, both physical and moral, and to heal all our hurts.[39] Thus, when our Lady gives birth without corruption of her virginity, she communicates, by her disposition of worship, the doctrine later set forth by her adoptive son in the opening verses of his Gospel: 'In the beginning was the Word, and the Word was with God, and the Word was God . . . And the Word was made flesh and dwelt among us' (John 1: 1–2, 14).

Finally, our Lady, by her vow of virginity and her whole life of perpetual virginity, gives honour to the Holy Spirit. Who but He could have inspired a maiden in Israel, where the bearing of many children is a religious duty,[40] to have vowed virginity from an early age?[41] It is by the overshadowing of the same Holy Spirit that the Virgin conceives her Son, just as, in docility to Him, she had given her consent. Her womb is the special sanctuary of the Holy Spirit, for there Christ's sacred flesh is formed, and so, says St Thomas, it would have been an offence against the Spirit, had she had relations with a man.[42]

The virginity of our Lady glorifies the Triune God, whom we hope to see in Heaven, but in a way it even anticipates the happiness of Heaven. When the angel Gabriel tells Mary that she is to conceive and give birth without loss of her virginity, he fulfils the prophecy of Zephaniah: 'Give praise, O daughter of Sion; shout, O Israel. Be glad and rejoice with all thy heart, O daughter of Jerusalem . . . [T]he king of Israel is in the midst of thee' (Zeph. 3: 14–15). Indeed He is in thy midst; He is coming to dwell, as a little child, in thy womb. The virginity *in partu* is likewise a joyful mystery, a kind of foretaste of heavenly bliss. By sparing His Blessed Mother any physical harm in childbirth, our Lord makes us all a promise of the gladness to come: when the Bridegroom is with us, and we with Him, there can be no fasting or gloom. Even when He plunges into the agony of His Passion, and a sword pierces His Mother's heart, the final goal is still joy, a happiness that in Heaven will flow like oil from the Head into the whole Mystical Body. The religion founded by the Virgin-born Son makes no cult of suffering for its own sake.

Super omnes speciosa: Our Lady's Beauty— From Conception to Assumption

Super omnes speciosa, 'Loveliest whom in Heaven they see. | Fairest thou where all are fair!' The blessed gaze upon the uncreated beauty of the Trinity in the Beatific Vision, and in that gaze, by reflection and participation, they are themselves made beautiful. They also behold the beauty of their Queen and Mother, whose created loveliness, in soul and body, surpasses theirs by far. *Tota pulchra es, Maria* . . . 'Thou art all fair, O Mary; the primal stain is not found in thee.'[43]

Blessed Denys the Carthusian devotes many pages of his works on our Lady to the praise and explanation of her beauty. This preoccupation should not surprise us, since Denys is one of the foremost exponents of what Hans Urs von Balthasar has called the 'theological aesthetic', that is, the perception of the beauty, the objective splendour, of what God has revealed and given to us in His Son.[44] As already mentioned, Denys the Carthusian is the author of a work explicitly devoted to this theme: *De venustate mundi et pulchritudine Dei*, 'On the Charm of the World and the Beauty of God'. With regard to our Lady, he says: 'Just as it was fitting for the Author of Nature, the fount of the beauty of the universe, the restorer of the corrupt and reformer of the deformed, to be born of an inviolate and utterly incorrupt virgin, so it was fitting that she should be beautiful, utterly immaculate.'[45] Denys argues that, just as her divine Son in His human nature is fairer in form than all the sons of men (cf. Ps. 44: 3), so Blessed Mary is lovelier, even in natural physical beauty, than those of her holy ancestors whose beauty is praised in the Scriptures (Rebecca, Rachel, Judith, and Esther), and the Christian maidens (Catherine, Agatha, Agnes, and the rest) praised in the acts of the early martyrs.[46]

At a first reading, these assertions of our exuberant Flemish Carthusian may seem unreasonable and unwarranted. But Denys, rigorous Scholastic philosopher and theologian that he is, never makes a statement without the support of Scripture, as interpreted by the Fathers, and careful reasoning from generally established principles. First, we should notice the unselfconscious and very Catholic affirmation of the goodness of the body that this celebration of our Lady's beauty presupposes; Denys is far removed from angelism or false spiritualism. Secondly, we need to learn a lesson from Denys about the importance and intellectual coherence of Scholastic arguments of 'convenience' or fittingness, which demonstrate the beautiful harmony between the works of God in creation and redemption.[47] In Mariology, such arguments take as their major premise the fitting correspondence of the privileges of the Blessed Mother with the divine dignity of her Child. Now Christ is the fairest of the sons of men (cf. Ps. 44: 3). Therefore, it is most fitting that His Blessed Mother should be 'the loveliest among the daughters of men'. For Scriptural proof, Denys cites texts from the Canticle, for, like many other theologians in the Tradition, he regards the Blessed Virgin as the most perfect realization of the Bride of Christ, the personification, as it were, of the Church as Bride.[48] Our Lady is related to her Son in the natural order as Mother, but she is related to Him in the supernatural order as Bride, as indeed is every Christian by faith and charity.[49] In his commentary on the forty-fourth Psalm, 'The queen stood on thy right hand' (Ps. 44: 9), Denys writes: 'She is the unique and supreme Queen standing always on the right hand of her Son, who ineffably delights the eternal Father, and beyond all comparison pleases her Spouse and Son, as the heavenly Bridegroom says to her [in the Canticle]: *Pulchra es* . . . "Thou art beautiful, O my love, sweet and comely" (S. of S. 6: 3).'[50] Because she is 'first' in so many ways, in her Christian believing and loving, and above all in the dignity of her divine motherhood, our Lady is the first to receive all the beautifying gifts that her Son wants to bestow upon His Bride the Church, making her 'glorious, not having spot or wrinkle . . . holy, and without blemish' (cf. Eph. 5: 27).

Bodily beauty is good, but spiritual beauty is better.[51] Natural beauty is a great thing, but supernatural beauty, whether of body or soul, is greater beyond measure. Now the Immaculate Conception and Assumption of our Lady are two kinds of supernatural beauty. The first concerns the supernatural beauty of grace, chiefly in her soul, while the second grants her the supernatural beauty of glory in both soul and body. Let us consider each of these in turn, for Quarton makes reference to them in his altarpiece.

Beauty of Soul: The Immaculate Conception

The mantle of Heaven's sweet Queen is royal blue, the colour of majesty, but still more of purity. She is *super omnes speciosa*, lovely above all, because of her freedom from sin, for sin is always unlovely, the soul's darkening, disordering, disintegration. To prepare her to be a human Mother worthy of divine Wisdom in His brilliance, she is preserved from ever falling into the darkness of actual sin, both mortal and venial, and spared even that disorder of desire, concupiscence, from which sin springs forth like a flame out of tinder. Moreover, from her conception, by a singular privilege from God, she is preserved from the moral disintegration, the spiritual death, that is Original Sin. At our conception we receive our human nature from Adam in the state in which he left it, deprived of the beauty of sanctifying grace. But as soon our Lady exists in her mother's womb, she is *tota pulchra*, all fair and full of God's better beauty, which is grace. 'Not for a single moment', says Blessed Columba Marmion, 'is the soul of Mary to belong to the devil; it will be radiant with purity; and that is why, from the morrow of the Fall of our first parents, God put absolute enmity between the devil and the chosen Virgin; it is she whose heel is to crush the infernal serpent.'[52]

Our altarpiece was painted at a time of growing understanding of the totality of spiritual beauty in the soul of the Mother of God. Fifteen years before Quarton took up his brush, the Council of Basel made the first official conciliar pronouncement on the Immaculate Conception: it said that the doctrine of our Lady's freedom from Original Sin was 'pious' and in accord with 'the liturgy of the Church, Catholic faith, sound reasoning, and Sacred Scripture'.[53] The trouble was that, by the time the proclamation was made, the Council had ceased to be in communion with the lawful pope, and so its teaching had no juridical authority. However, the proclamation was a milestone on the road to the dogmatic definition of 1854.

The teaching of the Council of Basel did not go unnoticed in Provence. From September 1457 to March 1458, four years after the painting of the Villeneuve altarpiece, a provincial council met in Avignon that ordered 'the decree of Basel on the Conception of the Blessed Virgin Mary to be observed inviolably and prohibited, under pain of excommunication, anyone from proposing anything contrary to it, whether in preaching or in public disputations'.[54] It would seem that the 'City of the Popes' was a centre of devotion to our Lady's privilege. In the same period, Denys the Carthusian clearly affirms the Blessed Virgin's freedom from Original Sin: 'Hail Mary,' he cries out, 'never didst thou contract Original Sin, just as thou didst not commit any actual sin'.[55] His words manifestly imply the Immaculate Conception. At no moment of her existence, he says, did our Lady contract Original Sin. But the sons and daughters of Adam contract Original Sin at their conception. Therefore, in her conception, our Lady was preserved from contracting Original Sin.

The final beautification of the Mother in Heaven takes place immediately above the Crucifixion of the Son on earth; thus a straight line connects His Heart in its piercing with her heart in its purity. The doctrinal lesson seems plain, or at least it does to those familiar with the dogmatic definition of the Immaculate Conception: it was 'in view of the merits of Christ Jesus, the Saviour of the human race' that the Mother of God was, 'in the first instant of her conception . . . preserved immune from all stain of Original Sin',[56] or, as the collect of the Solemnity puts it, she was kept from all stain 'by the foreseen death' of the only-begotten of the Father. As Blessed Denys says, the Blessed Virgin was preserved from Original Sin 'by the prevenient grace of her Son',[57] that is, by His grace 'coming before', working backwards in time from the hour of the Passion. The pattern in our Lady's gold of Ophir is made up of scarlet threads, as if to show that the beauty of her soul is an effect of the Precious Blood. The Lamb of God redeems other men by delivering them from Original Sin once they have contracted it, but He redeems His Mother by making sure she never contracts Original Sin. Thus the full Trinitarian pattern of the Immaculate Conception is disclosed: to the honour of the Blessed Trinity, and for the beautification of the Virgin Mother of God, from the first moment of her conception, by the anticipated merits of the Saviour-Son, she is filled with the sanctifying grace that adopts her as the beloved daughter of the Father and consecrates her as the temple of the Holy Spirit.

Radiant in Body: The Assumption

The Villeneuve Charterhouse wanted the altarpiece to show the valley of Josaphat in Jerusalem, in which, according to the contract, there was to be a church, 'where the tomb of our Lady is found, and above it an angel saying: *Assumpta est Maria ad ethereum thalamum in quo Rex Regum stellato sedet solio*, 'Mary has been taken up to the heavenly bridal chamber, in which the King of Kings sits on a starry throne'.[58] Thus Quarton includes in his painting a reference to the Assumption of our Lady, by which she entered Heaven in the glory of both body and soul. Moreover, he reminds us that Heaven is a nuptial mystery, the wedding feast of the kingly Lamb and His Bride, the Church Triumphant, whose immaculate heart is Mary.

The depiction of the tomb of our Lady reminds us of the truth taught by the overwhelming majority of the Fathers and Doctors of the Church, including Denys the Carthusian, namely, that, before being assumed into eternal life in both body and soul, the Blessed Virgin suffered the separation of body and soul. When he defined the dogma of the Assumption in 1950, Pope Pius XII left open the question of death, and spoke simply of the Mother of God being assumed into heavenly glory 'when the course of her earthly life was completed',[59] words that could certainly be taken to refer to death, but that might equally be compatible with the opinion of that small group of Catholic theologians who hold that our Lady was glorified without suffering death beforehand. More recently, in 1997, the present Holy Father, while stopping short of defining the matter, has not only affirmed the death of our Lady but also given it a more detailed exposition than it has ever received before from the Papal Magisterium.

To understand the Holy Father's teaching, we need to consider the nature of human death from three aspects. First, if we look only at the material body of man, then we have to say that death is natural. By nature, the human body, like every other material substance, is 'composed of contraries', that is, made up of different parts held together in unity. Now what is composed can also decompose; what comes together into unity can also come apart. Therefore, by its very nature, man's body can fall apart, be dissolved or corrupted.[60] Secondly, if we consider the spiritual soul of man, which is immortal, and if we consider that man is a unity of body and soul, then we have to say that, for the soul, the state of death is unnatural: 'It is against the nature of the soul to be without the body.'[61] Thirdly, if we look at man as fallen, that is, when we remember that Adam was endowed with a preternatural gift of bodily immortality for himself and for us, and that by his sin he lost that gift of bodily immortality for himself and for us, then we have to say that death is penal, a punishment or penal consequence of sin.[62] 'Sin came into the death through one man, and through sin death' (Rom. 5: 12). Death is at once natural, unnatural, and penal.

The body of our Lady, like every other human body, was in itself naturally subject to death. True, she is preserved from all stain of Original Sin from her conception, but this preservation was a 'singular grace and privilege' and therefore did not bring with it any entitlement to a preternatural gift of bodily immortality similar to Adam's.[63] Thus our Lady suffered bodily death, not as a consequence of Original Sin, but as a consequence of human nature, as natural to the human body, not as penal because of Adam's sin. And if we ask why the Blessed Trinity decreed that the Immaculate should be subject to this consequence of human nature, which for us is a consequence of Original Sin, we have to reply that it was in order to conform her to her Son, and thereby to enable her to co-operate with Him in the salvation of mankind. In the words of Pope John Paul:

It is true that in revelation death is presented as a punishment for sin. However, the fact that the Church proclaims Mary to be free from Original Sin by a unique privilege does not lead to the conclusion that she also received physical immortality. The Mother is not superior to the Son, who underwent death, giving it a new meaning and changing into a means of salvation. Involved in Christ's redemptive work, and associated in His saving sacrifice, Mary was able to share in His suffering and death for the sake of mankind's redemption.[64]

The Holy Father goes on to say, drawing on the teaching of St Francis de Sales, that the death of our Lady was due to a 'transport of love': 'she died of love for her Son Jesus'.[65] St John of the Cross likewise says that, when a soul has attained the high summit of the mystical life, being united to Christ in the spiritual marriage, their death, whatever its natural causes may be, comes about through a vehement act of charity, an act so full of love for the Bridegroom that it literally stops the heart of the human lover.[66] So it is for the saints, and so it was for that most loving of brides, the Queen of All Saints.

But, in its qualities of purity and gentleness, the death of the Immaculate was unlike any other death. It was a 'dormition', a falling asleep, a passing over to eternal life in the whole of her human person. Her soul was separated from a body for a short time (we do not know for how long, though some early narratives suggest it was for three days), but then her Son raised up her body and reunited it to her soul in glory. Once again it is our Lady's divine and virginal motherhood that is the reason for this most wonderful privilege. Pope Pius XII calls on the testimony of St John Damascene: 'It was fitting that she, who had kept her virginity intact in childbirth, should keep her own body free from all corruption even after death.'[67] Thus, as the venerable Pope concludes: '[J]ust as the glorious resurrection (*anastasis*) of Christ was an essential part and the final sign of [His] victory [over sin and death], so that struggle which was common to the Blessed Virgin and her divine Son should be brought to a close with the glorification of her virginal body, for the . . . Apostle says: "When this mortal thing hath put on immortality, then shall come to pass the saying that is written: Death is swallowed up in victory" (1 Cor. 15: 54).'[68]

According to the most venerable tradition, the dormition and resurrection of the Mother of God took place in Jerusalem, 'on Zion', says Damascene, 'glorious and renowned, where the law of the letter was fulfilled and the law of the Spirit proclaimed, where Christ the Lawgiver put an end to the figurative Passover, and the God of the Old and New Covenant handed over the true Passover'.[69] It is fitting that in the very city in which the Son died, rose, and ascended in His human flesh, the Mother, from whom

He took that flesh, should—through Him and with Him and in Him—die, rise again, and be taken up into glory. From the earthly city of David the King the Blessed Virgin Mary passed into the heavenly city of Christ the King, the Son and God of David, as a sign of hope for all the members of Christ. The happiness that God-made-man has in store for the righteous is not only for the soul but also for the body. On the last day, He will come again in order to conform our lowly bodies to be like His glorious body (cf. Phil. 3: 21). Then those whose minds are radiantly happy with the sight of the Trinity will also be radiantly happy in the flesh, as complete human persons. One human person, the purest and loveliest, already enjoys that totality of fulfilment, and, by her unceasing intercession, she prays that we pilgrims may share it with her for ever.

In his treatise 'On the Dignity and Praises of the Blessed Virgin', Blessed Denys lives up to his title of 'Ecstatic Doctor' with rapturous pages on the taking up of the Mother of God into the beatitude of the Trinity, the *supergloriosissima Trinitas*, as he likes to say, 'the superlatively glorious Trinity'. He speaks once again of the infinite happiness of the Three Divine Persons, who 'gaze on each other with superlative clarity, love each other with superlative fervour, and enjoy each other with superlative sweetness'.[70] He then goes on to say that 'the Virgin Mary pre-elected above all' is plunged into participation in these things: she is 'supremely, perfectly, and proximately immersed in the light of the Godhead, plunged into the abyss of the Trinity, made a partaker of glory'.[71] But then, as proof that even amidst rapture his theological intelligence does not forsake him, he adds this condition: 'so far as it could be given to, or befitted, a creature without hypostatic union and falling short of personal conjunction'.[72] In other words, the Blessed Virgin is glorified, in soul and body, without loss of her personhood, substantial change of her nature, or obscuring of her creatureliness. In his rapture over our Lady's glorified rest in Paradise, Denys does not forget her sanctified work on pilgrimage: '[J]ust as she abounded in fullness of grace and merits above all others in this vale of tears, and shared Christ's sufferings, serving Him bodily and spiritually in her own person, so in the celestial Paradise, she is incomparably full of glory, overflowing with rewards, glorified with Christ and closely joined to Him.'[73] The degree of our Lady's glory in Heaven is in proportion to the incomparable fullness of grace she was given as Mother of God. She is more closely united to the Most Holy Trinity than is any other created person; she enters more deeply into the secrets of the Godhead by her enjoyment of the Beatific Vision than does any other created person; and yet, essentially, the final goal she has reached, the resplendent city to which she has come, is the harbour to which all the faithful are travelling, on board the ship of Peter, across the roaring waters of this world.

Blessed Denys writes in order to enhance our devotion to the Queen of Heaven, but his aim is also to encourage us as we march towards the realm over which, under her Son, she reigns, or rather he wants us to see the devotion to our Mother and Queen as the most effective means of reaching the sweet and blessed country of our Father and King. Our Mother and Queen, in the sublimity of her glorification, is the most powerful helper we have after God: the clarity in her God-seeing mind enables her to perceive our needs, the charity in her God-fired heart moves her to meet them. The Mother of God is a 'Mother *to us* in the order of grace',[74] the Mediatrix who by her prayers brings us from God all the graces we require for entry through Jerusalem's gates. As Blessed Denys says in his commentary on the last verse of the *Ave maris stella*:

[O Mary] *Vitam praesta puram*, 'Grant us purer living', that is, a conversation [i.e. mode of life] acceptable to God, especially one that is free from mortal sins, so that 'our conversation may be in Heaven' (cf. Phil. 3: 20), by seeking and savouring the things that are above (cf. Col. 3: 1–2), not carnal and earthly things. *Iter para tutum*, 'Safer make our journey', that is, arrange secure access for us to thy Son, so that we may so live that without resisting we may be led to His presence and not be separated from Him. *Ut videntes Jesum*, 'That beholding Jesus' through the Beatific Vision, as regards His deity, and as regards the assumed nature for the reception of the principal accidental reward . . . *Semper collaetemur*, 'Ever we be joyful', that is, may we ever be merry in Him and with Him in the Fatherland, as the chief of the Apostles says in the first of his Canonical Epistles: 'Though now you see Christ not, you believe, but seeing Him you shall rejoice with joy unutterable and glorified, receiving the end of your faith, the salvation of your souls' (cf. 1 Pet. 1: 8–9).

Conclusion: *In patriam per Matrem*

Enguerrand Quarton painted an image of the Fatherland, of our Father's house, which has our Mother at its heart. The eyes of our blessed Lady look down, in humility before God and in charity for her children. She is interceding for us now and at the hour of our death, so that with her we may be happy for ever in the Trinity. How wonderful is God the Father who has not only given His Son to us to be our brother and Head, thereby making us His own adopted sons, but has also given the Mother of the Son to be our Mother, too! By our baptism we become by grace what Jesus is by nature: sons-in-the-Son, the children of both His heavenly Father and His human Mother.

Why has God the Father given us a spiritual mother, both to guide us on our journey and to welcome us when we arrive? The experience of life teaches us that the mother is the heart of the home. When our fathers are widowed, perhaps living long brave years on their own, we know, they themselves know and are the first to say, that the heart has gone out of the family home. It seems not to be so, or at least not to the same extent, when our mothers are widowed. But why am I saying all of this? Can the earthly experience serve as an analogy for Heaven? Can we really believe that what is true for us here below by nature, the presence of a mother in the home, applies also to our supernatural and supernal existence, to the home of our divine Father in

Paradise? Yes, we can and indeed must so believe, and when we ponder this truth of our faith, we shall see why Catholic Christianity is not just the only authentically divine religion, the one given to men by God, but also the only compassionately human religion, the religion revealed by God-*made-man*, which does not crush or diminish our humanity but elevates and perfects it. Consider in this regard these words of Father Louis Bouyer, a priest of the French Oratory with a vast knowledge of the monastic tradition and warm bonds of affection with the Benedictines of the English-speaking world. He argues that, just as there is a heresy of Docetism about the natural Son of God, the heresy that denies the reality of His humanity, so there can be a heresy of Docetism about ourselves as the adopted sons of God, a heresy that disregards our own humanity.

The attitude of the Christian who imagines that in the order of grace it is enough to have a heavenly Father, without any need of an earthly Mother, is a dubious attitude. Does it not imply that Christian life and life as such have to remain on parallel levels without having anything in common? There is no pipe dream more futile. There is no Christian life that is something different from life as such. Christian life is life as such placed under the immediate guidance of God, and yet without being in any way cut off from our historical roots.[75]

'Behold thy son, behold thy Mother' (cf. John 19: 26–7), says the Incarnate Word from the Cross. He wants the living waters of the Holy Spirit, which flow through His own pierced Heart from the divine Father, to pass also through the intercession of the human Mother, not by any absolute necessity, but as a fitting, a most beautiful gift. And as He came down from Heaven into the spotless womb of Mary, so He wants us to go up to Heaven through her immaculate heart, for in both directions the path is one of humility. In her motherhood both of Christ and of Christians, our Lady is proof that, in redeeming us, God does not undo, but rather fulfils, what He does in creating us. He respects and works with the freedom of the human will. When He assumes our lowly nature, He does not force Himself upon us, but rather invites us, in the person of the Blessed Virgin, freely to receive Him. He displays transcendent courtesy in His care for the frailty of human flesh. In leaving the spotless womb, He does no harm to His Mother's maidenly integrity, for He has come to cure mankind of corruption, not to inflict it. And in ordering His Mystical Body on earth and in Heaven, He ensures that the gift of natural motherhood should be elevated to a most beautiful supernatural form: he gives the whole Church and every individual Christian a Mother in the order of grace.

Grace presupposes and perfects nature, but glory, which is the consummation of grace, also builds upon and fulfils everything that is naturally human and therefore good. That is why the family on earth can be the Domestic Church, and the Church in Heaven is the glorified family. In the Kingdom, there is neither marrying nor being given in marriage in its transient, this-worldly form, and yet all the just are caught up into the transcendent and everlasting nuptials of the Lamb and His Bride, the ultimate reality signified by the Sacrament of Christian Marriage. Here, then, in this particular interconnection of our human intimacies and divine destiny is the general answer to the masters of suspicion who regard devotion to Heaven as a distraction from the lawful demands of earth. On the contrary, only those who, by the grace of the virtues and the gifts, keep their sights on the final goal of happiness with God in Heaven will use and order the goods of earth aright. To do anything else would be to worship false gods, and to take the road of eventual, indeed everlasting unhappiness. That, in summary, is the entire moral and political doctrine of St Thomas and indeed of the whole Catholic Tradition.[76] To see this temporal world *sub specie aeternitatis* is to see it aright, and to begin to live and work within it in an ordered way that will not corrupt whatever good it contains. And, in the end, on the last day of human history, when the Son of Man comes again to conform our lowly bodies to His glorious body (cf. Phil. 3: 21), and 'to hand over to His Father an eternal and universal kingdom' in the new heaven and earth, then we shall find that whatever is good here and now will then be immeasurably better, for, as the Catechism says, it will be 'cleansed from the stain of sin, illuminated, and transfigured'.[77]

The saints, those who seek God with heroic faith, hope, and charity, walk through this world as through a vale of tears, with the eyes of their minds on the heavenly City and the Lamb that is its light. Yet, by a strange paradox, they treasure this earth as God's creation with a tenderness of which the worldling is incapable. St John of the Cross, who clung to nothing but God (*nada, nada, nada*), loved to gaze at the beauty of the night sky. Of St Francis of Assisi, St Bonaventure says that 'in beautiful things he saw the Most Beautiful One, and through His vestiges imprinted on creation he followed his Beloved everywhere, making all things a ladder by which he might ascend and embrace Him who is utterly desirable'.[78] So much is true of the friars, and it is true of the monks as well. St Bede the Venerable, who spoke of the celestial Fatherland in almost every line of his theological writings, loved his native land on earth and wrote its first Christian history. While those who lived for carnal and worldly passions plunged Europe into darkness, he who in purity longed only to look on the face of Christ transmitted to the Middle Ages so much of the brilliant wisdom of Christian and pagan antiquity. Our friend, Blessed Denys the Carthusian, in his hermitage in the Charterhouse, wrote treatises on everything human and divine, from the military to the mystical. Precisely because of what he accepted by supernatural faith, he esteemed his natural reason and his sensory powers, and therefore all the truth, however limited, that man, by the light of reason and starting from his sense-experience, could attain. He makes our divine Saviour Himself, the Word through whom all things were made, speak thus of the vestiges of God among creatures: 'Behold, all the vastly lovable things in the entire world, all the goodness and sweetness to be found in created things, are but rivulets of the uncreated goodness and lovableness and sweetness, that is, of the divine essence or eternal Godhead.'[79]

With our Lady's help, monks such as Denys seek God in charity, and, for the love of God, they do not despise but rather admire the great movement of all creatures towards the good, even those without reason or sense. From the Triune God all things come, and to Him all in their proper order return. What Abbot Vonier liked to call the 'goalfulness' of all creatures,[80] even of the humblest, is a sign to the sons of Adam of the glorious supernatural final end that they are called to enjoy, through the blood of the Lamb and the intercession of the Virgin, in the Beatific Vision, the Communion of Saints, the Resurrection of the Body, and the Life Everlasting. Strangely, and yet for those who have Catholic faith in the Incarnation it is not strange, looking to the transcendent splendour above makes one attentive to the lesser glories below. For the one with ears to hear, the call of the Father and the Fatherland echoes through the hum of Dom Benedict's bees and the cry of the kestrel above the wooded hills.

NOTES

INTRODUCTION

1 'Natural appetite is nothing other than the ordering of anything to its end according to its proper nature' (St Thomas Aquinas, *In libros physicorum*, lib. 1 lect. 15).

2 The truths of psychology and ethics presuppose and do not contradict those of physics; indeed, there is a certain resemblance of ethical action to physical motion. That is why appetite and love can be physical as well as ethical and psychological concepts. St Augustine, uniting the sciences, says that love is in spirits what weight is in bodies. St Thomas explains the basis of this analogical use of words: both love and weight *incline* (cf. *De veritate* q. 24 a. 11 ad. 3).

3 St Thomas, *ST* 1a q. 6 ad. 1. '[A]ll things that come from God, as effect from cause, are by desire turned to Him as their proper cause. This would not be so, did all things not have some likeness to God, for everything loves and desires what is like itself' (St Thomas, *In Dionysii De divinis nominibus*, cap. 9 lect. 3).

4 'All things naturally desire God implicitly, though not explicitly. Evidence for this is to be seen in the fact that a secondary cause cannot influence its effect except insofar as it receives the power of the First Cause. Now just as the influence of the efficient cause is acting, so the influence of the final cause is being sought and desired. Therefore, just as the secondary agent only acts through the power of the First Agent existing in it, so the secondary end is only desired through the power of the principal end existing in it, inasmuch as it is ordered to it or has a likeness to it. Therefore, just as God, as first efficient [cause], acts in every agent, so, as ultimate end, He is desired in every end. Now this is to desire God implicitly' (St Thomas, *De veritate* q. 22 a. 2).

5 St Thomas, *ST* 1a q. 7 ad. 1.

6 Ibid. 1a q. 2 a. 3. 'While the fifth way is sometimes confused with an argument based on order and design and the need for a supreme designer, Thomas's text makes it clear that he really has in mind an argument based on final causality in nature' (John F. Wippel, *The Metaphysical Thought of Thomas Aquinas: From Finite Being to Uncreated*

Being (Washington DC: Catholic University of America Press, 2000), 480).

7 Dante Alighieri, *The Divine Comedy: Paradiso*, canto 1, lines 115–17; trans. Dorothy L. Sayers and Barbara Reynolds (Harmondsworth: Penguin Books, 1962), 56.

8 Cf. *La Règle de Saint Benoît*, vol. 1 cap. 58; ed. J. Neufville OSB, *SC* 181 (Paris: Éditions du Cerf, 1972), p. 456.

9 'The principal efficient cause of grace is God Himself, to whom the humanity of Christ is related as a conjoined instrument, whereas a sacrament is like a separated instrument. Therefore, it is necessary for salvific power to flow from the divinity of Christ, through His humanity, into the Sacraments themselves' (St Thomas, *ST* 3a q. 62 a. 5).

10 Cf. St Thomas, *ST* 2a2ae q. 184 a. 3; *The Catechism of the Catholic Church*, n. 1973.

11 'The profession of the evangelical counsels serves as a sign that can and should effectively attract all the members of the Church energetically to fulfil the duties of their Christian calling' (The Second Vatican Council, Dogmatic Constitution on the Church, *Lumen gentium*, n. 44; *Sacrosanctum oecumenicum concilium Vaticanum II: Constitutiones, decreta, declarationes* (Vatican City: Vatican Press, 1966), 176).

12 Cf. St Ignatius of Antioch, *Epistola ad romanos*, n. 7; ed. J. B. Lightfoot, *The Apostolic Fathers*, new edn. (London: Macmillan, 1907), 122.

13 St Augustine, *Sermo* 80, n. 7; *PL* 38. 497–8.

14 *La règle de Saint Benoît*, cap. 4; ed. Neufville 456.

15 Ibid. 456–7.

16 Ibid.

17 Ibid. cap. 5; p. 464.

18 Ibid. cap. 7; p. 472.

19 Ibid. prologus; p. 418.

20 Ibid. vol. 2, cap. 73; p. 674.

21 See the errors condemned by Pope Innocent XII in *Cum alias ad apostolatus* of 12 March 1699 (DS 1327–1349).

22 Cf. Aristotle, *Ars rhetorica* 1380^b35.

23 Cf. *ST* 1a2ae q. 26 a. 4.

24 Cf. *ST* 2a2ae q. 17 a. 8.

25 St Thomas, 3 *Sent.* d. 29, a. 4.

26 Joseph Mayol OP (+1704), *Praeambula ad Decalogum: De fide, spe, caritate*, q. 3, a. 1, n. 1; ed. J. P. Migne, *Theologiae cursus completus* (Paris: Migne, 1838), xiii. 1087–8.

27 In his *Reflections on the Psalms*, C. S. Lewis suggests that God did not reveal the reward of Heaven from the very inauguration of the Old Covenant, because He wanted to train the Jews into loving Him principally for His own goodness, His intrinsic lovableness, and only afterwards to expect a reward for so loving Him. 'It is surely, therefore, very possible that when God began to reveal Himself to men, to show them that He and nothing else is their true goal and the satisfaction of their needs, and that He has a claim upon them simply by being what He is, quite apart from anything He can bestow or deny, it may have been absolutely necessary that this revelation should not begin with any hint of future Beatitude or Perdition. . . . Later, when, after centuries of spiritual training, men have learned to desire and adore God, to pant after Him "as pants the hart", it is another matter. For then those who love God will desire not only to enjoy Him but "to enjoy Him for ever", and will fear to lose Him' (*Selected Books: Reflections on the Psalms* (London: HarperCollins, 2002), 330).

28 Jean Leclercq OSB, *The Love of Learning and the Desire for God: A Study of Monastic Culture*, trans. Catharine Misrahi, new edn. (New York: Fordham University Press, 1974), 66.

29 Columba Marmion OSB, *Christ in His Mysteries*, trans. Mother M. St Thomas of Tyburn Convent, new edn. (London: Sands & Co., 1939), 312.

30 *[F]ecisti nos ad te; et inquietum est cor nostrum, donec requiescat in te* (St Augustine, *Confessiones* lib. 1 cap. 1 n. 1; CCSL 27.1).

31 St Thomas, *In symbolum apostolorum*, art. 11.

32 St Thomas, *Super ad Hebraeos* cap. 13 lect. 2.

33 See J. and Y. Le Pichon, *Le Mystère du Couronnement de la Vierge* (Paris: Éditions Robert Laffont / Le Centurion, 1982), *passim*.

34 Ibid. 14 ff.

35 For a forthright defence of 'Thomism of the Strict Observance', see David Berger, *Thomismus: Grosse Leitmotive der thomistischen Synthese und ihre Aktualität für die Gegenwart* (Cologne: Editiones Thomisticae, 2001).

36 *Cuthbert's Letter on the Death of Bede*; ed. B. Colgrave and R. A. B. Mynors, *Bede's Ecclesiastical History of the English People* (Oxford: Clarendon, 1969), 585. St Bede himself writes: 'In that fatherland above, where the eyes of the saints see Christ in His beauty, only the grace of divine and fraternal charity shines through all' (St Bede, *De templo* lib. 1; CCSL 119A. 176).

37 Anselme Stoelen's article is still the best introduction to Denys's life (ed. C. Baumgartner SJ et alii, *Dictionnaire de spiritualité* (Paris: Beauchesne, 1957), iii. 430–49).

38 He was instructed there, he said, *in via Thomae*, 'in the way of Thomas' (1 *Sent.* d. 8 q. 7; *DCOO* 19. 408D). According to Kent Emery Jr., in the fifteenth century the University of Cologne incorporated a certain amount of theology into the arts course: 'Beside Aristotle and his philosophic commentators, it was the novel practice of the masters in the *via antiqua* at Cologne to introduce theological writings, especially of Thomas Aquinas, into the teaching of the liberal arts' (Kent Emery Jr., *Dionysius Cartusiensis opera selecta, prolegomena, Bibliotheca manuscripta, 1a: Studia bibliographica* CCCM (Turnholt, 1991), 16).

39 As Kent Emery has said: 'Dionysius Cartusiensis (1402–1471) was probably the most prolific writer of the entire Middle Ages . . . An old adage states that "he who reads Dionysius reads everything"' (Emery, *Dionysius Cartusiensis* 5).

40 *DCOO* 1–14.

41 *DCOO* 19–25.

42 *DCOO* 15–16.

43 *DCOO* 26.

44 *DCOO* 28.

45 *DCOO* 33. 21 ff, 105 ff.

46 *Summa fidei orthodoxae*; *DCOO* 17, 18.

47 *Expositio missae*; *DCOO* 35. 327 ff.

48 *Expositio hymnorum aliquot ecclesiaticorum*; *DCOO* 35. 17 ff.

49 For example, among many treatises, there is the *De praeconio sive laude ordinis cartusiensis*; *DCOO* 38. 411 ff.

50 *De laudabili vita coniugatorum*; *DCOO* 38. 55 ff.

51 *De laudabili vita viduarum*; *DCOO* 38. 119 ff.

52 *De vita et regimine principum*; *DCOO* 37. 373 ff.

53 Soldiers, says Denys, are appointed to fight for the defence of the commonwealth, the Catholic faith, widows, orphans, and the poor (*De vita militarium* aa. 1, 2; *DCOO* 37. 569A–570B).

54 Cf. St John Damascene, *De haeresibus*, n. 100; *Saint Jean Damascène: Écrits sur l'Islam*, ed. and trans. Raymond le Coz, SC, 383 (Paris: Éditions du Cerf, 1992), 211 ff.

55 Cf. *Contra perfidiam Mahometi* lib. 1, art. 4; *DCOO* 36. 242 ff.; *Dialogus disputationis inter christianum et sarracenum*; *DCOO* 36. 443 ff. Denys's stated purpose in writing the *Contra perfidiam* was 'the conversion and true salvation of the Saracens' (lib. 1 a. 9; *DCOO* 36. 2252c').

56 Cf. Blessed Denys's *Protestatio ad superiorem suum quo motivo sua in utrumque testamentum conscripserit commentaria, operaque reliqua*;

DCOO 41. 626B. He is also familiar with the rabbis and other Jewish philosophers and theologians: Josephus, Philo, Rabbi Akiba, and Moses Maimonides, whom he describes as 'a great theologian and outstanding philosopher' (*Enarratio in cap. 20 Numerorum*, a. 34; *DCOO* 2. 433B).

57 The two causes—the defence of Christendom against Muslim fanaticism and the renewal of the ordinary Christian's zeal for holiness—came together in Blessed Denys's private revelations, which showed him that Christians were being persecuted by the 'most perfidious Turks and Saracens' on account of the 'sins of Christians' (Blessed Denys, *Epistola ad principes catholicos*, prooemium; *DCOO* 36. 503). Denys urged the Christian princes 'promptly, boldly, magnanimously, and cheerfully to fight against the Turks and Saracens' (ibid. a. 10; *DCOO* 36. 513D ff.). In his own 'Scrutiny of the Koran' (n. 4), Nicholas of Cusa tells us something of the background to Denys's writings on Islam: 'I urged Brother Dionysius to write against the Koran. He did so and sent his huge work to Pope Nicholas' (Jasper Hopkins, *Nicholas of Cusa's 'De Pace Fidei' and 'Cribratio Alkorani': Translation and Analysis* (Minneapolis: The Arthur J. Banning Press, 1990), 76).

58 The definitive exposition of the *loci theologici* is the work of Melchior Cano OP, *De locis theologicis*.

59 Cf. St Thomas, *ST* 1a q. 32 a. 1.

60 Cf. St Thomas, *ST* 1a2ae q. 57 a. 3.

61 'Human beings act and move by the judgement of reason; for they confer about the things they have to do. But all brute beasts act and move by natural judgement. This is clear from the fact that all things of the same species operate in a similar way; for example, all swallows make the same kind of nest. Again, brute beasts have judgement for some determinate work, not for all things; for example, bees possess industriousness for making nothing other than honeycomb. The same is true of other animals. Therefore, it is apparent to anyone who rightly considers the matter that the way in which movement and action are attributed to inanimate natural things is the way in which judgement about things to be done is attributed to brute beasts. Just as heavy things and light things do not move themselves in such a way they are the cause of their own movement, so brute beasts do not make a judgement about their own judgement, but follow the judgement imparted to them by God' (St Thomas, *De veritate* q. 24 a. 1).

62 '[T]he form of the house comes first in the artist, not in its material being, in stones and timbers, but in the immaterial being it has in the

mind of the artist' (St Thomas, *In libros metaphysicorum* lib. 7, lect. 8, n. 15; cf. *Summa contra Gentiles* lib. 4, cap. 13 n. 10). St Thomas also points out that the grasping of universals is indispensable to the true artist: 'Although a man without universal knowledge can work well on some particular knowledge, still he who would become an artist must tend to the knowledge of the universal, so that in some way he knows it' (*Sententia libri ethicorum* lib. 10 lect. 15 n. 8).

63 Cf. St Thomas, *In libros metaphysicorum* lib. 1 lect. 15 n. 8.

64 Cf. St Thomas, *ST* 1a q. 79 a. 4.

65 True, the intellectual soul depends upon the bodily senses for the phantasms from which it abstracts its ideas, but this dependence is extrinsic and, so to speak, ministerial, like the dependence of electrical current on a lamp for the purpose of illuminating a room.

66 Cf. St Thomas, *ST* 1a q. 75 aa. 2, 6; *Summa contra Gentiles* lib. 2 cap. 79–81; *Compendium theologiae* lib. 1 cap. 84.

67 St Thomas, *Super 1 ad Corinthios 1–16* cap. 15 lect. 2.

68 Anscar Vonier OSB, *The Collected Works of Abbot Vonier*, i *The Incarnation and Redemption* (London: Burns & Oates, 1953), 52–3.

1 THE BLISSFUL SIGHT OF THE TRINITY

1 See *The Catechism of the Catholic Church*, nn. 476–7, 1159–62, 2129–32.

2 On the visible mission of the Holy Spirit, see St Thomas, *ST* 1a q. 43 a. 7. St Thomas does not present an argument concerning the artistic representation of the Holy Spirit; but such an argument is easily made, starting from the revealed truth that the Holy Spirit has been sent in the visible forms of a dove and a flame. Now what is visible can be represented in art. Therefore, the Holy Spirit can be represented in art in the forms of a dove and a flame.

3 Blessed Denys, *Enarratio in cap. 2 Epistolae 1 B. Pauli ad Corinthios*, a. 2; *DCOO* 13. 133CD'.

4 St Thomas, 3 *Sent.* d. 22 q. 2 a. 1C, ad. 3. Cf. Blessed Denys, *Enarratio in cap. 2 Genesis*, a. 19; *DCOO* 1. 72AC.

5 'Christ gave up the ghost before the thieves did, as is clear from St John's Gospel (cf. 19: 32–3). Thus He entered the Limbo of the Fathers before the soul of the [penitent] thief did. He enlightened the Fathers immediately with the Beatific Vision, and then a little time afterwards the soul of the thief when he arrived there. This Beatific Vision is the spiritual paradise of which our Lord speaks when He says: "This day thou shalt be with me in Paradise"' (Blessed Denys, *Expositio hymni:* Hic est dies verus Dei; *DCOO* 35. 45D).

6 St Thomas, 3 *Sent.* d. 10 q. 2 a. 2B ad. 1.

7 Ibid. 4 *Sent.* d. 4 4 q. 2 a. 2E.

8 Cf. St Thomas, *ST* 1a q. 66 a. 3.

9 Ibid.

10 Ibid. *sed contra.*

11 Cf. Blessed Denys, *Enarratio in cap. 1 Genesis* a. 6; *DCOO* 1. 18C.

12 St Thomas, *ST* 1a q. 66 a. 3.

13 Cf. St Thomas, 4 *Sent.* d. 44 q. 2 a. 3B.

14 Blessed Denys, *De quatuor hominis novissimis*, a. 64; *DCOO* 41. 586C'–587B'.

15 Cf. Blessed Denys, *Contra perfidiam Mahometi*, lib. 3 a. 8; *DCOO* 36. 381A.

16 Cf. St Thomas, 2 *Sent.* d. 2 q. 2 a. 1. Dante says that the Empyrean is 'not in space and has no pole' (*The Divine Comedy: Paradise*, canto 22, line 67; trans. Dorothy L. Sayers and Barbara Reynolds (Harmondsworth: Penguin Books, 1962), 251). 'This heaven it is which has no other "where" | Than the Divine Mind; 'tis but in that Mind | That love, its spur, and the power it rains inhere' (ibid. canto 27, lines 109–11; p. 294).

17 Cf. Blessed Denys, *In librum 2 Sententiarum* d. 2 q. 3; *DCOO* 21. 151B'.

18 Blessed Denys, *Enarratio in cap. 17 Lucae*, a. 40; *DCOO* 12. 137B'.

19 Jean Leclercq OSB, *The Love of Learning and the Desire for God: A Study of Monastic Culture*, trans. Catharine Misrahi, new edn. (New York: Fordham University Press, 1974), 67.

20 Ibid.

21 St Bede the Venerable, *In principium Genesis usque ad nativitatem Isaac*; 1344. lib. 3 cap. 12 line 1133.

22 Cf. Blessed Denys, *Commentarium in Ps. 26* a. 59; *DCOO* 5. 566C'.

23 'The same Church that now is militant will afterwards be triumphant, when death will be swallowed up in victory (cf. 1 Cor. 15: 54)' (Blessed Denys, *Enarratio in cap. 60 Isaiae* a. 88; *DCOO* 8. 726A). It is important for us to remember, as Jacques Maritain says, that '[t]he Church Triumphant and the Church Militant are but one single Church, a single and unique Mystical Body in two essentially different states: the Church Militant is *in time* and, as the Abbé Journet says, in the "crucified and pilgrim state"; the Church Triumphant is *in eternity*, in the state of glory' (Jacques Maritain, 'À propos de l'Église du ciel'; *Carnet de notes* (Paris: Desclée de Brouwer, 1965), 355).

24 Cf. St Thomas, *ST* 3a q. 8 a. 3.

25 'Like the ointment on the head that came down on to Aaron's beard, we have all received from His fulness (cf. John 1: 16). First,

then, we are anointed with a priestly unction as a figure of the Kingdom to come, for we shall be kings and free men. And since we still suffer from our enemies, we shall be afterwards anointed with actual glory, namely, the robe of glory in soul and body' (St Thomas, *In psalmos*, pars 26 n. 1).

26 St Thomas, *Super epistolam ad Ephesios*, cap. 1 lect. 8.

27 Blessed Denys, *Enarratio in cap. 21 Apocalypsis*, a. 22; *DCOO* 14. 365BC'.

28 Blessed Denys, *Enarratio in Psalmum 5 poenitentialem*, n. 20; *DCOO* 14. 449B. God is said 'in a special way to exist, dwell, operate, and listen to us' in the Empyrean heaven (cf. Blessed Denys, *Enarratio in cap. 31 libri secundi Paralipomenon* a. 30; *DCOO* 4. 258A).

29 St Augustine, *Enarratio in psalmum 30, Sermo 3* n. 8; CCSL 38. 218.

30 St Augustine, *Sermo 123* n. 3; *PL* 38. 685.

31 St Ambrose, *Expositio evangelii secundum Lucam 10*, 121; CCSL 14. 379.

32 Blessed Denys, *Enarratio in cap. 21 Apocalypsis*, a. 22; *DCOO* 14. 361CD'.

33 Ibid.

34 Cf. St Augustine, *De civitate Dei* lib. 20 cap. 14; CCSL 48. 724.

35 Cf. St Thomas, *Compendium theologiae* lib. 1 cap. 170.

36 See C. Trottman, 'Vision béatifique et intuition d'un objet absent: des sources franciscaines du nominalisme aux defenseurs scotistes de l'opinion de Jean XXII sur la vision différée', *Studi medievali* ser. 3 34 (1994), 653–715. X. Le Bachelet's article on 'Benoît XII' is still useful (*DTC* 2/1, 657–96).

37 Le Bachelet, *DTC* 2/1, 662.

38 *Benedictus Deus* (1336); DS 1000.

39 Cf. St Thomas, *ST* 1a2ae q. 2 a. 8.

40 See St Thomas *Summa contra gentiles* lib.3 cap. 63 and *In symbolum apostolorum* a. 12 on how the supernatural beatitude of Heaven fulfils all our desires.

41 Cf. St Thomas, *ST* 1a2ae q. 2 a. 8.

42 Blessed Denys, *Creaturarum in ordine ad Deum consideratio theologica*, a. 126; *DCOO* 34. 204BC.

43 Cf. Blessed Denys, *De lumine christianae theoriae*, lib. 2 a. 98; *DCOO* 33. 506D'–507A.

44 Cf. St Augustine, *Confessiones* lib. 1 cap. 1 n. 1; CCSL 27. 1.

45 St Thomas, *In symbolum apostolorum*, a. 12.

46 Cf. Aristotle, *Ethica Nicomachea* 1177ª12; St Thomas, *Sententia libri ethicorum* lib. 10 lect. 10; Blessed Denys, *Elementatio philosophica* prop. 76; *DCOO* 33. 85B'D'.

47 Cf. St Thomas, *ST* 1a2ae q. 5 aa. 3, 5.

48 'Since God is utterly incomprehensible, and altogether transcendent in His infinite excellence over every creature, no created mind can attain to the clear, face-to-face, and immediate vision of God by natural power and by one's natural resources alone. Nevertheless, the same super-best and super-sweetest God, wishing to communicate supernaturally and most abundantly His immense felicity and glory to intellectual creatures, instituted and created the rational creature for the obtaining of the clear vision of Himself *per speciem*, that is, for contemplating immediately and clearly His uncreated essence most deliciously in itself' (Blessed Denys, *Elementatio theologica* prop. 147; *DCOO* 33. 219c'd').

49 St Thomas, *ST* 1a q. 12 a. 4.

50 Cf. St Thomas, *Summa contra gentiles* lib. 3 cap. 52.

51 By the operations of natural reason, we can offer a rigorous philosophical proof of the *possibility* of the vision of God as Creator and Lord, but we cannot prove that such a vision is *actually* attainable (cf. R. Garrigou-Lagrange OP, 'La Possibilité de la vision béatifique peut-elle démontrer?' *Revue thomiste* 16 (1933), 669–88). And, of course, without revelation and faith, we cannot know that God, the Creator and Lord, is Three Persons in One Essence.

52 'Although man is naturally inclined to his final end, he cannot attain it naturally, but only by grace, and this is on account of the loftiness of this end' (St Thomas, *In Boethii De Trinitate*, pars 3 q. 6 a. 4 ad. 5).

53 'To see God by essence, in which the ultimate beatitude of the rational creature consists, is above the nature of *any created intellect*. Therefore, no rational creature can have the movement of his will ordered to that beatitude unless he is moved by a supernatural agent, and this we call "the help of grace",' St Thomas, *ST* 1a q. 62 a. 2). 'Since the Apostle says, "The grace of God, life everlasting" (Rom. 6: 23), it is evident that the vision of God, which is true happiness, surpasses the natural power of every rational creature; that is why *even before sin man could not, without grace, attain eternal beatitude*' (Blessed Denys, *Creaturarum in ordine ad Deum consideratio theologica*, a. 104; *DCOO* 34. 183d'–184A).

54 'Others undermine the "gratuitousness" of the supernatural order, when they say that God could not create beings endowed with intellect without ordaining and calling them to the beatific vision' (Pope Pius XII, *Humani generis* (1950); DS 3891).

55 St Thérèse de l'Enfant-Jésus et de la Sainte Face, *Le carnet jaune* (5 June 1897), n. 4; *Œuvres complètes* (Paris: Éditions du Cerf, 2001), 1009.

56 '"Show thy face", now by faith and grace, in the future by sight and glory, "and we shall be saved". This indicates most clearly that our salvation or beatitude consists in the showing or vision of the divine countenance, namely, in an act of the intellect' (Blessed Denys, *Commentarium in psalmum 78*, a. 3; *DCOO* 6. 282CD'). 'The "face of God" is to be understood to mean God Himself as present and known' (*Commentarium in psalmum 41*, a. 82; *DCOO* 5. 672C').

57 St Thomas, *ST* 1a q. 12 a. 3.

58 Blessed Denys, *Enarratio in cap. 5 Epistolae 2 B. Pauli ad Corinthios*, a. 5; *DCOO* 13. 229B'.

59 Cf. St Thomas, *Super ad Hebraeos* cap. 6, lect. 1; Blessed Denys, *Commentarium in psalmum 20*, a. 49; *DCOO* 5. 528B.

60 Blessed Denys, *De natura aeterni et veri Dei*, a. 1; *DCOO* 34. 13B–13A'.

61 Cf. St Thomas, *ST* 1a q. 12 a. 2. Blessed Denys likewise says: 'Every created essence, form, and species is infinitely outdone and over-shadowed by the super-substantial nature of God. Therefore, it is not able to represent the divine essence to the point where, through it, the divine essence would be seen in itself and essentially; indeed, the super-exalted purity of the First Truth shines in every created entity in such a defectible way that this very shining is infinitely distant from the limpidity of its fontal light. We have therefore demonstrated that the divine essence can be known in itself by no created species' (Blessed Denys, *De lumine christianae theoriae*, lib. 2 a. 57; *DCOO* 33. 455C'–456B).

62 Blessed Denys, *De lumine christianae theoriae*, lib. 2 a. 58; *DCOO* 33. 456C'–457A.

63 Blessed Denys, *De laudibus Dei*; *DCOO* 34. 410A'.

64 Anscar Vonier OSB, *The Collected Works of Abbot Vonier*, iii. *The Soul and the Spiritual Life* (London: Burns & Oates, 1953), 142.

65 Cf. the Council of Vienne, *Ad nostrum qui* (1312); DS 895.

66 Blessed Denys, *De lumine christianae theoriae*, lib. 2 a. 63; *DCOO* 33. 461D'.

67 Cf. St Thomas, *ST* 1a q. 12 a. 5.

68 Blessed Denys, *De lumine christianae theoriae*, lib. 2 a. 62; *DCOO* 33. 461B.

69 Ibid. a. 63; *DCOO* 33. 462B.

70 Anscar Vonier OSB, *Collected Works*, iii. 138–9.

71 Cf. St Thomas, *ST* 1a q. 12 a. 7 and ad. 1.

72 Blessed Denys, *De lumine christianae theoriae*, lib. 2 a. 59; *DCOO* 33. 458AB.

73 Cf. St Thomas, *ST* 1a q. 12 a. 7 ad. 3; *Summa contra gentiles*, lib. 3 cap. 55; *De veritate*, q. 8 a. 2 ad. 6. See also David Berger, *Thomismus: Grosse Leitmotive der thomistischen Synthese und ihre Aktualität für die Gegenwart* (Cologne: Editiones Thomisticae, 2001), 368–9.

74 Blessed Denys, *De passione Domini salvatoris dialogues*, a. 26; *DCOO* 35. 306BC.

75 '[The intellect] is the cause of love and interior *delectatio*, for love is based on the recognition of the true, and likewise interior *delectatio*. The will moves the intellect only in a secondary sense, in the sense, namely, that understanding is apprehended as good. For it is the intellect that proposes the thing understood to the will, and moves it by the way in which an end moves, since the good understood is an object of the will. In short, the best power of a being is that from which the definition of its species is derived. Now separate substances and the rational soul obtain their species from the intellect; wherefore it is necessary that felicity be appropriate to them according to intellect. For such substances are called "intelligences" by reason of the intellect. Principally, then, felicity is in the intellect, then in the will, which is also an immaterial and inorganic power and the most worthy one after the intellect. Now love is in the will. But since love is concerned about what one does not have as well as what one does, felicity does not consist principally in love, but rather in contemplation, which love follows. On account of which the Saviour says: "This is eternal life, that they know thee, the true God etc" (John 17: 3). Therefore, love is only perfect inasmuch as it is the love of something already possessed; it is not therefore perfect by reason of itself. But felicity is perfect *per se*. In truth, contemplation is contemplation only of what is already possessed, for the perfection of the intellect is according as the intelligible thing is united to it. The perfection of the will, however, consists in the union of itself to the thing willed; therefore love exists both in tendency and in terminus. In love that is only tending, there is no felicity; for such love is imperfect, nor does it render the appetite content. Again, the love of what is possessed and present is perfect by reason of the uniting (*unitio*). But this uniting of it is by reason of contemplation or rather it is contemplation itself, for we are already talking about intellectual love. It is clear, therefore, that *contemplation* is the more formal aspect of beatitude than love' (Blessed Denys, *De lumine christianae theoriae*, lib. 1 a. 45; *DCOO* 33. 286B'–287B).

76 Cf. *De civitate Dei*, lib. 22 cap. 30; CCSL 48. 866.

77 *The Divine Comedy: Paradise* canto 28, lines 109–11; trans. Sayers and Reynolds, 304.

78 *De distantia perfectionis divinae et humanae*, a. 29; *DCOO* 34. 288c–288a'.
79 Cf. Blessed Denys, *De fonte lucis ac semitis vitae*, a. 10; *DCOO* 41. 107bc.
    '[B]eatitude is essentially in the intellect, since it is the knowledge of
    God, as God Himself says, "This is eternal life, that they know thee,
    the only true God" (John 17: 3), but *by way of completion* in the will'
    (cf. *De contemplatione*, lib. 3 a. 15; *DCOO* 41. 270b').
80 Cf. St Thomas, *Super evangelium Johannis*, cap. 17 lect. 1.
81 Cf. St Thomas, 4 *Sent*. d. 44 q. 2 a. 4a.
82 Cf. St Thomas, *Summa contra Gentiles*, lib. 4 cap. 86 n. 5.
83 Columba Marmion OSB, *Christ, the Life of the Soul: Spiritual Con-*
    ference, trans. Mother M. St Thomas of Tyburn Convent, new edn.
    (London: Sands, 1922), 396.
84 Cf. *Benedictus Deus* (1336); DS 2305.
85 Dante Alighieri, *The Divine Comedy: Paradise*, Canto 14, lines 43–55,
    55–60; ET by Dorothy L. Sayers (Harmondsworth: Penguin Books,
    1962), 179–80. Blessed Denys says, commenting on 2 Cor. 5: 4: 'We
    groan because *we would not be unclothed*, that is, separated entirely
    and finally from union with the body, since it is natural for the soul
    to inform the body, and the saints in the Fatherland desire to be
    united to their glorious bodies, but rather *clothed upon*, that is, attain
    the immortality and glorification of the body' (*Enarratio in cap. 5 epis-*
    tolae 2 B. Pauli ad Corinthios, a. 5; *DCOO* 13. 229c).
86 Cf. St Thomas, *ST* 1a2ae q. 4 a. 5 ad. 4 and ad. 5.
87 Anscar Vonier OSB, *Collected Works*, iii. 319.
88 Marmion, *Christ, the Life of the Soul*, 97–8.
89 Le Pichon, *Le Mystère du Couronnement de la Vierge*, 16.
90 Blessed Denys, *De laudibus sanctissimae et individuae Trinitatis, per*
    modum horarum; *DCOO* 35. 142cd.
91 The 'operations *ad extra* of the most high and incomprehensible
    Trinity are utterly undivided' (Blessed Denys, *Expositio hymni: Con-*
    ditor alme siderum; *DCOO* 35. 19b).
92 'Thou the image of the Father, equal | Full and true and natural, |
    And exemplary cause | Of every being in the world' (Blessed Denys,
    De laudibus superlaudabilis Dei; *DCOO* 34. 441d).
93 Cf. the Athanasian Creed; DS 75.
94 Cf. Boethius, *De consolatione philosophiae*, lib. 5 prosa 6; *PL* 63. 858; St
    Thomas in *ST* 1a q. 10 a. 1.
95 St Bede the Venerable, *Homelia* I, 12, *In theophania seu epiphania*
    Domini; CCSL 122. 83.
96 Cf. St John Damascene, *Homilia 2 in dormitionem Beatae Virginis*
    Mariae, n. 2; SC 80. 126.

97 Marmion, *Christ, the Life of the Soul*, 102.

98 'If we are right to understand the Father to be the One who kisses, and the Son to be the One who is kissed, then it cannot be wrong to see the kiss as the Holy Spirit, for He is the imperturbable peace of the Father and the Son, their firm bond (*gluten firmum*), their undivided love, their indivisible unity' (St Bernard of Clairvaux, *Sermo 8 in Cantica*, n. 2; *S. Bernardi opera*, i, ed. J. Leclercq OSB, C. H. Talbot, and H. M. Rochais OSB (Rome: Editiones Cistercienses, 1957), 37).

99 *De laudibus superlaudabilis Dei*; *DCOO* 34. 442D'–443A.

100 The Council of Florence, *Decretum pro Graecis* (1439); DS 1300.

101 Le Pichon, *Le Mystère du Couronnement de la Vierge*, 81.

102 The Council of Florence, *Decretum pro Graecis* (1439); DS 1305.

103 Marmion, *Christ, the Life of the Soul*, 391.

104 Blessed Denys, *Enarratio in cap. 3 Exodi*, a. 5; *DCOO* 1. 498C. Cf. St Thomas, *ST* 1a q. 13 11; St John Damascene, *De fide orthodoxa*, lib. 1 cap. 9; *PG* 94. 836B.

105 Blessed Denys, *De venustate mundi et pulchritudine Dei*, prooemium; *DCOO* 34. 225. In some works, the rhapsodic theology becomes theological rhapsody: 'O eternal light, most super-splendid, and most super-beautiful (*superpulcherrima*), light that shines forth in thyself with infinite radiance; of thy beauty there is no end, and the splendour of thy loveliness is utterly immense, O super-simple, incomprehensible, uncircumscribed light! O adorable Trinity, thou pure, immense, fontal, super-substantial, eternal goodness' (Blessed Denys, *De laudibus sanctissimae et individuae Trinitatis, per modum horarum*; *DCOO* 35. 138D–139A).

106 Cf. St Thomas, *ST* 1a q. 39 a. 1.

107 Pope Pius XII, *Mystici corporis* (DS 3815). 'Then we shall most clearly understand whatever now we believe concerning thee, Lord God, for we shall then see, with supreme delight, how one person proceeds from the other in the Godhead, how thou, O Son, art begotten by God the Father, and how thou, O Holy Spirit, art spirated by both' (Blessed Denys, *De laudibus Dei*; *DCOO* 34. 410BC').

108 Blessed Denys, *Contra detestabilem cordis inordinationem in Dei laudibus*, a. 12; *DCOO* 40. 209A.

109 St Thomas quotes the words *Intra in gaudium Domini* when discussing everlasting life in his final conference on the Creed (cf. *In symbolum apostolorum*, a. 12).

110 Marmion, *Christ, the Life of the Soul*, 394.

111 Cf. Blessed Denys, *De venustate mundi et pulchritudine Dei*, a. 24; *DCOO* 34. 250AB.

112 In *Humani generis* (1950) Pope Pius XII condemns the opinion of those who hold that God cannot create an intellectual being without at the same time ordering and calling it to a supernatural final end (cf. DS 3891).

113 Blessed Denys, *De quatuor hominis novissimis*, a. 57; *DCOO* 41. 573D–573A'.

114 Cf. St Thomas, *ST* 2a2ae q. 24 a. 3 ad. 3.

115 Marmion, *Christ, the Life of the Soul*, 398.

116 This statement refers to the glorification of our Lord's complete humanity, body as well as soul. The summit of His human soul was, of course, glorified through the Beatific Vision from the first moment of His conception, but He freely prevented bliss and glory from overflowing from that high summit to the lower slopes of His human soul and thence into His body (see the discussion in the next chapter).

117 Marmion, *Christ, the Life of the Soul*, 388.

118 The Schoolmen, following St Augustine's exegesis of the six days of creation, make a distinction between 'morning' and 'evening' knowledge: morning knowledge is the knowledge of things in the Word; evening knowledge is the knowledge of them in their own nature (cf. St Thomas, 3 *Sent.* d. 31 q. 2 a. 1 qa. 1 ad. 4; *ST* 1a q. 58 a. 7).

119 Cf. St Thomas, *Quodlibeta* 8, q. 9 a. 2.

120 St Thomas, *Super ad Thess.* 1, cap. 1 lect. 1.

121 Cf. the Council of Florence, *Decretum pro Graecis* (1439); DS 1305.

122 Blessed Denys, *De mutua cognitione beatorum in patria*, a. 5; *DCOO* 36. 182BC.

123 Cf. St Thomas, *ST* 3a q. 10 a. 2.

124 Cf. St Thomas, *4 Sent.* d. 45 q. 3 a. 1. All the blessed know and see in God what they naturally desire to know (cf. Blessed Denys, *De mutua cognitione beatorum in patria*, a. 5; *DCOO* 36. 182B). Even apart from the Beatific Vision, separated souls know some individual things through the ideas that flow into them from God (cf. St Thomas, *ST* 1a q. 89 a. 4). Abbot Vonier has bequeathed us a beautiful summary of St Thomas's doctrine on the natural knowledge of the separated soul as expounded in *ST* 1a q. 89: 'The theory of St Thomas about the way a disembodied human soul acquires spirit-knowledge is wonderfully bold; at the same time it is exceedingly simple. The whole spirit-world constantly radiates knowledge, as the material world sends forth the stimuli of our senses. Spirits are incessantly at work, they never rest; and their activity is to impart

knowledge. Every spirit receives those communications in a measure dependent on his own capacity, his own power of grasping the thought. Nor is it in the power of a spirit to screen himself from the influence of those communications. The disembodied soul is thus filled with wide and sublime knowledge, as the bodily eye, when open, is filled with the vision of all that lies within its horizon. There is no distinction in this matter between holy and reprobate souls, for those spirit-communications are a law of their nature; they become the happiness of the upright, and the despair of the perverted will. The elect soul, of course, will be the object of further illumination of a higher order. But we are speaking . . . of the merely natural conditions, not of the privileged condition of the soul' (*Collected Works*, iii. 55–6).

125 Blessed Denys, *De mutua cognitione beatorum in patria*, a. 8; DCOO 36. 186B.

126 Cf. St Thomas, *4 Sent.* d. 45 q. 3 a. 1.

127 Jacques Maritain, 'À propos de l'Église du ciel'; *Carnet de notes* (Paris: Desclée de Brouwer, 1965), 357.

128 Ibid. 358.

129 Ibid. 357. On the freedom of the blessed, see Simon Gaine OP, *Will There be Free Will in Heaven? Freedom, Impeccability, and Beatitude* (London: T. & T. Clark, 2003).

130 Jacques Maritain, 'À propos de l'Église du ciel', 359.

131 Cf. St Thomas, *ST* 1a q. 108 a. 5 ad. 5.

132 Cf. Le Pichon, *Le Mystère du Couronnement de la Vierge*, 42.

133 Ibid. 17.

134 *Creaturarum in ordine ad Deum consideratio theologica*, a. 46; DCOO 34. 134D. Cf. St Thomas, *ST* 1a q. 108 a. 8.

135 Blessed Denys, *Enarratio in cap. 22 Matthaei*, a. 36; DCOO 11. 246D.

136 Cf. the hymn sung during the Divine Liturgy of St John Chrysostom in the Byzantine Churches.

137 Cf. the *Decretum pro Graecis* (1439); DS 1305; Blessed Denys, *Enarratio in cap. 3 Cantici canticorum* a. 9; DCOO 7. 351C'.

138 Cf. St Thomas, *ST* 1a q. 12 a. 6.

139 Cf. ibid.

140 St Thérèse of Lisieux, *Histoire d'une âme*, 19ᵛ; *Œuvres complètes* (Paris: Éditions du Cerf, 1992), 99.

141 Vonier, *The Collected Works*, ii. 144.

142 Dante, *The Divine Comedy: Paradise*, canto 3, line 85.

143 Marmion, *Christ, the Life of the Soul*, 400.

144 St Thomas, *In symbolum apostolorum*, a. 10.

145 Pope Leo XIII, *Mirae caritatis* (1902); DS 3363.

146 St Gregory the Great, *Homiliarum in Ezechielem liber* 2, n. 9; *PL* 76. 954A; cf. St Thomas, *ST* 2a2ae q. 180 a. 8 ad. 1. Contemplation 'will be perfect in the life to come, when we shall see Him face to face' (St Thomas, *ST* 2a2ae q. 180, a. 4).

147 '[C]ontemplation is a kind of *fides occulta*, a faith become, as it were, experiential through supernatural light' (Berger, *Thomismus*, 363).

148 Marmion, *Christ, the Life of the Soul*, 401.

149 Cf. Christopher Dawson, *Religion and the Rise of Western Culture*, new edn. (New York: Doubleday, 1958), 204.

150 Pope Leo XIII, *Exeunte iam anno* (1888); *Sanctissimi Domini nostri Leonis Papae XIII allocutiones, epistolae, constitutiones, aliaque acta praecipua*, iii. 1887–1889 (Bruges: Desclée, 1893), 191–2.

151 'Since such a great reward in heavenly happiness is promised to kings who conduct themselves well when they rule, they must watch themselves with diligent care, lest they lapse into tyranny. For nothing should be more acceptable to them than being transferred from the kingly honour in which they were exalted on earth to the glory of the Kingdom of Heaven. Tyrants go astray when they forsake justice for the sake of earthly advantages, thereby depriving themselves of the great reward that they could have obtained by ruling justly. No one but a fool or an infidel can fail to see how foolish it is to lose the greatest and everlasting goods for the sake of paltry and temporal goods of this kind. We should add that the very temporal advantages for which tyrants abandon justice more commonly accrue to monarchs when they serve justice' (*De regimine principum*, lib. 1 cap. 11).

152 The great Italian novelist, Eugenio Corti, who witnessed the horrors of Stalinist Russia during the Second World War, has devoted many of his writings to exposing the anti-human brutality of the Marxist pursuit of the perfect society: 'According to the Marxist-Leninist texts, the new society is attained in two phases or steps. The first (the lower step or first stage of Communism) is called Socialist society; from this there eventually develops a true and proper Communist society. Obviously the time for arriving at this last stage is not predetermined. However, Lenin predicted that the USSR would attain Communism by 1930, certainly by 1940 . . . The supreme goal of the Kmer Rouge is to construct a new society of "instantaneous peasant Communism" based on Mao's "faith in the land as a source of self-sufficiency"' (*Processo e morte di Stalin:*

Tragedia con altri testi sul communismo (Milan: Edizioni Ares, 1999), 143, 233).

153 Columba Marmion OSB, *Christ in His Mysteries*, trans. Mother M. St Thomas, new edn. (London: Sands & Co., 1939), 312, citing finally Pope St Gregory the Great.

2 OPENING HEAVEN'S GATES

1 Cf. St Thomas, *ST* 3a q. 52 a. 1 ad. 2.

2 Cf. 3a q. 49 a. 3 ad. 1.

3 *Pange lingua gloriosi* in M. Britt OSB, *The Hymns of the Breviary and Missal*, new edn. (London: Burns, Oates, & Washbourne, 1924), 127.

4 The Cross is '"lofty" in power, and dignity, and effects' (Blessed Denys, *Expositio hymni: Crux fidelis, inter omnes*; *DCOO* 35. 94c').

5 Blessed Denys speaks of this mysterious becoming without change as follows: 'While being the offspring of the Father's intellect, the Word is most truly born [as man]; but far be it from us to believe that He progresses from non-being to being; if He were to migrate in this way from potency to act, He would not be true God' (*De praeconio et dignitate Mariae*, lib. 1 a. 7; *DCOO* 35. 483B).

6 Pope St Leo the Great, *Epistola 'Lectis dilectionis tuae' ad [S.] Flavianum episcopum Constantinopolitanum, sive 'Tomus [I] Leonis*; DS 294.

7 Britt, *The Hymns of the Breviary and Missal*, 188; trans. J. M. Neale, adapted.

8 Blessed Denys, *Enarratio in cap. 15 epistolae 1 B. Pauli ad Corinthios*, a. 16; *DCOO* 13. 204B.

9 '[T]he union of the human and divine natures took place in the person and hypostasis and supposit, though with the distinction of the natures remaining. Thus there is the same person and hypostasis in the divine and human natures, with the properties of the natures being preserved. Therefore . . . the Passion is to be attributed to the supposit of the divine nature, not by reason of the divine nature, which is impassible, but by reason of the human nature. Therefore, in his synodical epistle, Cyril says: "If anyone does not confess the Word of God to have suffered and been crucified in the flesh, let him be anathema." Therefore, the Passion of Christ pertains to the supposit of the divine nature by reason of the passible assumed nature, not by reason of the impassible divine nature' (St Thomas, *ST* 3a q. 46 a. 12).

10 The suffering of Christ was the 'greatest among the sufferings of this present life' (cf. St Thomas, *ST* 3a q. 46 a. 6).

11 Blessed Denys, *Expositio hymni*: Vexilla Regis prodeunt; *DCOO* 35. 39D–39A'.

12 Pope St Leo the Great, *Epistola 'Lectis dilectionis tuae' ad [S.] Flavianum episcopum Constantinopolitanum, sive 'Tomus [I] Leonis*; DS 294.

13 'In Adam original sin, which is the sin of nature, is derived from his actual sin, which is a personal sin, because in him the person corrupts nature, and by means of this corruption, the sin of the first man is passed to his posterity, corrupt nature corrupting the person. But grace is not passed on from Christ to us by means of human nature, but by the personal action of Christ Himself alone. Therefore, we must not distinguish two graces in Christ, one corresponding to nature, the other to the person, in the way that in Adam there is a distinction between the sin of nature and the sin of the person' (St Thomas, *ST* 3a q. 8 a. 5 ad. 1). Commenting on this passage, Claude Sarrasin says: 'Such is the principle that alone has the power to surmount the isolation of the human person in relation to the first father and in relation to other men . . . If human nature in Christ played the role it plays in the transmission of Adam's sin, it would be purely and simply subject to corruption; it is precisely the grace of union that prevents this degradation' (*Plein de grâce et de vérité: Théologie de l'âme du Christ selon St Thomas d'Aquin* (Venasque: Éditions du Carmel, 1992), 113).

14 Cf. St Thomas, *ST* 3a, q. 8 a. 1.

15 Cf. ibid. a. 3.

16 Cf. ibid. q. 48 a. 2 ad. 1.

17 'Christ and His members are one mystical person, which is why the works of the Head are in a certain way the works of the members. Thus, when God gives us something on account of the merits of Christ, there is no contradiction of what is said in the Psalm: '[T]hou wilt render to every man according to his works' (Ps. 61: 13). Still, Christ's merits are of benefit to us in such a way that through the Sacraments they cause in us the grace by which we are stirred to perform meritorious works' (St Thomas, *De veritate* q. 29 a. 7 ad. 11).

18 Marmion, *Christ in His Mysteries*, 254. '"Thou hast said it", as if to say, "Thou hast said it in truth", namely, that I am the Christ, the Son of the living and blessed God' (Blessed Denys, *Enarratio in cap. 26 Matthaei*, a. 42; *DCOO* 11.298B').

19 Cf. St Thomas, *ST* 3a q. 15 a. 10. 'Christ was at once wayfarer and beholder: wayfarer, as regards the possibility of human nature and everything pertaining to it; beholder as regards the union of the divinity, according to which He enjoyed God most perfectly' (St Thomas, *Super evangelium Iohannis*, cap. 4 lect. 6).

20 Cf. Blessed Denys, *Elementatio theologica*, prop. 116; *DCOO* 33. 199D'–200A.

21 Cf. St Thomas, *ST* 3a q. 14 aa. 1, 2; q. 45 a. 2; q. 54 a. 2; Blessed Denys, *Elementatio theologica*, prop. 128; *DCOO* 33. 206A'.

22 One of the axioms of the mystical theology of St John of the Cross is that faith is 'the only proximate and proportionate means to union with God' (*The Ascent of Mount Carmel*, cap. 9 n. 1; *The Collected Works of St John of the Cross*, trans. Kieran Kavanaugh OCD and Otilio Rodriguez OCD, new edn. (Washington DC: Institute of Carmelite Studies, 1979), 129).

23 '"He has seen the Father" (John 6: 46), by a vision of perfect comprehension, inasmuch as He is God, and likewise by the vision of beatific enjoyment, inasmuch as He is man, from the beginning of the Incarnation' (Blessed Denys, *Enarratio in cap. 6 Joannis*, a. 17; *DCOO* 12. 398c').

24 *The Catechism of the Catholic Church*, n. 151.

25 *Decretum S. Officii* (5 June 1918); DS 3646.

26 Pope Pius XII, *Mystici corporis* (29 June 1943); DS 3812.

27 St Thomas, *ST* 3a q. 9 a. 2.

28 Ibid.

29 Cf. St Thomas, *ST* 3a q. 12 a. 2.

30 Cf. *The Catechism of the Catholic Church*, n. 473.

31 Cf. St Thomas, *ST* 3a q. 46 aa. 7, 8.

32 Pope John Paul II, *L'osservatore romano* (1988), English language edition, issue 49, p. 1.

33 Pope John Paul II, *Novo millennio ineunte*, n. 26; *AAS* 93 (2001), 283.

34 Cf. St Thomas, *ST* 3a q. 10 a. 2. St Thomas speaks here of Christ knowing all things 'in the Word' (*in Verbo*). Father Claude Sarrasin explains this statement as follows: '[T]he knowledge *in Verbo* that St Thomas considers in Christ is no more and no less than the knowledge that He has humanly in Himself' (*Plein de grâce et de vérité*, 173).

35 '[I]n the divinity to which it was united, His soul saw clearly all the sins of mankind, all the outrages committed against God's holiness and infinite love' (Marmion, *Christ in His Mysteries*, 252). 'Christ, in seeing God, sees also that the beatitude He enjoys is absent in us' (Sarrasin, *Plein de grâce et de vérité*, 181).

36 *The Catechism of the Catholic Church*, n. 478.

37 Pope John Paul II, Apostolic Letter, *Novo millennio ineunte*, n. 27; *AAS* 93. 283–4.

38 *The Catechism of the Catholic Church*, n. 1717.

39 Cf. St Thomas, *ST* 3a q. 48 aa. 1–4.

40 Cf. ibid. a. 1.

41 Cf. ibid. a. 2.

42 Ibid. a. 3.

43 Cf. ibid. a. 4.

44 Ibid. 49, a. 5.

45 A hymn of the Ambrosian tradition dating from the seventh century. The translation is a cento made by me from older versions.

46 Le Pichon, *Le Mystère du couronnement de la Vierge*, 18.

47 Marmion, *Christ in His Mysteries*, 289.

48 Cf. St Thomas, *Super epistolam ad Romanos*, cap. 6 lect. 2.

49 Cf. Blessed Denys, *Enarratio in cap. 20 Joannis*, a. 48; *DCOO* 12. 607BC.

50 '[He vanished] from their sight suddenly and as it were imperceptibly and most quickly through the gift of agility, thereby showing He had a glorified body. He did not, however, vanish like a ghost' (Blessed Denys, *Enarratio in cap. 24 Lucae*, a. 50; *DCOO* 12. 256A).

51 Pope St Gregory the Great, *Moralium liber* 14, cap. 55 n. 68; *PL* 75. 1075AB.

52 Pope St Gregory the Great, *Homiliarum in evangelia*, lib. 2, hom. 21; *PL* 76. 1172C. In his earlier works, St Thomas argues that the bodies of the saints were resurrected in glory on the first Easter Sunday. For example, in the commentary on St Matthew's Gospel, he writes as follows: '[The evangelist] says . . . "Many bodies of the saints that had slept arose". The question usually asked about these bodies is whether or not they were to die a second time. It is a fact that some people, such as Lazarus, were resurrected only to die later. But of [the saints] we can say that they did not rise and then die a second time, because they rose to manifest the Resurrection. Now it is certain that Christ, having risen from the dead, never dies again. Likewise, if [the saints] had risen [only to die again], no benefit would have been displayed, but only a disadvantage. Therefore, they rose so as to enter with Christ into Heaven' (*Super evangelium Matthaei*, cap. 27 lect. 2). Later, in the *ST*, Thomas seems to have reservations about this opinion and leaves open the question of the saints' resurrection (cf. 3a q. 53 a. 3). The most comprehensive modern study of the issue is H. Zeller SJ, '*Corpora sanctorum*: Eine Studie zu Mt 27: 52–53', *Zeitschrift für katholische Theologie* 71 (1949), 385–465.

53 Blessed Denys, *Enarratio in cap. 27 Matthaei*, a. 44; *DCOO* 11. 313B'. 'Christ desired to have companions and witnesses of His Resurrection: for if He had risen alone He might have been thought a phantom; but when He had others with Him, who rose at the same time

as He did, He could easily show that He could rise, because He could raise them' (John Maldonatus, *A Commentary on the Holy Gospels*, trans. George J. Davie, 2nd edn. (London: John Hodges, 1888), ii. 565–6).

54 Blessed Denys, *Enarratio in cap. 27 Matthaei*, a. 44; *DCOO* 11. 313D'.

55 Cf. St Thomas, *ST* 3a q. 48 a. 1. 'He merited everything that we lost in Adam (cf. Rom. 5: 15–20; Eph. 1: 3) . . . Therefore, He merited for us *sanctifying grace*, the infused virtues and the seven Gifts, and likewise all the *actual graces* by which we are prepared for justification, by which thereafter we perform meritorious works, and by which we persevere. He likewise merited *eternal life* or salvation, and even the final resurrection, or the lost preternatural gifts, immunity from death, suffering, concupiscence, and error' (R. Garrigou-Lagrange OP, *De Christo Salvatore* (Turin: Marietti, 1949), 414).

56 Cf. St Thomas, *ST* 3a q. 56 aa. 1–2.

57 Cf. ibid. a. 2 ad. 3.

58 Pope John Paul II, *Redemptor hominis*, n. 20; *AAS* 71 (1979), 310; cf. Pope John Paul II, *Ecclesia in Eucharistia*, n. 13; *AAS* 95 (2003), 442.

59 St Thomas, *ST* 3a q. 53 a. 1.

60 Cf. ibid. a. 4.

61 Cf 3a q. 50, a. 4.

62 Ibid. 53 a. 4.

63 See Blessed Denys's commentary on this hymn of St Ambrose's: *Expositio hymni: Optatus votes omnium*; *DCOO* 35. 49D'–50A.

64 Cf. St Thomas, 3 *Sent.* d. 22 q. 3 a. 1, SC 3. 'A place must be proportionate to the thing placed. Now, by His Resurrection, Christ has begun an immortal and incorruptible life. But the place where we live is a place of generation and corruption, whereas the heavenly place is a place of incorruption. Therefore, it was not fitting for Christ after His Resurrection to remain on earth, but it was fitting that He should ascend into Heaven' (St Thomas, *ST* 3a q. 57 a. 1).

65 The Ambrosian hymn *Aeterne rex altissime* in Britt, *The Hymns of the Breviary and Missal*, 158.

66 St Gregory the Great, *In primum Regum expositiones*, lib. 1 cap. 1 n. 45; *PL* 79. 45.

67 Marmion, *Christ in His Mysteries*, 319–20. 'His very presence, in the human nature brought into Heaven, is a kind of intercession for us, in the sense that, since God has thus exalted human nature in Christ, He also has mercy on those for whom the Son of God assumed human nature' (St Thomas, *ST* 3a q. 57 a. 6).

68 Blessed Denys, *Enarratio in cap. 8 epistolae B. Pauli ad Romanos,* a. 12; *DCOO* 13. 71CD.

69 Blessed Denys, *Expositio hymni: Ave, maris stella; DCOO* 35. 83D'.

70 '"And I shall prepare a place for you" (cf. John 14: 3), that is, I shall send the Holy Spirit to you, by whose power and grace you will be prepared for attaining the place of the heavenly mansion' (Blessed Denys, *Enarratio in cap. 14 Joannis,* a. 35; *DCOO* 12. 528BC).

71 Cf. St Thomas, *ST* 3a q. 57 a. 1 ad. 3.

72 Cf. Pope John Paul II, *Dominum et vivificantem,* n. 10; *AAS* 78 (1986), 819.

73 Marmion, *Christ, the Life of the Soul,* 104–5. 'Just as the generation of the Son is by way of internal mental utterance, so the procession of the Holy Spirit is by way of the most liberal and first gratuitous donation, by which love, that first gift, in which other gifts are given, flows forth from the Lover into the Beloved, and from the Beloved flows back into the Lover, as the mutual friendship of the two' (Blessed Denys, *Elementatio theologica,* prop. 38; *DCOO* 33. 141CD').

74 'It is necessary to attribute habitual grace to Christ, first, because of His soul to the Word of God. For the closer anything receptive is to the cause that flows into it, the more it will share in that inflow. Now the inflow of grace is from God . . . Therefore, it was supremely fitting for that soul to receive the inflow of divine grace' (St Thomas, *ST* 3a q. 7 a. 1).

75 The habitual grace that fills the soul of Christ is a 'plenitude of super-abundance', whereas His Blessed Mother's fullness of grace is a 'plenitude of prerogative' and St Stephen's (cf. Acts 7: 55) a 'plenitude of suffering' (cf. Blessed Denys, *Enarratio in cap. 4 Lucae,* a. 10; *DCOO* 11. 460B–460D).

76 Marmion, *Christ, the Life of the Soul,* 110. St Thomas says that 'the soul of Christ was most perfectly moved by the Holy Spirit' (*ST* 3a q. 7 a. 5).

77 St Thomas, *Super epistolam ad Hebraeos* cap. 9 lect. 3; cf. Blessed Denys, *Enarratio in cap. 9 epistolae B. Pauli ad Hebraeos,* a. 9; *DCOO* 13, 507A.

78 Cf. St Thomas, *ST* 3a q. 7 a. 1.

79 Ibid. a. 9.

80 Cf. Blessed Denys, *Enarratio in cap. 7 Joannis,* a. 20; *DCOO* 12. 420D–421A.

81 Ibid.

82 Cf. Pope John Paul II, *Dominum et vivificantem,* n. 24; *AAS* 78. 832.

83 St Thomas, *Super evangelium Iohannis,* cap. 7 lect. 5. St Thomas mentions another interpretation, that of St John Chrysostom, who

argues that the glorification in question is the Passion, for our Lord says on the evening of Holy Thursday, after Judas goes off to betray Him: 'Now is the Son of Man glorified' (John 13: 31). Now the Holy Spirit is the Gift *par excellence*, and gifts are not given to enemies. But before the Passion we were the enemies of God. 'It was therefore necessary for the Victim to be offered on the altar of the Cross, and for the enmity to be dissolved, so that, thus reconciled to God and made His friends by the death of His Son, we might receive the gift of the Holy Spirit' (ibid.).

84 St Bede the Venerable, *Homeliarum liber 2*, hom. 17; CCSL 122. 301.

85 Pope Leo XIII, *Divinum illud munus* (1897); DS 3331.

86 Cf. *The Catechism of the Catholic Church*, nn. 689–90.

87 See Marmion, *Christ, the Life of the Soul*, 111–12.

88 *The Catechism of the Catholic Church*, n. 1129.

89 Pope John Paul II, *Ecclesia in Eucharistia*, nn. 18–19; *AAS* 95. 448–9.

90 Cf. St Thomas, *ST* 3a q. 75 a. 2.

91 Ibid.

92 Cf. the Fourth Lateran Council, *Definitio contra Albigenses*; DS 802.

93 Cf. the Council of Trent, *Decretum de ss. Eucharistia*, cap. 4; DS 1642, 1652.

94 Cf. Pope John Paul II, *Ecclesia de Eucharistia*, n. 15; *AAS* 95. 443.

95 Cf. the Council of Trent, *Decretum de ss. Eucharistia*, cap. 3; DS 1640. Abbot Vonier says of 'concomitance': 'Though it has a very technical sound, it is in reality a most gracious word. Its Latin roots signify, with a redundance of adverb and verb, the act of walking along with someone as a companion—*concomitari*—the roots of which are *cum* (with) and *comes* (companion). The theological meaning is this, that the Eucharistic Body and the Eucharistic Blood of Christ are accompanied; they are not alone, they come, as it were, escorted by friends. Those holy things, Body and Blood, are like the centre of a group; they are surrounded by other holy things, without which they do not exist' (*Collected Works*, ii. *The Church and the Sacraments* (London: Burns & Oates 1952), 329).

96 Cf. the Council of Trent, *Decretum de ss. Eucharistia*, cap. 3; DS 1640.

97 Cf. St Thomas, *ST* 3a q. 75 a. 1.

98 Blessed Denys, *De sacramento altaris et missae celebratione dialogus*, a. 7; *DCOO* 35. 390C.

99 From the Roman Canon.

100 Blessed Denys, *Expositio missae* 21; *DCOO* 35. 356CD'.

101 Cf. St Thomas, *ST* 3a q. 83 a. 4 ad. 9.

102 Ibid.

103 The hymn *Verbum supernum prodiens*, by St Thomas Aquinas, in J. M. Neale's translation, in Britt, *The Hymns of the Breviary and Missal*, 188.

104 The origins of this devotional image in late medieval art are well summarized by Eamon Duffy: 'According to the legend, Pope Gregory, while celebrating Mass in the church of Santa Croce in Gerusalemme in Rome, had experienced a vision of Christ, seated on or standing in His tomb, displaying His wounds and surrounded by the implements of the Passion. The legend almost certainly derives from an early medieval Byzantine icon displayed in the church of Santa Croce, which had a chapel dedicated to St Gregory. The image became an object of pilgrimage, and from the fourteenth century was widely copied, first in Italy and then in France' (*The Stripping of the Altars. Traditional Religion in England, c. 1400– c. 1580* (New Haven: Yale University Press, 1992), 238).

105 Cf. *The Catechism of the Catholic Church*, n. 1367.

106 Cf. the Council of Trent, 22nd Session, *Doctrina de ss. Missae sacrificio* (1562), cap. 1, 2; DS 1739–43; Pope Pius XII, Encyclical Letter, *Mediator Dei* (1947); *AAS* 39 (1947), 549–50.

107 The Council of Trent, 22nd Session, *Doctrina de ss. Missae sacrificio* (1562), cap. 2; DS 1743.

108 '[O]n the altar, by reason of the glorious state of His human nature, "death shall have no more dominion over Him" (Rom. 6: 9), and so the shedding of His blood is not possible. Still, according to the plan of divine wisdom, the Sacrifice of our Redeemer is shown forth in an admirable manner by external signs which are the tokens of His death. For by the transubstantiation of bread into the Body of Christ and of wine into His Blood, His Body and Blood are both really present. Now the eucharistic species under which He is present symbolize the violent separation of His body and blood. Thus the commemorative representation of His death, which actually took place on Calvary, is repeated in every sacrifice of the altar, since Jesus Christ is signified and shown forth by separate tokens to be in the state of a victim' (Pope Pius XII, Encyclical Letter, *Mediator Dei*; *AAS* 39. 548–9).

109 The Council of Trent, 22nd Session, *Doctrina de ss. Missae sacrificio* (1562), cap. 1; DS 1741; Pope John Paul II, Encyclical Letter, *Ecclesia de Eucharistia*, n. 12; *AAS* 95. 441.

110 Cf. St Thomas, *ST* 3a q. 79 a. 2.

111 Pope Pius XII, *Mediator Dei*; *AAS* 39. 551.

112 Blessed Denys, *Expositio missae* a. 35; *DCOO* 35. 374A′.

113 St Thomas, 4 *Sent.* d. 8 q. 1 a. 1c.

114 Cf. St Thomas, *ST* 3a q. 73 a. 4.

115 Cf. ibid. 79 a. 3 ad. 1.

116 St Thomas, *Piae preces*, nn. 6, 8.

117 Cf. St Thomas, *Super evangelium Iohannis* cap. 6 lect. 7.

118 Cf. St Ignatius of Antioch, *Epistle to the Ephesians*, n. 20; *The Apostolic Fathers: Part 2, St Ignatius, St Polycarp*, ed. J. B. Lightfoot, new edn. (London: Macmillan, 1889), 87.

119 Marmion, *Christ, the Life of the Soul*, 286–7.

120 *La Règle de Saint Benoît*, i. prologus; ed. J. Neufville OSB, *SC* 181 (Paris: Éditions du Cerf, 1972), p. xxx.

121 Marmion, *Christ in His Mysteries*, 259.

122 Blessed Denys, *De passione Domini salvatoris dialogus*, a. 26; *DCOO* 35. 304D.

123 Ibid. 305BD.

124 Marmion, *Christ in His Mysteries*, 260–1.

125 Ibid. 261.

126 Pope John Paul II, *Salvifici doloris*, n. 20; *AAS* 76 (1984), 227.

127 *La Règle de Saint Benoît*, vol. 1 cap. 4; ed. J. Neufville OSB, *SC* 181 456–7.

128 *La Règle de Saint Benôit*, vol. 2 p. 612.

129 Pope St Gregory the Great, *Homiliarum in evangelia*, lib. 2 hom. 39; *PL* 76. 1300BD.

130 Walter Daniel, *The Life of Ailred of Rievaulx*, n. 28/xxix, ET (London, 1950), 36 ff.

131 Cf. Pope John Paul II, *Ecclesia de Eucharistia*, n. 15; *AAS* 95. 443.

132 Cf. St Thomas, *ST* 3a q. 79 a. 1 ad. 2; q. 79 a. 4 and ad. 1; q. 79 a. 8 ad. 2. 'Christ makes us sharers of His thoughts, and His sentiments; He communicates His virtues to us, but above all, He enkindles in us the fire that He came to cast upon earth (cf. Luke 11: 49), the fire of love, of charity: that is the result of this transformation produced by the Eucharist' (Marmion, *Christ, the Life of the Soul*, 286).

3 HEAVEN LOST AND HEAVEN LONGED FOR

1 Dante, *The Divine Comedy: Purgatory*, canto 1, line 6; trans. Sayers 73.

2 'Every human being having the use of free will is in a position to attain eternal life, because he can prepare himself for grace, by which one merits eternal life. Therefore, if he fails in this, his sorrow

will be very great, because he is losing something it was possible for him to have. Now infants [dying before Baptism] have never been in a position to have eternal life, because it is not owed to them by the principles of nature, since it surpasses all the power of nature, nor can they have acts of their own enabling them to attain such a great good. Therefore, they will not be at all sorrowful about their loss of the vision of God. On the contrary, they will rather rejoice at their great share in the divine goodness and in natural perfections' (St Thomas, 2 *Sent.* d. 33 q. 2 a. 2). 'Although unbaptized children are separated from God as regards the union that comes through glory, they are nevertheless not entirely separated from Him; on the contrary, they are united to Him through sharing in natural good, and so are even able to rejoice in Him by a natural knowledge and goodness' (ibid. ad. 5; cf. *De malo*, q. 5 a. 3).

3 Cf. *The Catechism of the Catholic Church*, n. 1261.

4 Commenting on the phrase *ab inferis resurrectionis*, Blessed Denys says: '[T]he soul of Christ was with the Fathers in the Limbo of Hell until the hour of the Resurrection, as we sing in the Psalm, "Because thou wilt not leave my soul in Hell, nor wilt thou give thy holy one to see corruption" (Ps. 15: 10)' (*Expositio missae*, a. 32; *DCOO* 35. 369c').

5 Cf. Blessed Denys's comments on the line *Excursus usque ad inferos* in the hymn *Venit Redemptor gentium* (*DCOO* 35. 31B).

6 Cf. St Thomas, *ST* 3a q. 52 a. 2.

7 *Paradise Lost*, bk. 1, 403; *The Poetical Works of John Milton*, ed. H. C. Beeching, new edn. (London: Oxford University Press, 1944), 191.

8 *The Catechism of the Catholic Church*, n. 1033.

9 These words are from Gerard Manley Hopkins's translation of St Thomas's *Adoro te devote* (Britt, *The Hymns of the Breviary and Missal*, 190; *The Poems of Gerard Manley Hopkins*, ed. W. H. Gardner and N. H. MacKenzie, new edn. (London: Oxford University Press, 1970), 211).

10 *The Catechism of the Catholic Church*, n. 1035.

11 See e.g. Hans Urs von Balthasar, *Was dürfen wir hoffen?* (Einsiedeln: Johannes Verlag, 1986). Balthasar's eschatology has been subjected to a searching critique by Germain Grisez in *The Way of the Lord Jesus*, iii. *Difficult Moral Questions* (Quincy, Ill.: Franciscan Herald Press, 1997), 21–8.

12 Cf. *The Catechism of the Catholic Church*, n. 1036.

13 Pope John Paul II, *Salvifici doloris*, n. 14; *AAS* 76 (1984), 215.

14 The translation of the *Dies irae* is my own adaptation of the version in *The English Hymnal*, new edn. (London: Oxford University Press, 1933), n. 351, 486 ff.

15 St Thomas Aquinas, *Catena Aurea: Commentary on the Four Gospels Collected out of the Works of the Fathers*, i. *St Matthew*, trans. John Henry Newman et al., new edn. (London: St Austin Press, 1997), 865.

16 *The Catechism of the Catholic Church*, n. 1037.

17 Ibid. n. 308.

18 Cf. St Thomas, *ST* 1a q. 105 a. 5.

19 Cf. ibid. 1a2ae q. 79 a. 2; *De malo* q. 3 a. 2.

20 As St Augustine says: '"There the workers of iniquity are fallen; they are cast out, and could not stand" (Ps. 35: 13). In impiety each one attributes to himself what is of God, and by that impiety he is cast out into his own darkness, which is what the "works of iniquity" are. It is plainly he himself who performs *these* works, and *for carrying them out he is self-sufficient*. But he does not do the works of justice unless he receives help from that fount and that light in which there is a life that wants for nothing, and where there is "no change, nor shadow of alteration" (Jas. 1: 17)' (*De spiritu et littera*, cap. 7 n. 11; *PL* 44. 206–7). Herbert McCabe OP makes the same point: 'The sinner's failure to choose happiness is just that—a failure, a not-doing, and this not-doing is not the work of God. The only thing there is the sinner's own failure. Sin and Hell, because they are failures, absences, undoings, are the only things that are uniquely and solely the work of human choice with which God has nothing whatever to do. *They are purely and simply the result of private enterprise and initiative*' (*God Still Matters* (London: Continuum Press, 2002), 185–6).

21 On the distinction between the *poena damni* and the *poena sensus* as corresponding to the twofold movement in mortal sin, see St Thomas's discussion in *ST* 2a2ae q. 79 a. 4 ad. 4 and *De malo*, q. 5 a. 2.

22 Cf. Blessed Denys, *De quatuor hominis novissimis*, art. 45; *DCOO* 41. 556BD'; St Thomas, *4 Sent.* d. 44 q. 3 a. 2 qa. 1; *Summa contra gentiles* lib. 4 cap. 90 n. 6.

23 Marmion, *Christ, the Life of the Soul*, 178.

24 Cf. St Thomas, *ST* 2a2ae q. 24 a. 10.

25 Columba Marmion OSB, *Christ—The Ideal of the Priest: Spiritual Conferences*, trans. M. Dillon, new edn. (St Louis, Mo.: Herder, 1952), 95.

26 Blessed Denys, in whose writings the note of beauty is so prominent, does not fail to emphasize the ugliness of Hell. 'As the fatherland of the blessed, the heavenly Paradise, is inestimably lovely, delightful, and sweet, so Hell is inconceivably and incomprehensibly hideous, desolate, and foul' (Blessed Denys, *De quatuor hominis novissimis*, art. 44; *DCOO* 41. 555CD).

27 Marmion, *Christ—The Ideal of the Priest*, 96.

28 Marmion, *Christ, the Life of the Soul*, 178.

29 Blessed Denys, *Enarratio in cap. 3 Matthaei*, art. 6; *DCOO* ii. 37D'.

30 Ibid. 38AB.

31 Cf. St Thomas, 4 *Sent*. d. 44 q. 3 a. 2A; St Bonaventure, 4 *Sent*. d. 44 a. 2 q. i.

32 Cf. St Thomas, 4 *Sent*. d. 44 q. 3 a. 2B.

33 This difficulty applies only to the present state of the souls of the damned. At Christ's Second Coming, the souls of the damned will be reunited to their bodies and will thus be capable of feeling the pain of sense in a bodily way (cf. St Thomas, 4 *Sent*. d. 43 q. i a. iB; d. 44 q. 3 a. iC).

34 Cf. Blessed Denys, *De particulari iudicio in obitu singulorum dialogus* a. 18; *DCOO* 41. 451C.

35 This is Denys's summary of the Thomistic explanation (cf. *De particulari iudicio in obitu singulorum dialogus*, a. 16; *DCOO* 41. 448D).

36 Vonier, *Collected Works*, iii. *The Soul and the Spiritual Life* (London: Burns & Oates, 1953), 109.

37 'Fear, pain (*dolor*), joy, and the like, as passions, cannot exist in the demons. As such, they are proper to the sensitive appetite, which is a power in a bodily organ. However, as denoting simple acts of the will, they can exist in the demons. We must say that there is pain in them, for pain, as signifying a simple act of the will, is nothing other than the resistance of the will to what is or is not. Now it is evident that the demons wish many things not to be that are, and many things to be that are not, for, out of envy, they would wish others to be damned who are saved. Consequently, pain must be said to exist in them, and especially because it is of the very essence of punishment for it to be repugnant to the will. They are even deprived of the happiness that they desire naturally; and their wicked will is curbed in many respects' (St Thomas, *ST* ia q. 64 a. 3).

38 Cf. St Thomas, *Summa contra gentiles*, lib. 4 cap. 90 nn. 5–6.

39 Cf. Blessed Denys, *De sacra communione frequentanda*, art. 4; *DCOO* 35. 446C'.

40 Marmion, *Christ, the Life of the Soul*, 179.

41 Ibid. 179–80.

42 Ibid. 180.

43 Ibid.

44 Marmion, *Le Christ, idéal du moine*, new edn. (Paris: Desclée, 1926), 463.

45 Marmion, *Christ—The Ideal of the Priest*, 96–7.

46 'All who die in God's grace and friendship, but still imperfectly purified, are indeed assured of their eternal salvation; but after death

they undergo purification, so as to achieve the holiness necessary to enter the joy of Heaven' (*The Catechism of the Catholic Church*, n. 1030).

47   Blessed Denys, *Enarratio in cap. 22 Apocalypsis*, art. 23; DCOO 14. 373AB'.

48   Cf. R. Garrigou-Lagrange OP, *Life Everlasting and the Immensity of the Soul*, trans. P. Cummins, new edn. (Rockford: Tan Books, 1991), 179. In his book on the Four Last Things, Blessed Denys reports the story of a vision experienced by a monk of Eynsham in England, as recorded by Adam, sub-prior of Eynsham and chaplain of St Hugh of Lincoln, the great Carthusian bishop. According to this vision, certain souls in Purgatory are uncertain of their final destiny. Elsewhere Denys makes it clear that he himself does not adhere to this opinion. For example, commenting on the words in Job, 'I will say to God: Do not condemn me' (Job 10: 2), he says: 'This seems not to apply to the souls in Purgatory, since they are certain of glory' (*Enarratio in cap. 10 Job*, art. 26; DCOO 4. 460AB). If Denys is at fault in *De quatuor hominis novissimis*, then it is a fault of imprudence in including an alarming narrative rather than of promoting a positive doctrinal error.

49   The Council of Florence, *Decretum pro graecis*; DS 1304.

50   The Council of Trent, 25th Session, *Decretum de purgatorio* (1563); DS 1820.

51   'Fish's *Supplicacyon* with Foxe's Sidenotes'; *The supplycacyon of soulys Made by syr Thomas More knyght councellor to our souerayn lorde the Kynge and chauncellor of hys Duchy of Lancaster: Agaynst the supplycacyon of beggars*; *The Complete Works of St Thomas More*, ed. F. M. Manley, G. Marc'hadour, R. Marius, and C. H. Miller (New Haven: Yale University Press, 1990), vii. 412.

52   *The supplycacyon of soulys Made by syr Thomas More*, 228, III. Blessed Denys says that the souls in Purgatory are to be 'loved as [our] neighbours' (*De perfectione caritatis dialogus* a. 9; DCOO 41. 358D').

53   *The supplycacyon of soulys*, 202.

54   Ibid. 219.

55   *Hamlet* I. i. 130–2.

56   *The supplycacyon of soulys*, 179 ff.

57   Ibid. 181.

58   'If anyone says that the whole punishment is not always remitted by God at the same time as the guilt, and that the satisfaction of penitents is nothing other than the faith by which they apprehend that Christ has made satisfaction for them, let him be anathema' (the Council of Trent, 14th Session, *Canones de sacramento paenitentiae*, 12; DS 1712).

59 The Latin word *poena* can be translated into English by either word. 'Pain' comes from *poena* via the medieval French *peine*.

60 Cf. St Thomas, 2 *Sent.* d. 30 a. 1 ad. 6.

61 St Thomas, *De malo*, q. 1 a. 4.

62 *The Catechism of the Catholic Church*, n. 1472.

63 Cf. St Thomas, *ST* 1a2ae q. 87 a. 6; 2a2ae q. 108 a. 4.

64 St Thomas, *De veritate* q. 28 a. 2.

65 'The powers of human nature are not sufficient to do away with this offence: the gift of divine grace is needed' (St Thomas, *De veritate* q. 28 a. 2).

66 Cf. St Thomas, *ST* 3a q. 48 a. 2.

67 Cf. ibid. ad. 1.

68 The Council of Trent, 14th Session, *Doctrina de sacramento paenitentiae*, cap. 8; DS 1691.

69 Ibid.

70 St Thomas, *ST* 3a q. 48 a. 2 ad. 1; cf. *Super ad Galatas* cap. 6 lect. 1. In the commentary on the Sentences, he mentions an example from the 'lives of the Fathers', according to which one brother, out of charity, did penance for a sin he had not committed for the good of another brother, who had committed the sin (cf. 4 *Sent.* d. 20 q. 1 a. 2c ad. 1).

71 The relevant texts in the works of St Augustine are discussed by Father Emile Mersch in *The Whole Christ: The Historical Development of the Doctrine of the Mystical Body in Scripture and Tradition*, trans. (Milwaukee: Bruce Publishing, 1938), 424 ff.

72 Pope Pius XII, *Mystici corporis* (1943); DS 3805.

73 Pope Paul VI, *Indulgentiarum doctrina* (1967); ed. J. Neuner SJ and J. Dupuis SJ, *The Christian Faith in the Doctrinal Documents of the Catholic Church*, new edn. (London: Collins, 1983), 485 (n. 1687).

74 Ibid. 486 (n. 1690/1); cf. *The Catechism of the Catholic Church*, n. 1472.

75 The Council of Trent, 14th Session, *Doctrina de sacramento paenitentiae*, cap. 8; DS 1690.

76 St Thomas says that 'it more glorious for man to purge away by plenary satisfaction the sin he has committed than for him to be forgiven without satisfaction, just as it is more glorious for man to possess eternal life from his merits than for him to attain it without merits, because what someone merits he somehow has from himself, inasmuch as he has merited' (3 *Sent.* d. 20 a. 1B).

77 'At this point the Eternal Truth proceeded to show her that, though He had created us without ourselves, He would not save us without ourselves' (St Catherine of Siena, *The Dialogue*, trans. A. Thorold

(London: Burns, Oates, & Washbourne, 1925), ch. 23, p. 44). St Augustine's exact words are: 'He who made you without you does not justify you without you' (*Sermones*, 169 cap. 11 n. 13; *PL* 38. 923).

78 '[Satisfactory penances] heal the after-effects of sin and destroy evil habits, acquired through an evil life, by acts of virtue opposed to them' (The Council of Trent, 14th Session, *Doctrina de sacramento paenitentiae*, cap. 8; DS 1690).

79 Cf. A. Tanquerey, *Synopsis theologiae dogmaticae*, iii. *De Deo sanctificante et remuneratore seu De gratia, De sacramentis et De novissimis*, new edn. (Paris: Desclée, 1938), 766 (n. 1132).

80 Vonier, *Collected Works*, iii. *The Soul and the Spiritual Life*, 126.

81 John Henry Newman, *Prayers, Verses, and Devotions*, new edn. (San Francisco: Ignatius Press, 1989), 718.

82 *The Catechism of the Catholic Church*, n. 1031.

83 L. Ott, *Fundamentals of Catholic Dogma*, new edn. (Cork: Mercier Press, 1963), 485.

84 Blessed Denys, *Enarratio in cap. 3 Exodi*, art. 5; *DCOO* 1. 494c'.

85 'I believe no happiness can be found worthy to be compared with that of a soul in Purgatory except that of the saints in Paradise; and day by day this happiness grows as God flows into these souls, more and more as the hindrance to His entrance is consumed' (St Catherine of Genoa, *Treatise on Purgatory and The Dialogue*, trans. C. Balfour and H. D. Irvine (London: Sheed & Ward, 1946), 18–19).

86 Ibid. 17 ff and *passim*.

87 Cf. St Thomas, *ST* 3a q. 89 a. 1 ad. 3.

88 St Catherine of Genoa, *Treatise on Purgatory and The Dialogue*, 17 ff and *passim*.

89 The Council of Trent, 25th Session, *Decretum de purgatorio* (1563); DS 1820.

90 The Council of Trent, 22nd Session, *Doctrina de sanctissimae Missae sacrificio* (1562), cap. 2; DS 1743.

91 'We must pray fervently for the dead. First, because they cannot help themselves, as they are not in the state of meriting or demeriting. Secondly, since when they attain to happiness, they pray most faithfully for those whose intercessions have helped them. Thirdly, since they have a twofold pain, namely, of loss and sense, and both are greater than any pain of this present life' (Blessed Denys, *Expositio missae* a. 35; *DCOO* 35. 374c).

92 *La règle de Saint Benoît*, vol. 1, cap. 4; ed. Neufville, 460.

93 Ibid. cap. 5; p. 464.

94 Ibid. prologus; p. 414.

95 Ibid. cap. 7; pp. 488–9.

96 Ibid. prologus; p. 424.

97 Ibid. prologus; p. 412.

98 The purgation of the mind is the 'the mind's withdrawal from those things which are contrary to charity and likeness with God' (Blessed Denys, *De ecclesiastica hierarchia*, cap. 1 a. 4; DCOO 15. 362C); cf. Blessed Denys, *De caelesti hierarchia*, cap. 7 a. 36; DCOO 15. 133CD'.

99 John Chapman OSB, *The Spiritual Letters* (London: Sheed & Ward, 1935), 146.

100 'Just as the spirits suffer purgation there so as to be able to see God through clear vision in the next life, souls in their own way suffer purgation here on earth so as to be able to be transformed in Him through love in this life' (St John of the Cross, *The Living Flame of Love*, stanza 1 n. 24; *The Collected Works of St John of the Cross*, trans. Kieran Kavanaugh OCD and Otilio Rodriguez OCD, new edn. (Washington DC: Institute of Carmelite Studies, 1979), 589).

4 AVE REGINA CAELORUM

1 These geometrical observations are a development of the commentary of Jean and Yan le Pichon (cf. *Le Mystère du Couronnement de la Vierge* 42 ff.).

2 Ibid. 44.

3 The Second Vatican Council, Dogmatic Constitution on the Church, *Lumen gentium*, n. 65; *Sacrosanctum oecumenicum concilium Vaticanum II: Constitutiones, decreta, declarationes* (Vatican City: Vatican Press, 1966), 202.

4 The translation of the *Ave regina caelorum* is Father Caswall's (Britt, *The Hymns of the Breviary and Missal*, 87).

5 R. de Vaux OP, *Ancient Israel: Its Life and Institutions*, trans. J. McHugh (London: Darton, Longman, & Todd, 1961), 117 ff.

6 Blessed Denys, *De dignitate et laudibus B. V. Mariae*, prooemium; DCOO 36. 105A'.

7 Blessed Denys, *Commentarium in psalmum 44*, a. 87; DCOO 6. 12A.

8 See e.g. the painting of this scene by Bergognone, late fifteenth century, now hanging in the National Gallery, London.

9 Pope Pius XII, *Ad caeli reginam*; AAS 36 (1954), 635.

10 Cf. St Thomas, *In salutationem angelicam*, a. 1.

11 Blessed Denys, *De perfectione caritatis dialogues*, a. 49; DCOO 41. 412D'–413A.

12 Blessed Denys, *De praeconio et dignitate Mariae* lib. 2 a. 14; *DCOO* 35. 521A.

13 Ibid. 520D'.

14 See Ch. 1.

15 Blessed Denys, *De praeconio et dignitate Mariae*, lib. 4 a. 6; *DCOO* 35. 571B.

16 Ibid. 571CD.

17 'We know that the Blessed Virgin is the Queen of Heaven and Earth, but she is more Mother than Queen' (St Thérèse de l'Enfant-Jésus et de la sainte-face, *Le carnet jaune* (21 August 1897), n. 2; *Œuvres complètes*, 1103).

18 Cf. St Thomas, *De malo*, q. 8 a. 3 ad. 9.

19 Cf. Blessed Denys, *De praeconio et dignitate Mariae*, lib. 3 a. 21: *DCOO* 35. 555CD'.

20 Blessed Denys, *De quatuor hominis novissimis*, a. 59; *DCOO* 41. 575C'.

21 Ibid. a. 61; 582D.

22 *Christ, the Life of the Soul*, 371.

23 Ibid.

24 St Thomas, *ST* 3a q. 30 a. 1.

25 Blessed Denys, *De quatuor hominis novissimis*, a. 61; *DCOO* 41. 582D.

26 '[T]he confession that Mary is *Deipara*, or the Mother of God, is that safeguard wherewith we seal up and secure the doctrine of the Apostle from all evasion, and that test whereby we detect all the pretences of those bad spirits of "Antichrist which have gone out into the world". It declares that He is God; it implies that He is man; it suggests to us that He is God still, though He has become man, and that He is true man though He is God . . . If Mary is the Mother of God, Christ must be literally Emmanuel, God with us. And hence it was, that, when time went on, and the bad spirits and false prophets grew stronger and bolder, and found a way into the Catholic body itself, then the Church, guided by God, could find no more effectual and sure way of expelling them than that of using this word *Deipara* against them; and, on the other hand, when they came up again from the realms of darkness, and plotted the utter overthrow of Christian faith in the sixteenth century, then they could find no more certain expedient for their hateful purpose than that of reviling and blaspheming the prerogatives of Mary, for they knew full well that, if they could once get the world to dishonour the Mother, the dishonour of the Son would follow close. The Church and Satan agreed together in this, that Son and Mother went together; and the experience of three centuries has confirmed their

testimony, for Catholics, who have honoured the Mother, still worship the Son, while Protestants, who now have ceased to confess the Son, began then by scoffing at the Mother' (John Henry Newman, 'The Glories of Mary for the Sake of her Son', *Discourses Addressed to Mixed Congregations*, new edn. (London: Longman's, 1891), 347).

27 The hymn to the Mother of God sung during the Liturgy of St Basil the Great in the Byzantine Church.

28 Blessed Denys, *De quatuor hominis novissimis*, a. 61; *DCOO* 41. 582B'.

29 Ibid. 582C'. Among these joys of the accidental reward Blessed Denys includes the happiness of seeing the sacred humanity of the Son of God; this happiness, too, surpasses the joy of seeing the Mother of God.

30 Vonier, *Collected Works*, i *The Incarnation and Redemption*, 375.

31 Ibid.

32 Ibid. 375–6.

33 Cf. St Thomas, *ST* 3a q. 28 a. 1.

34 'Relation in the Godhead is not like an accident inhering in a subject, but is the divine essence itself; that is why it is subsistent, just as the divine essence subsists. Therefore, just as the Godhead is God, so divine Fatherhood is God the Father, who is a divine person. A divine person, therefore, signifies a relation as subsistent' (St Thomas, *ST* 1a q. 29 a. 4).

35 According to the Gloss, 'glory is clear knowledge with praise' (cf. St Thomas, *3 Sent.* d. 18 a. 4)

36 Pope St Gregory the Great, *Moralium libri sive expositio in librum Iob*, lib. 18 cap. 52 n. 85; *PL* 76. 90.

37 Cf. St Thomas, *ST* 3a q. 28 a. 3.

38 Of course, the *content* of the idea and the utterance may be morally corrupting.

39 Cf. St Thomas, *ST* 3a q. 28 a. 2.

40 Cf. ibid. a. 4.

41 St Bede says of our Lady's words, 'How shall this be done, because I know not man?' (Luke 1: 34): 'She reverently disclosed the intention of her mind, namely, to have decided to lead a virginal life' (*In Lucae evangelium expositio* [loc. cit.]; *CCSL* 120. 33).

42 Cf. St Thomas, *ST* 3a q. 28 a. 3.

43 The Alleluia chant from the Mass of the Immaculate Conception in the Roman Missal. The words are an adaptation of the Canticle (cf. S. of S. 4: 7).

44 For an explanation of the concept of the theological aesthetic, see

the first volume of Balthasar's *Herrlichkeit: Eine theologische Ästhetik* (Einsiedeln: Johannes Verlag, 1961), *passim*.

45 Blessed Denys, *De dignitate et laudibus B. V. Mariae*, lib. 1 a. 34; *DCOO* 36. 61c.

46 Ibid. 61cd.

47 See G. Narcisse OP, *Les Raisons de Dieu: argument de convenance et ésthetique théologique selon St Thomas d'Aquin et Hans Urs von Balthasar* (Fribourg: Éditions universitaires, 1997).

48 'The Bride of Christ is threefold: universal, which is the Church; particular, namely, the faithful soul; and singular, the divine [i.e. divinized] Virgin' (Blessed Denys, *Commentarium in psalmum 44*, a. 87; *DCOO 6*. 11c).

49 Cf. Blessed Denys, *Commentarium in psalmum 44*, a. 87; *DCOO 6*. 11b.

50 Ibid. 11c.

51 'God's better beauty, grace' ('To what serves Mortal Beauty?', *The Poems of Gerard Manley Hopkins*, ed. W. H. Gardner and N. H. MacKenzie, new edn. (London, Oxford: Oxford University Press, 1970), 98).

52 Marmion, *Christ, the Life of the Soul*, 374.

53 Ed. J. D. Mansi, *Sacrorum conciliorum nova et amplissima collectio*, xxix (Florence, 1788), col. 183bc.

54 Le Pichon, *Le Mystère du Couronnement de la Vierge*, 84.

55 Blessed Denys, *De perfectione caritatis dialogus*, a. 49; *DCOO* 41. 412d.

56 Blessed Pope Pius IX, *Ineffabilis Deus* (1854); DS 2803.

57 Blessed Denys, *Commentarium in psalmum* 118, a. 29; *DCOO 6*. 543d.

58 Le Pichon, *Le Mystère du Couronnement de la Vierge*, 18.

59 Pope Pius XII, *Munificentissimus Deus* (1950); DS 3903.

60 Cf. St Thomas, *ST* 2a2ae 164, 1 ad. 1.

61 Cf. St Thomas, *Summa contra Gentiles* lib. 4 cap. 79.

62 Cf. St Thomas, *ST* 2a2ae 164, 1.

63 Cf. J. P. Carol OFM, *Fundamentals of Mariology* (New York: Benziger, 1956), 177.

64 Pope John Paul II, General Audience address, 25 June 1997.

65 Ibid. 'What death, think you, the Holy Virgin died, if not the death of love?' ('Sermon pour la fête de l'Assomption de la Sainte Vierge', 15 août 1618; *Œuvres de Saint François de Sales*, ix. *Sermons*, pt. 3 (Annecy: Niérat, 1897), 182).

66 Cf. St John of the Cross, *The Living Flame of Love*, stanza 1 n. 30; *The Collected Works of St John of the Cross*, trans. Kavanaugh and Rodriguez, 591–2.

67 Pope Pius XII, *Munificentissimus Deus*; *AAS* 32 (1950), 761.

68 Ibid. 768.

69 St John Damascene, *Homilia 2 in dormitionem Beatae Virginis Mariae Deiparae*, n. 4; *SC*, 80, 136.

70 Blessed Denys, *De dignitate et laudibus B. V. Mariae*, lib. 4 a. 9; *DCOO* 36. 160C.

71 Ibid. 160D.

72 Ibid. 160C.

73 Ibid. 160B'.

74 The Second Vatican Council, Dogmatic Constitution on the Church, *Lumen gentium*, n. 61; *Sacrosanctum oecumenicum concilium Vaticanum II: Constitutiones, decreta, declarationes* (Rome: Vatican Press, 1966), 199.

75 Louis Bouyer, *Le trône de la sagesse: Essai sur la signification du culte marial*, new edn. (Paris: Éditions du Cerf, 1987), 240.

76 According to the definition supplied by a present-day Thomist: 'Moral theology is the part of theology that studies human acts so as to order them, by means of grace, the virtues, and the gifts, and in the light of revelation and reason, towards the loving vision of God, which is true and complete beatitude and the final end of man' (S. Pinckaers OP, *Les Sources de la moral chrétienne: Sa méthode, son contenu, son histoire* (Fribourg: Éditions universitaires, 1990), 18–19).

77 *The Catechism of the Catholic Church*, n. 1050, citing the Second Vatican Council, Pastoral Constitution on the Church in the Modern World, *Gaudium et spes*, n. 39.

78 St Bonaventure, *Legenda maior*, cap. 9 n. 1; *Doctoris seraphici S. Bonaventurae opera omnia* (Quaracchi: Typographia collegii S. Bonaventurae, 1898), viii. 530.

79 Blessed Denys, *De passione Domini salvatoris dialogues*, a. 2; *DCOO* 35. 272CD'.

80 Vonier, *Collected Works*, iii. 312.

BIBLIOGRAPHY

AQUINAS, ST THOMAS, *S. Thomae Aquinatis opera omnia*, ed. Roberto Busa SJ (Stuttgart: Frommann-Holzboog, 1980).

BENOÎT, SAINT, *La Règle de Saint Benoît*, i; ed. J Neuville OSB, *SC* 181 (Paris: Éditions du Cerf, 1972).

BRITT OSB, MATTHEW, *The Hymns of the Breviary and Missal* (London: Burns, Oates & Washbourne, 1922).

DANTE ALIGHIERI, *The Divine Comedy: Hell, Purgatory, Paradise*, trans. Dorothy L. Sayers and Barbara Reynolds (Harmondsworth: Penguin Books, 1949, 1955, 1962).

DENYS THE CARTHUSIAN, BLESSED, *Doctoris ecstatici D. Dionysii Cartusiani opera omnia* (Montreuil-sur-mer: Typis Cartusiae S. M. de Pratis, 1896–1913).

JOHN OF THE CROSS, ST, *The Collected Works of St John of the Cross*, trans. Kieran Kavanagh OCD and Otilio Rodriguez OCD, new edn. (Washington DC: Institute of Carmelite Studies, 1979).

LECLERCQ OSB, JEAN, *The Love of Learning and the Desire for God: A Study of Monastic Culture*, trans. Catherine Misrahi, new edn. (New York: Fordham University Press, 1974).

MARMION OSB, BLESSED COLUMBA, *Christ, the Life of the Soul: Spiritual Conferences*, trans. Mother M. St Thomas of Tyburn Convent, new edn. (London: Sands & Co., 1922).

—— *Le Christ, idéal du moine: Conférences spirituelles sur la vie monastique et religieuse* (Paris: Desclée, 1926).

—— *Christ in His Mysteries*, trans. Mother M. St Thomas of Tyburn Convent, new edn. (London, Sands & Co., 1939).

—— *Christ—The Ideal of the Priest: Spiritual Conferences*, trans. M. Dillon, new edn. (St Louis, Mo.: Herder, 1952).

MORE, ST THOMAS, *The supplycacyon of soulys Made by syr Thomas More knyght councellor to our souerayn lorde the Kynge and chauncellor of hys Duchy of Lancaster: Against the supplycacyon of beggars; The Complete Works of St Thomas More*, vii, ed. F. M. Manley, G Marc'hadour,

R. Marius, and C. H. Miller (New Haven: Yale University Press, 1990).

PICHON, JEAN AND YANN LE, *Le Mystère du Couronnement de la Vierge* (Paris: Éditions Robert Laffont/Le Centurion, 1982).

VONIER, ANSCAR, *The Collected Works of Abbot Vonier* (London: Burns & Oates, 1953), 3 vols.

INDEX